LEADERSHIP, ETHICS,
AND THEIR CIRCUMSTANCES

LYNCHBURG COLLEGE SYMPOSIUM READINGS

Third Edition

2010

Volume X

LEADERSHIP, ETHICS, AND THEIR CIRCUMSTANCES

Edited by

Maria Louise Nathan, Ph.D.

Library of Congress Control Number: 2010902878
ISBN: Hardcover   978-1-4500-5329-7
                        Softcover   978-1-4500-5328-0

To order additional copies of this book, contact:
Xlibris Corporation
1-888-795-4274
www.Xlibris.com
Orders@Xlibris.com
23039

CONTENTS

SECTION VI: LEADERSHIP AND ETHICS

Acknowledgements

Reprinted from ON HEROES, HERO-WORSHIP, AND THE
HEROIC IN HISTORY by Thomas Carlyle, edited by Carl
Neimeyer, published by the University of Nebraska Press.
"The Power of Leadership" (pp. 23-8) from LEADERSHIP
by JAMES MACGREGOR BURNS. Copyright © 1978 by
James MacGregor Burns. Reprinted by Permission of
HarperCollins Publishers.
From ON BECOMING A LEADER by WARREN BENNIS ©
1989 by Warren Bennis, Inc., Reprinted by permission of
Basic Books, a member of the Perseus Books Group.
From BAD LEADERSHIP, WHAT IT IS, HOW IT HAPPENS,
WHY IT HAPPENS by Barbara Kellerman © copyright
2004 by Barbara Kellerman. Harvard Business School
Publishing. Boston. MASS. Used by permission.
Reprinted with permission of the publisher—Berett-Koehler

From *Creating Leaderful Organizations: How to Bring out
Leadership in Everyone.* © Joseph A. Raelin 2003. Berrett-
Koehler Publishers, Inc., San Francisco, CA. All right
reserved. www.bkconnection.com.

From *The New Superleadership: Leading Others Lead
Themselves.* © C. Manz and H. Sims, 2001. Berrett-
Koehler Publishers, Inc., San Francisco, CA. All right
reserved. www.bkconnection.com.

LYNCHBURG COLLEGE SYMPOSIUM READINGS SENIOR SYMPOSIUM AND THE LCSR PROGRAM

The ten-volume series, Lynchburg College Symposium Readings, has been developed by Lynchburg College faculty for use in the Senior Symposium and the Lynchburg College Symposium Readings Program (SS/LCSR). Each volume presents primary source material organized around interdisciplinary, liberal arts themes.

In 1976, the College developed the Senior Symposium as a two-hour, interdisciplinary course, required of all graduating seniors. On Mondays, students in all sections of the course come together for public lectures, given by invited guest speakers. On Wednesdays, Symposium students meet in their sections for student-led discussions and presentations on associated readings from the LCSR series. The course requires students, who have spent their later college years in narrowing the scope of their studies, to expand their fields of vision within a discussion group composed of and led by their peers. Students can apply analytical and problem-solving capabilities learned in their major fields of study to issues raised by guest speakers and classical readings.

This approach works against convention in higher education, which typically emphasizes the gradual exclusion of subject areas outside of a student's major field. But Senior Symposium leads students, poised for graduation, into their post-college intellectual responsibilities. They gain experience in taking their liberal education into real world problems, using it to address contemporary problems thoughtfully and critically. In order to do this successfully, students must abandon their habitual posture as docile receptors of authoritative information for a much more skeptical attitude toward opinion, proof, reasoning, and authoritative experience. The effort to think constructively through a variety of conflicting opinions—on a weekly basis—prepares them well for the mature, independent, well-reasoned points of view expected of educated adults.

The LCSR Program's primary goals are to foster an appreciation of the connection between basic skills and interdisciplinary knowledge, and to promote greater cross-disciplinary communication among faculty and students. General education core courses or courses that serve other program requirements may be classified as "LCSR," as long as they fulfill certain speaking and writing activities connected to LCSR readings. The effect of the program has been to help create the atmosphere of a residential academic community; shared learning creates a climate in which teaching and learning take root more forcefully.

Since its inception, the SS/LCSR Program has helped create opportunities for faculty interaction across the disciplines in "pre-service" and "in-service" workshops. Each May, the LCSR Program sponsors a four-day pre-service workshop to which all new full-time and part-time faculty members are invited. Participants receive individual sets of the Lynchburg College Symposium Readings, which they make their own by using them during the workshop in exercises designed to promote familiarity with a wide variety of the readings. The goals of the workshop are several: for those unfamiliar with the program, to begin planning an LCSR course; for new faculty, to become acquainted with those they have not met and to get to know their acquaintances better; for other faculty of various experiential levels, to share their pedagogical successes; for new teachers, to ask questions about teaching, about the College, and about the students in an informal setting; for experienced teachers to re-visit some of their assumptions, pedagogies, and strategies; to inspire strong scholarship, creative teaching, risk-taking, and confidence among all participants.

Another opportunity comes with the "in-service" workshops, which occur each month during the school year. The LCSR Program sponsors luncheons and dinners at which faculty teaching in the program give informal presentations on their use of specific teaching strategies or reading selections. Attendance is voluntary, but many try to be present for every session. For those involved in the LCSR program, teaching has become what Lee Schulman, President of the Carnegie Foundation, calls "community property."

On the Lynchburg College campus, there is evidence of a systematic change in teaching effectiveness as well as sustained faculty commitment to the program. By the 2002-2003 academic year, nearly two-thirds of all full-time faculty members and more than half of all part-time faculty members had completed the workshop at some time during their time at Lynchburg College. In any given semester, roughly ten to fifteen percent of the total class enrollments are in LCSR courses, not counting the required Senior Symposium. An important feature of this program is that participation is voluntary on the part of the faculty and, except for the required Senior Symposium, on the part of students. The program's influence quietly pervades the campus community, improving teaching and scholarship. Many see the LCSR Program as the College's premier academic program.

The Senior Symposium/LCSR program publishes *Agora*, an in-house journal that features the best of student writings responding to LCSR texts. The journal selections by students must integrate classical ideas and issues with contemporary ones. Faculty may also submit writings that address innovative teaching strategies. The journal takes its title from the marketplace at the heart of classical Athens, where much of Athenian public life was carried on: mercantile exchange, performance, political debate, athletic contests, and the public worship of deities all took place within the hustle and bustle of the Athenian agora. Similarly, the journal seeks to be a marketplace for compelling ideas and issues. Faculty members and students serve together on the editorial committee.

Since 1976, the Senior Symposium and the LCSR Program have affected the academic community both within and beyond the Lynchburg College campus. In 1991, Professor Richard Marius from Harvard University's writing center in reviewing the program favorably said, "I have seldom in my life been so impressed by an innovation in college education. I suppose the highest compliment that I could pay to the program was that I wished I could teach in it." Also in 1991, Professor Donald Boileau of George Mason University's Communication Studies department wrote, "what I discovered was a sound program that not only enriches the education of students at Lynchburg College, but what I hope can be a model for many other colleges and universities throughout our country." In spring 2003, in an article titled, "Whither the Great Books," Dr. William Casement described the LCSR program as the "most fully organized version" of the recent growth of great-books programs that employ an "across-the-disciplines structure." According to him, this approach perhaps encourages the use of the great books across the curriculum, which can be less isolating than even interdisciplinary programs. The Senior Symposium and LCSR Programs have received national acclaim in such publications as Loren Pope's *Colleges That Change Lives* and Charles Sykes and Brad Miner's *The National Review of College Guide, America's 50 Top Liberal Arts Schools.*

Leadership, Ethics, and their Circumstances is the tenth and final volume in this series. It is a newly created volume on leadership and ethics, topics timely for our times. The Senior Symposium was the creation of Dr. James Huston, Dean of the College, *Emeritus* (1972-1984). With Dr. Michael Santos, professor of history, he co-founded the LCSR program. Dean Huston served as the first series editor, and with Dr. Julius Sigler, co-edited the second series. All three remain committed to the program today, and for this we are grateful.

Peggy Pittas, Ph.D.
Series Managing Editor
Katherine Gray, Ph.D.

INTRODUCTION

Most people will act as leaders in some capacity at some point in their lives (e.g., in the home, the community, a church, a business, or an organization). At other times, these same people will act as followers, playing another integral role in the leadership process. This volume provides opportunities for both aspirant and incumbent leaders to reflect upon leadership and its circumstances.

The works selected for this volume will assist current and future leaders to become familiar with key thinkers' concepts of leadership; to think critically about first-rate leadership and its circumstances; to gain inspiration from the lives of great leaders; to examine their own ideas, underlying assumptions, and experiences of leadership; to shape their own personal theories of leadership; and to reflect upon the desired results of leadership. In this way, readers can use this volume to become both effective leaders and effective followers of others' leadership.

These readings were chosen according to the following criteria: (1) comprehensive treatment of the subtleties of leadership; (2) both classical and current sources; (3) both eastern and western world perspectives; (4) varied contexts, such as business, government, social movements, religions, peace and wartime, crisis and calm; (5) varied levels of analysis, such as individual, dyad, team, organizational, national, and cross-national; (6) males and females, both as authors and leaders.

Each of the six sections of this volume begins with an introduction, addressing the leadership-related theme. Then each set of readings is organized by chronological dates of authorship. Excerpts from recent books and journal articles are also included because the scholarly study of leadership began in earnest only in the twentieth century. Each reading is preceded by a brief introduction, giving information about the writer and his/her time so that the reader can appreciate the key concepts of leadership illustrated in each reading.

The book is divided into six sections: (1) leadership defined, (2) personal qualities of the leader, (3) what leaders do, (4) the circumstances of leadership, (5) leadership and strategic change, and (6) leadership and ethics.

Section I explores some of the hundreds of definitions of leadership. Plato focuses on the philosopher king, while Carlyle studies the ablest man as the hero in history. Bennis differentiates the transformational, change-enhancing leader from the transactional manager, who capably maintains the status quo. Kellerman questions the assumption that leadership is necessarily good by providing an ample supply of real-world examples of bad leaders who were weak, ineffectual, and sometimes evil. Finally, Raelin constructs an alternate view of leadership in which an organization is found to have abundant leaders at all levels who manage themselves and others—"leaderful" organizations.

Section II explores the personal qualities possessed by those distinguished as great, memorable, and effective leaders. Included in this section are formal discussions of the traits of leaders as well as time-favored stories about admirable individuals who have led effectively. Some of the qualities of leadership explored in Section II may not fit the conventional definition of a strong leader. Instead, we see that some leaders are quiet, reflective, humble, selfless, loving, and even vulnerable. The recollections and letters of Robert E. Lee, prepared by his son, create a fascinating study of one hero's softer, more personal side. Section II also considers the question of leadership being innate or learned behavior. Von Clausewitz's bold leader in battle (*On War*) would seem to have natural propensities of mind and body. On the other hand, Nehemiah prayed and obeyed as he took on his challenging leadership task. Miyamoto Musashi (*Book of Five Rings*) expects the leader to return to his/her original or true mind when facing a challenge. The excerpt from Sophocles' play *Ajax* is a cautionary tale of negative qualities that can cause even a hero to derail. Thus, Section II looks at instructive traits of the leader.

In Section III, the behaviors of the leader—what he or she actually does (and doesn't do)—are studied. The exemplars of leadership behavior in this section take us one step closer to results. The ancient Chinese sage Lao-tzu advised that the leader should act as a mid-wife who helps to bring new life into the world but who then steps aside to give full credit to the one who gave birth to this new life. Shackleton, captain of the *Endurance*, is often applauded for his leadership under highly adverse circumstances because of all that he did to keep his crew alive. However, in the passage found in this volume we see a different, more vulnerable Shackleton in the aftermath of his second Antarctic expedition.

Section III also explores the self-work that must precede intelligent and self-aware leadership behavior. Sashkin and Senge both speak of the need for the leader first to confront his/her own deficiencies and insecurities before taking on the challenge of getting others to change and grow. Manz and Sims create a new role for the leader as hero-maker who helps followers to lead themselves. Wheatley challenges us to consider a more naturalistic basis for leader behaviors that is more attuned to the current-day understanding within the natural sciences.

Change is never easy: plans get derailed, followers resist, mistakes are made, twice the time is needed than was allowed, yet the ability to make change happen is a key defining feature of leadership. "Leadership" is about strategic change, while "management" is about maintenance of the status quo. Section IV examines this integral component of leadership—strategic change. The readings in this section offer both "how to" and "how it was done" advice. Nelson Mandela and Betty Friedan speak volumes not only through their lives but also through their inspiration as thought leaders. These leaders were effective change agents because they understood their social milieu and boldly considered how to change it appropriately. Betty Friedan, offering ample data and speaking from her own personal experience, forged new vistas for young females as they contemplated their futures. She challenged women to reflect upon the disquiet many of them experienced as housewives and to reconsider what it means to "have it all." Mandela, like Martin Luther King, Jr., wrote from a prison cell, to challenge us to think again about what adverse circumstances can produce.

Does leadership depend upon the circumstances? Should more highly educated people be led differently from those less well educated? Are some leaders more effective in some circumstances than in others? How might great leaders be born of the trials of crisis? Section V studies the circumstances of leadership. Tolstoy suggested that rulers are actually history's slaves, doing only what they must do in their given circumstances with far less discretion than we might assume. In this section, Jermier and Kerr explore the idea that sometimes "substitutes" for leadership may make leadership less necessary and less relevant to followers. Furthermore, after international studies researcher Geert Hofstede looked at a large sample of managers from all around the world, he found many different leadership styles, depending upon the national origin. Burns explores this theme from yet a different angle. He found that leaders in developing and turbulent economies are regarded as heroes by their people in direct proportion to the severity of the followers' needs. Thus, American-generated theories of leadership may not necessarily apply in other countries and other contexts. Finally, the leadership story is not complete without the study of the leader-follower dyad and the effect of followership. Leadership is not just about the leader! Ira Chaleff studies courageous followership of those who enhance the organization. Courageous followers will not permit the leaders to do wrong; they will uphold high standards that further support their leaders. Such insights permit the reader to gain deeper insight into how leadership is bounded by circumstances.

Section VI, the final section of the volume, seeks to explore the fundamental relationship between leadership and ethics. As in previous sections of this volume, some selections are conceptual, examining the relationship between the fundamentals of leadership and ethics; other readings demonstrate through parables (the Parable of the Sadhu, the Sermon on the Mount), while yet another (Machiavelli) shockingly reveals some of the darkest views of human nature. If a choice had to be made, would a leader prefer to be feared or loved? Machiavelli says it is better to be feared. However, not everyone agrees with him, as is clear in Lao-tzu's selection in Section III.

To understand leadership, the reader must do soul work; to understand leadership and its relationship to ethics, the reader must make the journey to self-understanding. Johnson asks readers to explore their dark sides as one means to this end. Additional self-questions posed by other authors in this section include: "What are my values, and how do my values relate to the major decisions I've made in my life?" "Does character matter? Is it destiny?" "What do I think about human nature? (For example, are people basically good, bad, amoral)?" "Why and in what ways will I be limited by my lack of self-understanding?" "What is the value of a human life?" and "Why do I want to lead?" Greenleaf's servant leader challenges those who are in it for the prestige, the money, or the need to prove themselves.

Warren Bennis (2003), whose work is included in Section I, asked the profound question, "Where have all of the leaders gone?" He noted that eighteenth century America was noted for geniuses; the nineteenth century was noted for adventurers, entrepreneurs, investors, scientists, writers, titans of the Industrial Revolution, and explorers who opened the world and defined us as a nation, like Thomas Edison, Eli Whitney, Lewis and Clark, Whitman, Twain, all people of vision who led us in the march to higher productivity. But what of today? Has the challenge of leadership in current times become too daunting? A more hopeful view is that our understanding of leadership has become more advanced (in the form of new ideas such as transformational leadership, servant leaders, self leadership, authentic leadership, leaderful organizations, and more) so that we are better equipped for leadership than ever. Those who read this volume must decide if they are willing to submit their understanding of what it means to be a leader to the ultimate test-application in the real world.

Source:

Bennis, W. (2003). *On becoming a leader.* New York: Addison-Wesley.

Section I

Leadership Defined

Leadership has intrigued historians and philosophers since ancient times. The scientific study of leadership is much more recent, beginning only in the twentieth century. Leadership, like beauty, is hard to define, yet we know it when we see it. More than 350 definitions of leadership have been offered over time, so leadership is among the most studied yet least understood phenomena. The meaning of leadership may depend on the kind of institution in which it is practiced. Leadership has been conceived as a focus of group processes, a means of inducing compliance, the exercise of influence, certain behaviors, certain forms of persuasion, and a power relationship instrumental in achieving goals, among numerous other definitions.

Leadership is a social influence process shared among all members of a group. Thus, followers too are part of the leadership process. Furthermore, leadership has varied formats. For example, the term "thought leadership" describes the influence of a speaker and/or writer who transforms the way a public looks at a phenomenon. Betty Friedan, whose writing is included in Section IV, wrote about the typical American woman of the 1960s, who was supposed to be fully satisfied in the role of wife and mother. Friedan became a "thought leader" and influenced many people when she wrote from the heart, expressing women's need to do much more with their lives.

Source:

Bennis, W. G. & Nanus B. (1985). *Leaders: The strategies for taking charge.* New York: Harper & Row.

PLATO

427-347 B.C.E.

The Republic of Plato

ca. 360 B.C.E.

Plato, famous student of Socrates, was the son of wealthy and influential Athenians. Plato begins his masterpiece, *The Republic*, with a conversation between Socrates, Glaucon, and Adeimantus, who discuss justice, wisdom, courage, and moderation as applied to both individuals and society. Note that each new paragraph indicates a change of speaker. In the following excerpt, Plato argues that philosophers should be the rulers, and he outlines the requirements for the ideal leader of the ideal state (the philosopher king).

Selection from:

Plato. (1935). *The republic of Plato.* (J.L Davies & D. J. Vaughan, Trans.) (pp. 186-188, 201-204, 215-218). London: Macmillan and Co. (Original work written *ca.* 360 B.C.E.)

Book V

Then our next step apparently must be, to endeavour to search out and demonstrate what there is now amiss in the working of our states, preventing their being regulated in the manner described, and what is the smallest change that would enable a state to assume this form of constitution, confining ourselves, if possible, to a single change; if not, to two; or else, to such as are fewest in number and least important in their influence.

Let us by all means endeavour so to do.

Well, I proceeded, there is one change by which, as I think we might shew, the required revolution would be secured; but it is certainly neither a small nor an easy change, though it is a possible one.

What is it?

I am now on the point of confronting that very statement which we compared to the huge wave. Nevertheless it shall be spoken, even if it is to deluge me, literally like an exploding wave, with laughter and infamy. Pay attention to what I am going to say.

Say on, he replied.

Unless it happen either that philosophers acquire the kingly power in states, or that those who are now called kings and potentates, be imbued with a sufficient measure of genuine philosophy, that is to say, unless political power and philosophy be united in the same person, most of those minds which at present pursue one to the exclusion of the other being peremptorily debarred from either, there will be no deliverance, my dear Glaucon, for cities, nor yet, I believe, for the human race; neither can the commonwealth, which we have now sketched in theory, ever till then grow into a possibility, and see the light of day. But a consciousness how entirely this would contradict the common opinion made me all along so reluctant to give expression to it: for it is difficult to see that there is no other way by which happiness can be attained, by the state or by the individual.

Whereupon Glaucon remarked: The language and sentiments, Socrates, to which you have just given utterance, are of such a nature, that you may expect large numbers

of by no means contemptible assailants to rush desperately
upon you without a moment's delay, after throwing off their
upper garments, as it were, and grasping, in that state, the
first offensive weapon that comes in their way, to do signal
execution upon you: so that if you fail to repel them with the
weapons of argument, and make your escape, you will certainly
suffer the penalty of being well jeered.

Well, I said, was it not you that brought all this upon me?

Yes, and I did quite right. But I promise not to desert
you; on the contrary, I will assist you with the weapons at
my disposal, which are, good-will and encouragement; and
perhaps in my answers I may shew more address than another.
Therefore, relying on this assistance, endeavour to shew to the
incredulous that what you say is true.

I must make the attempt, I said, since you offer me such a
valuable alliance. Now, if we are to have a chance of escaping
from the assailants you speak of, I think it essential to give
them our definition of 'philosophers,' and shew whom we
mean, when we venture to assert that such persons ought
to govern; in order that, their character having been made
thoroughly apparent, we may be able to defend ourselves by
demonstrating that it is the natural province of these men
to embrace philosophy, and take the lead in a state, and the
province of all others to let philosophy alone, and follow the
lead of the former . . .

[***]

Then can you find any fault with an employment which
requires of a man who would pursue it satisfactorily, that nature
shall have given him a retentive memory, and made him quick
at learning, lofty-minded and graceful, the friend and brother
of truth, justice, fortitude, and temperance?

No, he replied; the very Genius of criticism could find no
fault with such an employment.

Well, can you hesitate to entrust such characters with the sole management of state affairs, when time and education have made them ripe for the task?

Here Adeimantus interposed and said; It is true, Socrates, that no one can dispute these conclusions; but still, every time that such theories are propounded by you, the hearers feel certain misgivings of the following kind. They fancy that, from want of practice in your method of question and answer, they are at each question led a little astray by the reasoning, until, at the close of the discussion, these little divergences are found to amount to a serious false step, which makes them contradict their original notions. And, as unskilful draught-players are in the end hemmed into a corner by the skilful, till they cannot make a move, just in the same way your hearers conceive themselves to be at last hemmed in and reduced to silence by this novel kind of draughts, played with words instead of counters. For they are not at all the more convinced that the conclusion to which they are brought is the true one. And, in saying this, I have the present occasion before my eye. For at this moment a person will tell you, that though at each question he cannot oppose you with words, yet in practice he sees that all the students of philosophy, who have devoted themselves to it for any length of time, instead of taking it up for educational purposes and relinquishing it while still young, in most cases become exceedingly eccentric, not to say quite depraved, while even those who appear the most respectable are notwithstanding so far the worse for the pursuit which you commend, that they become useless to their country.

When he had said this, I replied;—Then do you think this objection untrue?

I am not sure, he answered; but I should be glad to hear what you think of it.

Let me tell you, that I hold it to be a true objection.

How then can it be right to assert that the miseries of our cities will find no relief, until those philosophers who, on our own admission, are useless to them, become their rulers?

You are asking a question, I replied, which I must answer by the help of an illustration.

And you, I suppose, have not been in the habit of employing illustrations.

Ah! you rally me, do you, now that you have got me upon a subject in which demonstration is so difficult? However, listen to the illustration, that you may see still better how stingy I am with the work. So cruel is the position in which those respectable men are placed, in reference to their states, that there is no single thing whose position is analogous to theirs. Consequently I have to collect materials from several quarters for the imaginary case which I am to use in their defence, like painters when they paint goat-stags and similar monsters.

Figure to yourself a fleet, or a single ship, in which the state of affairs on board is as follows. The captain, you are to suppose, is taller and stronger than any of the crew, but rather deaf, and rather short-sighted, and correspondingly deficient in nautical skill; and the sailors are quarrelling together about the pilotage,—each of them thinking he has a right to steer the vessel, although up to that moment he has never studied the art, and cannot name his instructor, or the time when he served his apprenticeship; more than this, they assert that it is a thing which positively cannot be taught, and are even ready to tear in pieces the person who affirms that it can: meanwhile they Crowd incessantly round the person of the captain, begging and beseeching him with every importunity to entrust the helm to them; and occasionally, failing to persuade him, while others succeed better, these disappointed candidates kill their successful rivals, or fling them overboard, and, after binding the high-spirited captain hand and foot with mandragora or strong drink, or disabling him by some other contrivance, they remain masters of the ship, and apply its contents to their own purposes, and pass their time at sea in drinking and feasting, as you might expert with such a crew; and besides all this, they compliment with the title of 'able seaman,' 'excellent pilot,' 'skilful navigator,' any sailor that can second them cleverly in either persuading or forcing the captain into installing them in command of the ship, while they condemn as useless every one whose talents are of a different order,—having no notion that the true pilot must devote his attention to the year and its seasons, to the sky, and the stars, and the winds, and all that concerns his art, if he intends to be really fit to command a ship; and thinking it impossible to acquire and practise, along with the pilot's art, the art of maintaining the pilot's authority whether some of the crew like it or not. Such being the state of things on board, do you not think that the pilot who is really master of his craft is sure to be called a useless, star-gazing babbler by the mariners who form the crews of ships so circumstanced?

Yes, that he will, replied Adeimantus.

Well, said I, I suppose you do not require to see my illustration passed in review, to remind you that it is a true picture of our cities in so far as their disposition towards philosophers is concerned; on the contrary, I think you understand my meaning.

Yes, quite.

That being the case, when a person expresses his astonishment that philosophers are not respected in our cities, begin by telling him our illustration, and endeavour to persuade him that it would be far more astonishing if they were respected.

Well, I will.

And go on to tell him that[1] he is right in saying that the most respectable of the proficients in philosophy are of no use to the world; only recommend him to lay the fault of it not on these good people themselves, but upon those who decline

---

[1]   Reading τἀληθῆ λέγει.

their services. For it is not in the nature of things that a pilot should petition the sailors to submit to his authority, or that the wise should wait at the rich man's door. No, the author of that witticism was wrong: for the real truth is, that, just as a sick man, be he rich or poor, must attend at the physician's door, so all who require to be governed must attend at the gate of him who is able to govern,—it being against nature that the ruler, supposing him to be really good for anything, should have to entreat his subjects to submit to his rule. In fact, you will not be wrong, if you compare the statesmen of our time to the sailors whom we were just now describing, and the useless visionary talkers, as they are called by our politicians, to the veritable pilots.

You are perfectly right.

Under these circumstances, and amongst men like these, it is not easy for that noblest of occupations to be in good repute with those to whose pursuits it is directly opposed. But far the most grievous and most obstinate misconstruction, under which Philosophy labours, is due to her professed followers; who are doubtless the persons meant by the accuser of Philosophy, when he declares, as you tell us, that most of those who approach her are utterly depraved, while even her best pupils are useless:—to the truth of which remark I assented, did I not?

Yes, you did.

We have explained the reason why the good are useless, have we not?

Certainly we have.

Would you have us proceed next to discuss the question, why the majority are inevitably depraved, and to endeavour to shew, if we can, that of this also philosophy is guiltless?

Yes, by all means.

[***]

At present, those who pursue philosophy at all are mere striplings just emerged from boyhood, who take it up in the intervals of housekeeping and business; and, after just dipping into the most abstruse part of the study, (by which I mean Dialectic), abandon the pursuit altogether, and these are the most advanced philosophers; and ever afterwards, if, on being invited, they consent to listen to others whose attention is devoted to it, they think it a great condescension, because they imagine that philosophy ought to be made a mere secondary occupation; and on the approach of old age, all but a very few are extinguished far more effectually than the sun of Heracleitus[2], inasmuch as they are not, like it, rekindled.

And pray what is the right plan? he asked.

Just the opposite. In youth and boyhood they ought to be put through a course of training in philosophy, suited to their years; and while their bodies are growing up to manhood, especial attention should be paid to them, as a serviceable acquisition in the cause of philosophy. At the approach of that period, during which the mind begins to attain its maturity, the mental exercises ought to be rendered more severe. Finally, when their bodily powers begin to fail, and they are released from public duties and military service, from that time forward they ought to lead a dedicated life, and consecrate themselves to this one pursuit, if they are to live happily on earth, and after death to crown the life they have led with a corresponding destiny in another world.

Well, indeed, Socrates, I do not doubt your zeal. But I expect most of your hearers, beginning with Thrasymachus, to oppose you with still greater zeal, and express their unqualified dissent.

Do not make a quarrel between me and Thrasymachus, when we have just become friends;—though I do not mean to say that we were enemies before. I shall leave nothing untried, until I have either won him over to my way of thinking, along with the rest, or have achieved something for their good in that

---

2   Heracleitus is said to have believed that the sun was extinguished every evening and rekindled every morning.

future state, should they ever happen, in a second existence, to encounter similar discussions.

Truly a trifling adjournment! he exclaimed.

Rather speak of it as a nothing, compared with all time. However, it need not surprise us that most people disbelieve in my doctrines; for they have never yet seen our present theory realized. No, what is much more likely is, that they have met with proposals somewhat resembling ours, but forced expressly into appearing of a piece with one another, instead of falling spontaneously into agreement, as in the present case. They have never yet seen, in either one or more instances, a man moulded into the most perfect possible conformity and likeness to virtue, both in words and in works, reigning in a state as perfect as himself. Or do you think they have?

No, indeed I do not.

And further, my dear friend, they have not listened often enough to discussions of an elevated and liberal tone, confined to the strenuous investigation of truth by all possible means, simply for the sake of knowing it; and which therefore will, both in private disquisitions and in public trials, keep at a respectful distance from those subtleties and special pleadings, whose sole aim it is to prolong debate, and elicit applause.

You are right again.

It was for these reasons, and in anticipation of these results, that, notwithstanding my fears, I was constrained by the force of truth on a former occasion to assert, that no state, or constitution, or individual either, can ever become perfect, until these few philosophers, who are at present described as useless though not depraved, find themselves accidentally compelled, whether they like it or not, to accept the charge of a state, which in its turn finds itself compelled to be obedient[3] to them; or until the present sovereigns and kings, or their sons, are divinely inspired with a genuine love of genuine philosophy. Now to assert the impossibility of both or either

---

[3]   Reading κατηκόω.

of these contingencies, I for my part pronounce irrational. If they are impossible, we may fairly be held up to derision as mere visionary theorists. Am I not right?

You are.

If, then, persons of first-rate philosophical attainments, either in the countless ages that are past have been, or in some foreign clime, far beyond the limits of our horizon, at the present moment are, or hereafter shall be, constrained by some fate to undertake the charge of a state, I am prepared to argue to the death in defence of this assertion, that the constitution described has existed, does exist, yea and will exist, wherever the Muse aforesaid has become mistress of a state. For its realization is no impossibility, nor are our speculations impractical; though their difficulty is even by us acknowledged.

THOMAS CARLYLE

1795-1881

On Heroes, Hero-Worship, and the Heroic in History

1966 (Original work published 1841)

Thomas Carlyle was a Scottish Victorian-era essayist, satirist, and historian. His belief in the importance of heroic leadership was developed in his book *On Heroes, Hero-Worship, and the Heroic in History,* in which he compared different types of heroes, who flourished by using creative energy in the face of difficulty.

Carlyle (1966) believed that government should come from those most able: "Find in any country the Ablest Man that exists there; raise him to the supreme place, and loyally reverence him: you have a perfect government for that country; no ballot-box, parliamentary eloquence, voting, constitution-building, or other machinery whatsoever can improve it a whit. It is in the perfect state; an ideal country" (p. 197). Also Carlyle (1966) said, "Universal History the history of what man has accomplished in this world, is at bottom the History of the Great Men who have worked here . . . All things that we see standing accomplished in the world are . . . the other material result . . . of Thoughts." (p. 1).

In the series of lectures found in his book, Carlyle alternately construed the hero as a divinity, prophet, poet, priest, man of letters, and king. The following selection focuses on the leader as divine. Any one of these portraits of heroism could have been chosen as a means of illustrating Carlyle's "great man" perspective of leadership.

Source:

Carlyle, T. (1966). *On heroes, hero-worship, and the heroic in history.* Lincoln: University of Nebraska Press. (Original work published 1841.)

Selection from:

Carlyle, T. (1966). *On heroes, hero-worship, and the heroic in history.* (pp. 24-26, 28). Lincoln: University of Nebraska Press. (Original work published 1841.)

Lecture 1
The Hero as Divinity

[***]

How the man Odin came to be considered a *god*, the chief god?—that surely is a question which nobody would wish to dogmatise upon. I have said, his people knew no *limits* to their admiration of him; they had as yet no scale to measure admiration by. Fancy your own generous heart's-love of some greatest man expanding till it *transcended* all bounds, till it filled and overflowed the whole field of your thought! Or what if this man Odin,—since a great deep soul, with the afflatus and mysterious tide of vision and impulse rushing on him he knows not whence, is ever an enigma, a kind of terror and wonder to himself,—should have felt that perhaps *he* was divine; that he was some effluence of the 'Wuotan', '*Movement,*' Supreme Power and Divinity, of whom to his rapt vision all Nature was the awful Flame-image; that some effluence of *Wuotan* dwelt here in him! He was not necessarily false; he was but mistaken, speaking the truest he knew. A great soul, any sincere soul, knows not what he is, —alternates between the highest height and the lowest depth; can, of all things, the least measure— Himself! What others take him for, and what he guesses that he may be; these two items strangely act on one another, help to determine one another. With all men reverently admiring him; with his own wild soul full of noble ardours and affections, of whirlwind chaotic darkness and glorious new light; a divine Universe bursting all into godlike beauty round him, and no man to whom the like ever had befallen, what could he think himself to be? 'Wuotan?' All men answered, 'Wuotan!'—

And then consider what mere Time will do in such cases; how if a man was great while living, he becomes tenfold greater when dead. What an enormous *camera-obscura* magnifier is Tradition! How a thing grows in the human Memory, in the human Imagination, when love, worship, and all that lies in the human Heart, is there to encourage it. And in the darkness, in the entire ignorance; without date or document, no book, no Arundel-marble; only here and there some dumb monumental cairn. Why, in thirty or forty years, were there no books, any great man would grow *mythic*, the contemporaries who had seen him, being once all dead. And in three-hundred years, and in three-thousand years—!—To attempt *theorising* on such matters would profit little: they are matters which refuse to be *theoremed* and diagramed; which Logic ought to know that she *cannot* speak of. Enough for us to discern, far in the uttermost distance, some gleam as of a small real light shining in the centre of that enormous camera-obscura image; to discern that the centre of it all was not a madness and nothing, but a sanity and something.

[***]

To me there is something very touching in this primeval figure of Heroism; in such artless, helpless, but hearty entire reception of a Hero by his fellow-men. Never so helpless in shape, it is the noblest of feelings, and a feeling in some shape or other perennial as man himself. If I could show in any measure, what I feel deeply for a long time now, That it is the vital element of manhood, the soul of man's history here in our world,—it would be the chief use of this discoursing at present. We do not now call our great men Gods, nor admire *without* limit; ah no, *with* limit enough! But if we have no great men, or do not admire at all,—that were a still worse case.

JAMES MACGREGOR BURNS

1918-

Leadership

1978

James MacGregor Burns is a recognized pioneer and authority on leadership studies. The Academy of Leadership at the University of Maryland bears his name in honor of his many contributions in leadership studies, political science, as well as his work as a presidential biographer. He received a Pulitzer Prize and National Book Award in 1971 for *Roosevelt: Soldier of Freedom 1940-1945*. He is an *emeritus* professor of political science at Williams College.

Burns' important contributions in the theory of leadership include his focus on the traits of great men, on transactional or contractual leadership, and on the interaction of leaders and followers to their mutual benefit. He is an early contributor to an influential theory of leadership—transformational leadership: Wrote Burns (1978), "[Transformational] leadership occurs when one or more persons *engage* with others in such a way that leaders and followers raise one another to higher levels of motivation and morality" (20). In the piece found in this volume, Burns contemplates when leadership **is not** leadership.

Source:

James MacGregor Burns. Retrieved from http://www.
jamesmacgregorburns.com/
Burns, J. M. (1978). The power of leadership. In *Leadership.*
(p. 20). New York: Harper & Row.

Selection from:

Burns, J. M. (1978). The power of leadership. In *Leadership.*
(pp. 23-28). New York: Harper & Row.

THE POWER OF LEADERSHIP
What Leadership Is Not: Closing the Intellectual Gap

It may seem puzzling that after centuries of experience
with rulers as power wielders, with royal and ecclesiastical
and military authority, humankind should have made such
limited progress in developing propositions about *leadership*—propositions that focus on the role of the ruled, the
power recipients, and the followers. The first, and primary,
explanation lies in a blind alley in the history of political
thought; a second, in an inadequacy of empirical data. Plato's
parable of the ship epitomizes the first.

"Imagine then," said Plato, "a fleet or a ship in which there
is a captain who is taller and stronger than any of the crew, but
he is a little deaf and has a similar infirmity in sight, and his
knowledge of navigation is not much better." A furious quarrel
breaks out among the crew; everyone thinks he has a right
to steer, no matter how untrained in navigation. The sailors
throng around the captain, begging him to commit the helm
to them; when he refuses, they take over the ship and make
free with the stores. "Him who is their partisan and cleverly
aids them in their plot . . . they compliment with the name of
sailor, pilot, able seaman . . . but that the true pilot must pay
attention to the year and seasons and sky and wind . . . and that

he must and will be the steerer, whether other people like it or not—the possibility of this union of authority with the steerer's art has never seriously entered into their thoughts . . ." And the true pilot, Plato added, would be dismissed as a prater, a stargazer, a good-for-nothing.

Plato was apotheosizing a certain kind of authority—that of the true philosopher, artist, expert. Yet in derogating the sailors who would dismiss the navigator he was defending the status of philosopher-kings and of those in their courts. He was also ignoring the rightful concerns of the crew—their suspicion of experts, their difficulties with *this* expert, their doubts about *his* destination for the ship, their own needs and aspirations and destinations. For centuries after Plato his kind of expert embodied authority, but scientific revolutions later brought much learned authority under attack. It was discovered that captains and navigators pretended to an intellectual authority that often turned out to be false. Doctors and scientists and theologians are still treated as "authority" though their expertise may be challenged, their doctrines overturned, and the purposes to which they lend their expertise may be found to diverge from the public's own purposes.

For philosophers and kings, however, authority came to stand for much more than expertise. It was the intellectual and often the legal buttress of the power of the father in the family, the priest in the community, the feudal lord in the barony, the king in the nation-state, the Pope in Western Christendom. Authority was seen as deriving from God or, later, from the innate nature of man. Authority was even more fundamental than the state for it was the source and the legitimation of state power. In the tumultuous Western world the power of authority was the means of preserving order; it was necessary in an "unquiet world," Hooker said. It would compel men to regulate their conduct, Hobbes wrote. Church and state combined to furbish authority. It carried formal legitimacy, religious sanction, and physical force.

Typically authority was perceived and used as a *property*. Rulers were symbolically invested with authority through things—crowns, scepters, maces, scrolls, robes, badges. Such rulers were objects of awe for their subjects, until rivals seized the armaments of office or substituted their own. To the extent that authority was a *relationship* between monarch and subjects it was a relationship of gross inequality, of the ruler and the ruled. But authority was sharply distinguished from naked power, force, coercion. Rulers must be *legitimate*. They must inherit or assume office through carefully established procedures; they must assume certain responsibilities under God, and for the people.

Authority, in short, was legitimated power. But it was legitimated by tradition, religious sanction, rights of succession, and procedures, not by mandate of the people. Authority was quite one-sided. Rulers had the right to command, subjects the obligation to obey. Only a few complained. The fundamental need of the people was for order and security; obedience seemed a fair exchange for survival. In the seventeenth and eighteenth centuries, however, the concept of authority was undermined. Thinkers and preachers, riding new intellectual currents of innovation and iconoclasm, rebelled against the old canons of authority that were founded so often in the past, the dead, or the patriarchs. Spreading through Europe and America, powerful new doctrines proclaimed the rights of individuals against rulers, set forth goals and values beyond those of simple order or security, and called for liberty, equality, fraternity, even the pursuit of happiness.

Authority did not crumble under the impact of these forces; revolutionary disturbances and excesses like the French terror confirmed its importance. But it could not be re-established on the old foundations, for now it was supposed to be derived from the people and hence ultimately lie in their hands—at least in the hands of those people who were not poor, slaves, or women. A new secular basis of authority was needed: In response, the old "substantive" authority gave way to procedural. Since the citizenry now embodied authority, since the people had to be protected against themselves, and since authority had to be protected against shifting majorities and volatile popular movements, constitutions were adopted to safeguard the people against themselves. Under the constitutions, authority was concentrated in judges, legislative upper chambers, local governments, in doctrines of due process, protection of property, and in judicial review.

The upshot was this: the doctrine of authority came into the modern age devitalized, fragmentized, and trivialized; it became a captive of the right, even of fascism. Mussolini substituted authority, order, and justice for liberty, equality, fraternity. Hannah Arendt in this century could mourn that the entire concept of leadership had lost its validity; almost everyone could agree that the concept had been emptied of meaning and definition. The loss was not simply of a stricken concept—doctrines, like empires, grow, flourish, and decline—but of authority that was not transformed into a doctrine suitable for the new age. No new, democratized, and radicalized doctrine arose to salvage the authentic and the relevant in authority and link these strengths to a doctrine of leadership that recognized the vital need for qualities of integrity, authenticity, initiative, and moral resolve. Max Weber, Carl Friedrich, and others tried to pump new vitality and relevance into the concept, without marked success; Vilfredo Pareto's famous concept of the "circulation of the elites" focused chiefly on the problem of bringing fresh talent or expertise to the top. They, like the shapers of the grand tradition in earlier centuries, typically looked at the ruler-ruled relationship from the top down, not upward from the peasant's sward or the worker's bench. In the end, in a more democratic age, authority was never turned on its head.

The resulting intellectual gap—that is, the absence of a doctrine of leadership with the power and sweep of the old doctrine of authority but now emphasizing the influence of followers on leaders—was especially evident in America. The pilgrims' voyage to Plymouth in 1620 has been contrasted with Plato's parable of the ship most arrestingly by Norman Jacobson. The goal of the settlers was Virginia but they lost their way. Facing rebellion, and with their authority undermined, the leaders had to grant the demands of the rest of the party for a compact among all the members. Under this declaration no person or group was empowered to assume authority, nor was any one person seen as commanding special expertise. The compact idea was restated in the Declaration of Independence. By the time of the constitutional convention of 1787, however, in the wake of Shays' rebellion in Massachusetts, the Federalist leadership had become fearful of popular unrest and of electoral majorities that represented the turbulent masses. Under the new constitution, authority was derived from the people, but direct popular action was frustrated by an elaborate system of federalism, separation of powers, and checks and balances.

What would happen in a nation that made the people sovereign, that elevated Jeffersonian and Jacksonian and Lincolnian leaders who orated about government by the people, but a nation that hedged in popular majorities *and their leaders* with checks and balances that constituted probably the most elaborate and well-calculated barriers in constitutional history? As usual, the Americans tried to have the best of both ways. They maintained their system of restraints on leaders almost intact, but they encouraged the emergence of a powerful executive, especially in the twentieth century. American Marxists contended that not leaders but technicians—simple administrative functionaries, in Engels' words, "watching over the true interests of society"—would run the state. American Progressives looked on leadership as "bossism" and sponsored successfully such anti-leadership devices as the initiative, referendum and recall, and the destruction of parties. The failure was also intellectual. Historians and political scientists admired individual leaders, especially Presidents, who could break through legislative and judicial barriers. Some of them—notably Woodrow Wilson—moralized about the need for leaders in education and politics. No one advanced a grand theory of *leadership*.

Perhaps such a theory was impossible in any event, in the absence of hard and detailed data about the people, the public, the masses, the voters, the followers. Earlier thinkers had by no means ignored the psychology of the ruler's subjects. Hobbes and Locke, Rousseau and Bentham, and others, had offered some remarkable insights into human nature. These insights were based on observation and speculation, not on scientific data. In recent decades advances in theories of opinion formation, the revolution in the technique and technology of analyzing public attitudes, aspirations and goals in depth, and above all the impressive work of psychologists in analyzing the formation, structure, qualities, and change in persons' opinions, attitudes, values, wants, needs, and aspirations, have made possible an understanding of followers' response to leadership impossible only half a century ago. Cross-cultural research and analysis in popular motives and values at last permits us to avoid parochial notions of authority and power and to identify broad patterns of leadership-followership interaction as part of a broader concept of social causation. At last we can hope to close the intellectual gap between the fecund canons of authority and a new and general theory of leadership.

Such a general theory demands the best of several disciplines. Historians and biographers typically focus on the "unique" person with more or less idiosyncratic qualities and traits confronting particular sets of problems and situations over time. Psychologists scrutinize genetic factors, early intrafamily relationships, widening arcs of personal interaction, changing constellations of attitudes and motivations. Sociologists view the developing personality as it moves through a series of social contexts—family, school, neighborhood, workplace—and undergoes powerful socializing forces in the process. Political scientists emphasize the social and political institutions impinging on developing leaders, changes in political leaders as they learn from their experience, the eventual impact of leadership on policy and on history. And most of these various investigators wander into one another's fields, pouncing on insights, borrowing data, filching concepts.

We, too, will poach as required, but the initial emphasis will be heavily dependent on theories of personality development. As a political scientist I am sensitive to the impact of social and political entities—of homes, schools, regimens, constitutions, and political systems. I see that leaders operate in many contexts for many purposes. Why then is my central emphasis on "psychology"? The principal limitation of institutional or systemic analysis is that the kind of transferability of power or leadership that we can assess in gross terms (the influence of Indian Brahmins, the electoral power of a steel union, the discipline of the British Labour party) is not directly transferable to the calculating of influences on, or the influence of, particular leaders at particular times in particular circumstances. The power of the institution must be translated into discernible forces that immediately influence the behavior of leaders. In the past the exercise has often been fruitless because we lacked deep understanding of motivational forces. Modern developmental theory and data can help us to grasp the psychological forces immediately working on or in leaders and the dynamic psychological factors moving persons to new levels of motivation and morality.

The study of leadership in general will be advanced by looking at leaders in particular. The development of certain leaders or rulers is described not in order to "solve" leadership problems or necessarily to predict what kind of leader a person might become, but to raise questions inherent in the complexity of leadership processes. In singling out, among others, four twentieth-century "makers of history," Woodrow Wilson, Mahatma Gandhi, Nikolai Lenin, and Adolf Hitler—the first two of these leaders in my sense, the third a leader whose theory of leadership had a fatal flaw, the fourth an absolute wielder of brutal power—we can compare the origins and development of four men who took different routes to power and exercised power in different ways. We will note in these cases and others that authoritarian rulers can emerge from relatively benign circumstances, and democratic leaders from less benign ones. This will only enhance our sense of humility, complexity, and mystery (useful intellectual inhibitions in the explorations of leadership).

We might also note, in shunning simplistic theories, that the German crown prince who was endlessly mortified and savagely punished by his wrathful father grew up to be Frederick the Great, one of the most masterful—by contemporary standards—constructive and successful rulers in recent times. He who had been abused by power bore it with equanimity. "The passions of princes," Frederick wrote toward the end, "are restrained only by exhaustion."

WARREN BENNIS

1925-

On Becoming a Leader

1989

Warren Bennis is widely regarded as a pioneer in leadership studies. A one-time MIT professor and former president of the University of Cincinnati, Bennis has also served as advisor to four presidents of the United States. As the Founding Chairman of the Leadership Institute at the University of Southern California, he currently serves as a Distinguished Professor of Business Administration. His book, *An Invented Life*, was nominated for a Pulitzer Prize. In the following reading, Bennis identifies some fundamental properties of leadership and distinguishes leadership from management.

Source:

University of Southern California Center for Excellence in Teaching: Distinguished Fellows, Warren Bennis (2008). Retrieved from http://cet.usc.edu/faculty/bennis.html.

Selection from:

Bennis, W. (1989). Understanding the basics. *On becoming a leader.* (pp. 44-51). Menlo Park: Addison-Wesley.

Chapter 2
Understanding the Basics

[***]

Leaders, Not Managers

I tend to think of the differences between leaders and managers as the differences between those who master the context and those who surrender to it. There are other differences, as well, and they are enormous and crucial:

- The manager administers; the leader innovates.
- The manager is a copy; the leader is an original.
- The manager maintains; the leader develops.
- The manager focuses on systems and structure; the leader focuses on people.
- The manager relies on control; the leader inspires trust.
- The manager has a short-range view; the leader has a long-range perspective.
- The manager asks how and when; the leader asks what and why.
- The manager has his eye always on the bottom line; the leader has his eye on the horizon.
- The manager imitates; the leader originates.
- The manager accepts the status quo; the leader challenges it.

- The manager is the classic good soldier; the leader is his own person.
- The manager does things right; the leader does the right thing.

To reprise Wallace Stevens, managers wear square hats and learn through training. Leaders wear sombreros and opt for education. Consider the differences between training and education:

EDUCATION	TRAINING
inductive	deductive
tentative	firm
dynamic	static
understanding	memorizing
ideas	facts
broad	narrow
deep	surface
experiential	rote
active	passive
questions	answers
process	content
strategy	tactics
alternatives	goal
exploration	prediction
discovery	dogma
active	reactive
initiative	direction
whole brain	left brain
life	job
long-term	short-term

change	stability
content	form
flexible	rigid
risk	rules
synthesis	thesis
open	closed
imagination	common sense

THE SUM: LEADER   MANAGER

If the list on the left seems strange to you, it's because that isn't the way we are usually taught. Our educational system is really better at training than educating. And that's unfortunate. Training is good for dogs, because we require obedience from them. In people, all it does is orient them toward the bottom line.

The list on the left is of all the qualities that business schools don't encourage, as they opt for the short-run, profit-maximizing, microeconomic bottom line. Bottom lines have nothing to do with problem-finding. And we need people who know how to find problems, because the ones we face today aren't always clearly defined, and they aren't linear. Modern architects are moving away from the divinity of the right angle to rhomboids, to rounded spaces and parabolas. For a leader to develop the necessary competencies, he must start to think about rhomboids.

Leaders have nothing but themselves to work with. It is one of the paradoxes of life that good leaders rise to the top in spite of their weakness, while bad leaders rise because of their weakness. Abraham Lincoln was subject to fits of serious depression, yet he was perhaps this country's best president, guiding this country through its most severe crisis. On the other hand, Hitler imposed his psychosis on the German people, leading them through delusions of grandeur into the vilest madness and most horrific slaughter the world has ever known.

What is true for leaders is, for better or for worse, true for each of us: we are our own raw material. Only when we know what we're made of and what we want to make of it can we begin our lives—and we must do it despite an unwitting conspiracy of people and events against us. It's that tension in the national character again. As Norman Lear put it, "On the one hand, we're a society that seems to be proud of individuality. On the other hand, we don't really tolerate real individuality. We want to homogenize it."

For Oscar-winning movie director Sydney Pollack, the search for self-knowledge is a continuing process. "There's a sort of monologue or dialogue going on in my head all the time," he said. "Some of it's part of a fantasy life, some is exploratory. Sometimes I can trick myself into problem-solving by imagining myself talking about problem-solving. If I don't know the answer to something, I imagine being asked the question in my head. Faulkner said, 'I don't know what I think until I read what I said.' That's not just a joke. You learn what you think by codifying your thinking in some way."

That's absolutely true. Codifying one's thinking is an important step in inventing oneself. The most difficult way to do it is by thinking about thinking—it helps to speak or write your thoughts. Writing is the most profound way of codifying your thoughts, the best way of learning from yourself who you are and what you believe.

Newspaper editor Gloria Anderson added, "It's vital for people to develop their own sense of themselves and their role in the world, and it's equally vital for them to try new things, to test themselves and their beliefs and principles. I think we long for people who will stand up for what they believe, even if we don't agree with them, because we have confidence in such people."

Scientist Mathilde Krim agreed. "One must be a good explorer and a good listener, too, to take in as much as possible but not swallow anything uncritically. One must finally trust his own gut reactions," she said. "A value system, beliefs, are important so you know where you stand, but they must be your own values, not someone else's."

If knowing yourself and being yourself were as easy to do as to talk about, there wouldn't be nearly so many people walking around in borrowed postures, spouting secondhand ideas, trying desperately to fit in rather than to stand out. Former Lucky Stores CEO Don Ritchey said, on the need for being oneself, "I believe people spot phonies in very short order, whether that be on an individual basis or a company basis. As Emerson says, 'What you are speaks so loudly I cannot hear what you say.'"

Once Born, Twice Born

Harvard professor Abraham Zaleznik posits that there are two kinds of leaders: once-borns and twice-borns. The once-born's transition from home and family to independence is relatively easy. Twice-borns generally suffer as they grow up, feel different, even isolated, and so develop an elaborate inner life. As they grow older, they become truly independent, relying wholly on their own beliefs and ideas. Leaders who are twice born are inner-directed, self-assured, and, as a result, truly charismatic, according to Zaleznik.

Once-borns, then, have been invented by their circumstances, as in the case of Johnson, Nixon, and Carter, while twice-borns have invented themselves, as in the case of Roosevelt and Truman.

A couple of studies underscore the benefits, even the necessity, of self-invention. First, middle-aged men tend to change careers after having heart attacks. Faced with their own mortality, these men realize that what they've been doing, what they've invested their lives in, is not an accurate reflection of their real needs and desires.

Another study indicates that what determines the level of satisfaction in post-middle-aged men is the degree to which they acted upon their youthful dreams. It's not so much whether they were successful in achieving their dreams as the honest pursuit of them that counts. The spiritual dimension in creative effort comes from that honest pursuit.

There is, of course, evidence that women, too, are happier when they've invented themselves instead of accepting without question the roles they were brought up to play. Psychologist and author Sonya Friedman said, "The truth of the matter is that the most emotionally disturbed women are those who are married and into traditional full-time, lifetime homemaker roles. Single women have always been happier than married women. Always. And there isn't a study that has disproved that."

Staying single has historically been the only way most women were free to invent themselves. Nineteenth-century poet Emily Dickinson, a reclusive woman who never married and who surely invented herself, is supposed to have said to one of the rare visitors to her room, "Here is freedom!"

Fortunately, the changing times have meant changes in relationships, too. Many of the women leaders I talked with have managed to invent themselves even though married—as has Friedman herself.

I cannot stress too much the need for self-invention. To be authentic is literally to be your own author (the words derive from the same Greek root), to discover your own native energies and desires, and then to find your own way of acting on them. When you've done that, you are not existing simply in order to live up to an image posited by the culture or by some other authority or by a family tradition. When you write your own life, then no matter what happens, you have played the game that was natural for you to play. If, as someone said, "it is the supervisor's role in a modern industrial society to limit the potential of the people who work for him," then it is your task to do whatever you must to break out of such limits and live up to your potential, to keep the covenant with your youthful dreams.

Norman Lear would add to this that the goal isn't worth arriving at unless you enjoy the journey. "You have to look at success incrementally," he said. "It takes too long to get to any major success . . . If one can look at life as being successful on a moment-by-moment basis, one might find that most of it is successful. And take the bow inside for it. When we wait for the big bow, it's a lousy bargain. They don't come but once in too long a time."

Applauding yourself for the small successes, and taking the small bow, are good ways of learning to experience life each moment that you live it. And that's part of inventing yourself, of creating your own destiny.

To become a leader, then, you must become yourself, become the maker of your own life. While there are no rules for doing this, there are some lessons I can offer from my decade of observation and study. And we'll turn to those lessons now.

BARBARA KELLERMAN

1939-

Bad Leadership
What It Is, How It Happens, Why It Matters

2004

Barbara Kellerman is the James MacGregor Burns Lecturer in Public Leadership at Harvard University's John F. Kennedy School of Government. She previously taught at Fordham, Tufts, Fairleigh Dickinson, George Washington, and Uppsala Universities, and she was the director of the Center for the Advanced Study of Leadership at the James MacGregor Burns Academy of Leadership at the University of Maryland in 1998. At Maryland, she helped establish the International Leadership Association. She also authored *Reinventing Leadership: Making the Connection between Politics and Business*, which provided a bridge between business and political leadership; this work has been prescient in urging leaders from all sectors to work together to solve the nation's problems. In the following selection, Kellerman explores the dark side of leadership.

Source:

Harvard Kennedy School. John F. Kennedy School of Government. (2009). *Barbara Kellerman.* Retrieved from http://www.

hks.harvard.edu/about/faculty-staff-directory/barbara-kellerman

Selection from:

Kellerman, B. (2004). Claiming the bad side. In *Bad leadership what it is, how it happens, why it matters*. (pp. 3-14). Boston: Harvard Business School Press.

CHAPTER ONE
CLAIMING THE BAD SIDE

WHEN HE WAS INSTALLED as president of Harvard University in October 2001, Lawrence Summers delivered a speech in which he declared that "in this new century, nothing will matter more than the education of future leaders and the development of new ideas."[1] In this single sentence the new head of Harvard made at least two important assumptions: that people can be educated in ways that relate to being leaders, and in ways that relate to being *good* leaders.

This kind of positive thinking explains why leadership education has become a big business. The "leadership industry"—so tagged because in recent years it has grown so big so fast—is dedicated to the proposition that leadership is a subject that should be studied and a skill that should be taught. To meet the burgeoning demand for leadership education and training, a cadre of experts has emerged. These leadership scholars, teachers, consultants, trainers, and coaches work on the optimistic assumption that to develop leaders is to develop a valuable human resource.

The academic work that supports the leadership industry generally shares this positive bias. The titles of many of the best and most popular leadership books of the past twenty

---

[1] Lawrence H. Summers, "Installation Address of Lawrence H. Summers," Harvard University, 12 October 2001.

years send messages that make the point. Targeted primarily at those in the corporate sector, they include Thomas J. Peters and Robert H. Waterman's *In Search of Excellence: Lessons from America's Best-Run Companies*;[2] Rosabeth Moss Kanter's *The Change Masters: Innovation & Entrepreneurship in the American Corporation*;[3] Warren Bennis and Burt Nanus's *Leaders: The Strategies for Taking Charge*;[4] John Kotter's *A Force for Change: How Leadership Differs from Management*;[5] Noel Tichy's *The Leadership Engine: How Winning Companies Build Leaders at Every Level*;[6] and Jay Conger and Beth Benjamin's *Building Leaders: How Successful Companies Develop the Next Generation.*[7] Each of these books assumes that people can learn to be leaders and that to be a leader is to be a person of competence and character.

Good cheer of this kind is in even greater evidence among those who write for the general public. Authors such as Steven Covey, Kenneth Blanchard, and Spencer Johnson continue to sell tens of millions of books that suggest that you too can learn how to be a (good) leader, and in no time flat.[8]

By now such optimism has come to pervade not only American schools of business but also American schools of government. On the reasonable assumption that if leadership education makes sense for graduate students entering the private sector, it also makes sense for those entering the

[2]   Thomas J. Peters and Robert H. Waterman Jr., *In Search of Excellence: Lessons from America's Best-Run Companies* (New York: Warner, 1982).

[3]   Rosabeth Moss Kanter, *The Change Masters: Innovation & Entrepreneurship in the American Corporation* (New York: Simon and Schuster, 1983).

[4]   Warren Bennis and Burt Nanus, *Leaders: The Strategies for Taking Charge* (New York: Harper & Row, 1985)

[5]   John P. Kotter, *A Force for Change: How Leadership Differs from Management* (New York: Free Press, 1990).

[6]   Noel Tichy with Eli Cohen, *The Leadership Engine: How Winning Companies Build Leaders at Every Level* (New York: Harper Business, 1997).

[7]   Jay Conger and Beth Benjamin, *Building Leaders: How Successful Companies Develop the Next Generation* (San Francisco: Jossey-Bass, 1999).

[8]   See, for example, Spencer Johnson and Kenneth Blanchard, *The One Minute Manager* (New York: Morrow, 1982).

public and nonprofit sectors, schools of government now offer courses on how to manage and how to lead. Moreover, even though bad political leadership is as ubiquitous as bad business leadership, the prevailing view of leadership is rather relentlessly positive. As John Gardner wrote in the first of a series of highly influential leadership essays, "In our culture popular understanding of the term [leadership] distinguishes it from coercion—and places higher on the scale of leadership those forms involving lesser degrees of coercion."[9]

In this book I argue that there's something odd about the idea that somehow leadership can be distinguished from coercion, as if leadership and power were unrelated. In the real world, in everyday life, we come into constant contact not only with good leaders and good followers doing good things but also with bad leaders and bad followers doing bad things. In fact, anyone not dwelling in a cave is regularly exposed, if only through the media, to people who exercise power, use authority, and exert influence in ways that are not good. Still, even after all the evidence is in—after the recent corporate scandals, after the recent revelations of wrongdoing by leaders of the Roman Catholic Church, and before, during, and after political leadership all over the world that is so abhorrent it makes us ill—the idea that some leaders and some followers are bad, and that they might have something in common with good leaders and followers, has not fully penetrated the conversation or the curriculum.

The positive slant is recent. Historically, political theorists have been far more interested in the question of how to control the proclivities of bad leaders than in the question of how to promote the virtues of good ones. Influenced by religious traditions that focused on good and evil, and often personally scarred by war and disorder, the best political thinkers have had rather a jaundiced view of human nature.

---

9   John Gardner, *Leadership Papers #1: The Nature of Leadership* (Washington, D.C.: Independent Sector, 1986), 6.

Machiavelli provides perhaps the best example. He did not wrestle with the idea of bad—as in coercive—leadership. He simply presumed it. He took it for granted that people do harm as well as good, and so his advice to princes, to leaders, was to be ruthless. Consider this morsel about how leaders should, if need be, keep followers in line: "Cruelties can be called well used (if it is permissible to speak well of evil) that are done at a stroke, out of the necessity to secure oneself, and then are not persisted in but are turned to as much utility for the subjects as one can. Those cruelties are badly used which, though few in the beginning, rather grow with time."[10]

As the Gardner quotation makes plain, today leaders who use coercion are generally judged to be bad. But to Machiavelli, the only kind of bad leader is the weak leader. Machiavelli was a pragmatist above all, familiar with the ways of the world and with a keen eye for the human condition. And so, to him, the judicious use of cruelty was an important arrow in the leader's quiver.

Although it seems counterintuitive, America's founders thought like Machiavelli, at least insofar as they also believed that people required restraint. They were products of the European Enlightenment, but as they saw it, their main task was to form a government that was for and by the people but that would simultaneously set limits on the body politic and on those who would lead it.

To be sure, the emphasis was different. Whereas Machiavelli was concerned primarily with the question of how to contain followers, the framers of the U.S. Constitution were concerned primarily with the question of how to contain leaders. Alexander Hamilton, for example, was, in comparison with his peers, a proponent of a strong executive. But even he considered it ideologically important as well as politically expedient to focus not on the possibilities of presidential power but on its limits.

---

[10] Niccolo Machiavelli, *The Prince* (Chicago: University of Chicago Press, 1998), 37, 38.

In *The Federalist Papers*, Hamilton acknowledged America's "aversion to monarchy"—to leaders who inherit great power. He dedicated an entire essay to distinguishing between the proposed president, on the one hand, and the distant, detested British monarchy, on the other, an essay that made one main point: The U.S. Constitution would absolutely preclude the possibility that bad leadership could become entrenched. The very idea of checks and balances grew out of the framers' presumption that unless there was a balance of power, power was certain to be abused. Put another way, the American political system is the product of revolutionaries familiar with, and therefore wary of, bad leadership.

But as sociologist Talcott Parsons observed, on matters that relate to the importance of power and authority in human affairs, American social thought has tended toward utopianism.[11] For whatever reasons, most students of politics shy away from the subject of bad leadership and especially from really bad leaders, such as Stalin and Pol Pot. In other words, no matter how great and obvious its impact on the course of human affairs, "tyranny as such is simply not an issue or a recognized term of analysis."[12]

The question is, why do we tend toward utopianism on matters relating to the importance of power and authority in human affairs?[13] Why do we avoid the subject of tyranny in our leadership

---

[11]   Talcott Parsons, introduction to *The Theory of Social and Economic Organization*, by Max Weber (Free Press, 1947), 36.

[12]   Mark Lilla, "The New Age of Tyranny," *The New York Review of Books*, 24 October 2002, 29.

[13]   There are some exceptions to this general rule. See, for example, Christine Clements and John B. Washbush, "The Two Faces of Leadership: Considering the Dark Side of Leader-Follower Dynamics," *Journal of Work-place Learning: Employee Counseling Today* 11, no. 5 (1999); M.F.R. Kets de Vries, *Prisoners of Leadership* (New York: John Wiley & Sons, 1989); *Leaders, Fools and Imposters: Essays on the Psychology of Leadership* (San Francisco: Jossey-Bass, 1993); *The Leadership Mystique: An Owner's Manual* (London: Pearson, 2001), especially chapters 4 and 7; Jean Lipman-Blumen, "Why Do We Tolerate Bad Leaders: Magnificent Uncertitude,

curricula, thereby presuming that tyrannical leadership is less relevant to the course of human affairs than democratic leadership? Why does the leadership industry generally assume that a bad leader such as Saddam Hussein has nearly nothing in common with a good leader such as Tony Blair, or that the Nazis were one species and the Americans another? Is Bernard Ebbers really so very different from Louis Gerstner Jr.? How did *leadership* come to be synonymous with *good* leadership?[14] Why are we afraid to acknowledge, much less admit to, the dark side? These are the questions to which I now turn.

The Light Side

We want to read books about good leaders such as John Adams, Jack Welch, and Nelson Mandela. We don't want to read books about bad leaders such as Warren Harding, David Koresh, and Robert Mugabe.

This preference is natural. We go through life accentuating the positive and eliminating the negative in order to be as healthy and happy as possible. As Daniel Goleman put it, "[O]ur emotional and physical well-being is based in part on artful denial and illusion." In other words, for us to cultivate an "unfounded sense of optimism" serves a purpose. It is in our self-interest.[15]

In the leadership industry, this disposition has now moved from the level of the individual to the level of the collective.

Anxiety, and Meaning" in *The Future of Leadership: Today's Top Leadership Thinkers Speak to Tomorrow's Leaders*, eds. Warren Bennis, Gretchen M. Spreitzer, and Thomas G. Cummings (San Franciso: Jossey-Bass, 2001), 125-138; and Craig E. Johnson, *Meeting the Ethical Challenges of Leadership: Casting Light or Shadow* (Thousand Oakes, CA: Sage, 2001).

14   Edward Rothstein, "Defining Evil in the Wake of 9/11," *New York Times*, 5 October 2002, B7.

15   Daniel J. Goleman, "What is Negative About Positive Illusions? When Benefits for the Individual Harm the Collective," *Journal of Social and Clinical Psychology* 8 (1989): 191.

Those of us engaged in leadership work seem almost to collude to avoid the elephant in the room—bad leadership.[16] We resist even considering the possibility that the dynamic between Franklin Delano Roosevelt and his most ardent followers had anything in common with the dynamic between Adolph Hitler and his most ardent followers; or that John Biggs, the admired former CEO of TIAA/CREF, has skills and capacities similar in some ways to those of Richard Scrushy, the disgraced former CEO of HealthSouth.

As we have seen, the human predisposition to denial and optimism does not stop everyone from assuming the role of the hard-nosed pragmatist. Machiavelli and Hamilton understood that the human animal cannot be relied on to be good, and they prescribed accordingly. So what happened in the recent past to explain why the leadership industry and the general public have become positively disposed?

Reason 1: The Use of Language

In 1978 James MacGregor Burns, a Pulitzer Prize-winning historian and political scientist of impeccable repute, published *Leadership*, a book now widely regarded as seminal. The time was right. Even in higher education, there was growing support for the idea that "great men" mattered; and in the wake of Vietnam and Watergate and the assassinations of John Kennedy, Robert Kennedy, and Martin Luther King, Jr., Americans were increasingly persuaded that there was a "crisis of leadership."

Because the book itself was impressive, because for decades there had been nearly no good work on leadership per se, and because *Leadership* was published just as questions about governance in America became urgent, Burns's work had considerable impact. In fact, his two types of leadership—transactional and

---

16   Eviatar Zerubavel, "The Elephant in the Room," in *Culture in Mind*, ed. Karen A. Cerulo (New York: Routledge, 2002), 21.

transformational—became part of the leadership lingo among those interested in both political and corporate leadership.

Thus the way in which Burns chose to define the words *leader* and *leadership* mattered. "Leadership over human beings is exercised when persons with certain motives and purposes mobilize . . . resources so as to arouse, engage, and satisfy the motives of followers," he wrote. "This is done in order to realize goals mutually held by leaders and followers." Burns was unwilling to call those who "obliterate" followers "leaders." Instead he labeled them "power wielders." "Power wielders," Burns argued, "may treat people as things. Leaders may not."[17]

The fact that Burns's book came out just when the leadership industry was beginning to grow also explains his strong impact on how people understood the word *leadership*. Even now it is Burns's particular definition of leadership—a definition that excludes leaders who, even though they may exercise power, authority, or influence, fail to "arouse, engage, and satisfy the motives of followers"—that dominates the field. Warren Bennis, one of the gurus of corporate leadership, has taken a semantic stance similar to Burns's. In the new (2003) introduction to his classic *On Becoming a Leader*, Bennis restates the position he took when the book was first published (1989): that leaders engage others by creating shared meaning, speaking in a distinctive voice, demonstrating the capacity to adapt, and having integrity. In other words, like Burns, Bennis generally assumes that to become a leader is to become a good leader.[18]

Reason 2: Business Trumps Everything Else

During the last quarter of the twentieth century the leadership industry developed primarily in response to the demands of American business. The reason was simple: By

---

[17]   James MacGregor Burns, *Leadership* (New York: Harper & Row, 1978), 18.

[18]   Warren Bennis, introduction to the revised edition, *On Becoming a Leader* (Cambridge, MA: Perseus, 2003,) xxi, xxii.

the mid-1970s, American business was in trouble. As Rosabeth Moss Kanter put it in *The Change Masters*, published in 1983, "Not long ago, American companies seemed to control the world in which they operated." Now, she went on, they were in a much scarier place, one in which factors such as the control of oil by OPEC, foreign competition (especially from Japan), inflation, and regulation "disturb[ed] the smooth workings of corporate machines and threaten[ed] to overwhelm us."[19]

In response to the growing concern, American business (and American business schools) began pouring millions of dollars into developing a cadre of people who might fix what was wrong. The content of the behavioral sciences changed, and a new area of study developed with remarkable rapidity: leadership as a business management skill. Scholars, teachers, and consultants were now being paid very well indeed to teach people to lead companies that ran smoothly—and turned a profit.

Thus, during the past few decades corporate America and the schools that study and serve it started slowly to equate the learning of leadership with the learning of good leadership. It can be argued that this new definition of the word *leadership* accounts more than anything else for the explosive growth of the leadership industry. In particular, in keeping with the spirit of American capitalism, programs and curricula that claim to grow (good) leaders fill seats—and coffers.

Reason 3: The American National Character

The leadership industry is an American product—an American seed planted in American soil and harvested almost entirely by American experts. It is small wonder that the industry mirrors the American experience, in particular its self-help optimism.

Repeatedly, America's great leaders have given voice to this sense of the possible. In his Farewell Address, George Washington foretold an America that would "give to mankind

---

19   Kanter, *The Change Masters*, 17, 18.

the magnanimous and too novel example of a people always guided by an exalted justice and benevolence."[20] In his second inaugural address, Abraham Lincoln spoke of binding "the nation's wounds," [21] even though North and South had not yet finished fighting their excruciating Civil War. On the steps of the Lincoln Memorial, Martin Luther King, Jr., described his dream, in which his children would "one day live in a nation where they will be judged not by the color of their skin but by the content of their character."[22] And both John Kennedy and Ronald Reagan borrowed from John Winthrop the picture of America as a city on a hill. As Reagan put it while running for president the first time, "We can meet our destiny—and that destiny is to build a land here that will be, for all mankind, a shining city on a hill."[23]

Our newfound belief in the individual and collective benefits of leadership learning originates from this wellspring. We presume that to be a leader is to do good and to be good. We presume that all of us can, and that some of us will, build "a shining city on a hill."

The Dark Side

But the leadership industry has a problem that years ago I named Hitler's ghost.[24] Here is my concern. If we pretend that there is no elephant and that bad leadership is unrelated to good leadership, if we pretend to know the one without knowing

---

[20]   George Washington, Farewell Address, 17 September 1796.

[21]   Abraham Lincoln, second inaugural address, 4 March 1865, Washington, DC.

[22]   Dr. Martin Luther King, Jr., "I Have a Dream" speech, 28 August 1963, Washington, DC.

[23]   Ronald Reagan, the Anderson-Reagan presidential debate, 21 September 1980, Baltimore, MD. John Kennedy used the phrase in a speech delivered to the Massachusetts legislature on 9 January 1961, and Reagan also used it earlier, in a speech he delivered in 1974.

[24]   Barbara Kellerman, "Hitler's Ghost: A Manifesto" in *Cutting Edge: Leadership 2000*, eds. Barbara Kellerman and Larraine Matusak (College Park, MD: Burns Academy of Leadership, 1999), 65-68.

the other, we will in the end distort the enterprise. We cannot distance ourselves from even the most extreme example—Hitler—by bestowing on him another name, such as "power wielder." Not only was his impact on twentieth-century history arguably greater than anyone else's, but also he was brilliantly skilled at inspiring, mobilizing, and directing followers. His use of coercion notwithstanding, if this is not leadership, what is?

Similarly, it makes no sense to think of corporate lawbreakers as one breed, and corporate gods as another. Why would we preclude people at the top of the Enron hierarchy—chairman Kenneth Lay, CEO Jeffrey Skilling, and CFO Andrew Fastow—from being labeled leaders just because they did not "realize goals mutually held by leaders and followers"? The fact is that Lay, Skilling, and Fastow were agents of change. What they did affected the lives and pocketbooks of tens of thousands of Americans, many of whom were not Enron employees. Let's be clear here. These men were not just a few rotten apples. Rather, they created, indeed encouraged, an organizational culture that allowed many apples to spoil and, in turn, ruin others.

Thus the fundamental proposition of this book: To deny bad leadership equivalence in the conversation and curriculum is misguided, tantamount to a medical school that would claim to teach health while ignoring disease. Some might argue that the differences are merely semantic—that although Burns and Bennis equate the word *leadership* with good leadership, the rest of us are free to define leadership as we see fit. But words matter. Inevitably, the fact that the overwhelming majority of leadership experts use *leadership* to imply *good* leadership affects how we think about a subject that is far more complex, and frightening, than this dewy-eyed view would suggest.

Limiting leadership to good leadership presents three major problems.

It is confusing. Try telling the average undergraduate, or a non-American, or the proverbial man on the street, that the most reviled of recent American presidents, Richard Nixon, was something other than a leader. Most folks use the word *leader* as it has always been used: to refer to any individual who uses power, authority, and influence to get others to go along. *The New York Times* does not refer to former Liberian president Charles Taylor as a "power wielder," even though he stands accused of murder, rape, abduction, and other crimes against humanity. Nor is L. Dennis Kozlowski, the astonishingly successful former CEO of Tyco, considered by most people to be any the less a corporate leader because it was finally revealed that he was greedy to the point of being corrupt.

It is misleading. As Bernard Bass has observed, "[T]here are almost as many different definitions of leadership as there are persons who have attempted to define the concept."[25] For example, leadership can be considered the exercise of influence, or a power relation, or an instrument of goal achievement, or a differentiated role. The point is that each of these definitions is value-free. It makes no sense therefore to distinguish between leaders and power wielders. In fact, to compare them is not to compare apples and oranges, but apples and apples.

It does a disservice. All of us want good leadership—to live in a world of good leaders and good followers. We want good leadership at home, at work, and in the various communities of which we are members. One way to increase the probability of good leadership is to encourage as many people as possible to study it, teach it, and practice it. But another way is to encourage as many people as possible to explore bad leadership. How will we ever stop what we refuse to see and study?

Americans are familiar, of course, with bad leadership. We are not strangers to ineffective leaders and followers, nor to unethical leaders and followers. But it is also true that at

---

[25] Bernard Bass, *Stogdill's Handbook of Leadership: A Survey of Theory and Research* (New York: Free Press, 1981), 7.

the highest national level, the United States has never had a leader who was bad in the extreme. Unlike people in most of the rest of the world, Americans have never suffered under authoritarian rule, and so the dark side of public leadership has remained at a remove. Our bad leaders tend to disappoint because they are inept or corrupt, and not because they are despots. Even the worst of our national leaders, presidents such as James Buchanan, Warren Harding, or even Nixon, who resigned before he could be impeached, tend to be judged stupid, maladroit, sleazy, or ignoble rather than tyrannical.

But the American experience is not everything. Leaders and followers can be bad in ways that are of a different magnitude. In a foreword to *The Black Book of Communism: Crimes, Terror, Repression*, Martin Malia identifies several regimes by the brutal tyrants who led them: "Stalin's Gulag, Mao Zedong's Great Leap Forward and his Cultural Revolution, and Pol Pot's Khmer Rouge." Malia reminds us, in the event we need reminding, that Communism was a "tragedy of planetary dimensions"; its victims are estimated to number between 85 and 100 million. Moreover, he makes clear that it is impossible to understand what happened without understanding those who were immediately responsible.[26]

Those who are immediately responsible for bad leadership include bad followers just as much as bad leaders. Like leaders, followers run the gamut. At the extreme, there are those who commit "crimes of obedience." Herbert Kelman and Lee Hamilton demonstrated that such crimes take place not only in contexts of conflict—for example, when members of the military engage in sanctioned massacres—but also in political and bureaucratic settings. They point out that the burglars were the "foot soldiers of political espionage" in the original Watergate crime, and that the wrongdoing in Nixon's White

---

[26] Martin Malia, "Foreword: The Uses of Atrocity," in Stephane Courtois et al., *The Black Book of Communism: Crimes, Terror, Repression* (Cambridge, MA: Harvard University Press, 1999), x.

House continued in a series of "cover-up actions" that reached all the way down the chain of command to the clerical staff.[27]

So bad leadership is not solely the fault of a few bad leaders. We are all, every one of us, in this together.

Archbishop Desmond Tutu has said that his experience of South Africa taught him "two contradictory things." On the one hand, we "have an extraordinary capacity for good." But on the other hand, we have "a remarkable capacity for evil—we have refined ways of being mean and nasty to one another [through] genocides, holocausts, slavery, racism, wars, oppression and injustice."[28]

Because leadership makes a difference, sometimes even a big difference, those of us who desire to make the world a better place must do what Tutu did. We must come to grips with leadership as two contradictory things: good and bad.

---

[27] Herbert C. Kelman and Lee Hamilton, *Crimes of Obedience: Toward a Social Psychology of Authority and Responsibility.* (New Haven, CT: Yale University Press, 1989), 26.

[28] Desmond Tutu, "Let South Africa Show the World How to Forgive," *Knowledge of Reality* 19 (2000).

JOSEPH A. RAELIN

1948-

Creating Leaderful Organizations:
How to Bring Out Leadership in Everyone

2003

Joseph A. Raelin holds the Asa S. Knowles Chair of Practice-Oriented Education at Northeastern University. He was formerly Professor of Management at the Boston College Wallace E. Carroll School of Management. A prolific writer in the areas of leadership and management, Raelin has written many books and over one hundred journal articles. His books, *The Clash of Cultures: Managers Managing Professionals* (Harvard Business School Press, 1991), and *Creating Leaderful Organizations: How to Bring Out Leadership in Everyone,* are considered to be important readings in management.

In the following selection, he explores a qualitatively different way of looking at leadership that is more in line with twenty-first century organizational and group demands for self-leadership, leaderless groups, and shared leadership. A "leaderful" organization is one in which responsibility for leadership is distributed across all of the members of a community.

Joseph A. Raelin

Source:

Northeastern University, Center for Work and Learning. *About Us: Joe Raelin.* Retrieved from http://www.northeastern. edu/poe/about/raelin.htm

Selection from:

Raelin, J. A. (2003). *Creating leaderful organizations: how to bring out leadership in everyone.* (pp. 10-16). San Francisco: Berrett-Koehler.

The Tenets of Leaderful Practice

[***]

What Is Conventional Leadership?

Having identified what leadership represents, we next consider the dominant approach to effecting leadership. As the reigning paradigm, conventional leadership has qualities that are considered commensurate with leadership itself. As we shall see, there is an emerging recognition that this dominant approach may be limiting as we prepare to manage twenty-first-century organizations. There are four tenets of conventional leadership.

Leadership is *serial.* Once one achieves the office of leadership, that position continues at least for the duration of the term of office. Only when one completes his or her term—or vacates or is forced to leave the office—does leadership transfer to the next leader, though it may return at times to the original person. Leaders are thus always in a position of leadership and do not cede the honor to anyone else. Upon acquiring power, most leaders attempt to sustain or increase it. Giving up or sharing power with others would be seen as abdicating one's responsibility.

Leadership is *individual*. That a leader is one person signifies leadership's solitary role. An enterprise has only one leader and normally such a person is designated as the authority or position leader. It would weaken or at least confuse leadership to talk about having more than a single leader or to share leadership because there would not be a concrete end-role for making decisions and directing actions.

Leadership is *controlling*. The conventional leader believes it is his or her ultimate duty to direct the enterprise and engender the commitment of community members. To ensure smooth coordination of functions, the leader acts as the spokesperson for the enterprise. The subordinate role is to follow the guidance of the leader and to help him or her successfully accomplish the enterprise's mission. Leaders may choose to share their deepest beliefs but only with their closest associates.

Leadership is *dispassionate*. Although the leader may recognize that employees have feelings, the leader must make the tough decisions for the enterprise in a dispassionate manner. Tough decisions may result in not satisfying (or may even hurt) particular stakeholders, including employees, but accomplishing the mission of the enterprise must come first. Leaders are also the authoritative source when the operation faces problems, and they tend to exude a confidence that they are in charge and that subordinates can rely upon them to handle any challenge.

What Does It Mean to Be "Leaderful"?

In the opening vignette, Jamie Waters cautioned against calling groups leader*less*. In leader*less* groups, there is no longer a need for a leader, or even a facilitator, because the group has learned to conduct its affairs on its own. It no longer has, or needs, leadership. The problem with this idea is that it suggests a group may at times be devoid of leadership. It can go on for a while, albeit tenuously, until there's a crisis. At that point, a leader may need to emerge to settle things down. Consider, though, that some groups don't lose their leadership when they work in sync like a well-oiled machine. Leadership at this point becomes distributed across all members of the community. It is not leader*less*; it is leader*ful!* As Jamie noted, it is full of leadership since everyone shares the experience of providing leadership.

Leading in Your Community I would like to make a new reference to the unit that receives or conducts leadership. Let's refer to it as a *community*. A community is any setting where people congregate to accomplish work together. Hence, it can be a small group, an office, a plant, or a large organization. It can be in the private, public, or civil (nonprofit) sectors. I prefer to use the word *community*, rather than *group* or *organization*, because it is more hospitable to a notion of leadership that applies to the whole rather than to the parts or their sum. It also allows me to refer to leadership within any interpersonal context, rather than having to distinguish whether it refers to team or managerial or strategic settings. To say that leaderful practice occurs within a community comes with one qualifier: I am drawing attention to leadership's interpersonal character. The community is a unit in which members already have or may establish human contact with others. In this sense, it is a social structure that extends beyond the self, that links people together for some common purpose. Most of us can see ourselves as belonging to a number of communities. Some of them may not necessarily entail work; for example, people may assemble for recreational or spiritual purposes. In this book, I am most concerned with leadership that helps our communities work better together.

Some groups don't lose their leadership when they work in sync like a well-oiled machine. Leadership at this point becomes

distributed across all members of the community. It is not leader*less*; it is leader*ful*.

The Four C's of Leaderful Practice Leaderful leadership offers an alternative approach to conventional leadership that is ripe for the requirements of our communities in the current era. It is an integrative model that has been in the making for some time but for its coherence. In other words, it contains historical traditions that, without integration, have not been able to supplant the dominant heroic paradigm. Leaderful leadership can also accomplish the four processes of leadership in more settings and with more pervasive effectiveness than the conventional approach. Let's consider how the four tenets of conventional leadership can be replaced with what I have labeled the four C's. Leaderful managers are concurrent, collective, collaborative, and compassionate.

Figure 1-2 displays the two leadership approaches as a set of continua. I have chosen continua because most of us are not completely settled in one approach or the other. As much as I would wish for my readers to create fully leaderful organizations, it takes some practice to get there, as chapter 3 will point out. As such, some of you will find yourselves more leaderful compared to others but will also find that you vary in your leaderful tendencies across the tenets. For example, you may be a compassionate leader but believe firmly that leadership of the enterprise should gravitate to you as the ultimate single decision maker. Further, you may find that you embrace leaderful practice only under particular circumstances, such as when your colleagues are ready to share leadership with you. Otherwise, perhaps you tend to take control of the community.

As I expect that few readers will consider themselves entirely leaderful at this point, in this book I will attempt to both make the case on behalf of leaderful practice and illustrate some practical methods to help you become more so. It is not that I believe conventional leadership is invalid; it has served us well. I simply see the leaderful leadership approach as more practical and useful in managing communities in our new century.

The first tenet of leaderful practice, that leadership is *concurrent*, is perhaps the most revolutionary. It suggests that in any community, more than one leader can operate at the same time, so leaders willingly and naturally share power with others. Indeed, power can be increased by everyone working together. Since leaders perform a variety of responsibilities in a community, it is pointless to insist that only one leader operates at any one time. For example, an administrative assistant who "knows the ropes" and can help others figure out who is knowledgeable about a particular function may be just as important to the group as the position leader. However, this same position leader need not "stand down" nor give up his or her leadership as members of the community turn their attention to the administrative assistant. These two, as well as many others, can offer their leadership to the community at the same time.

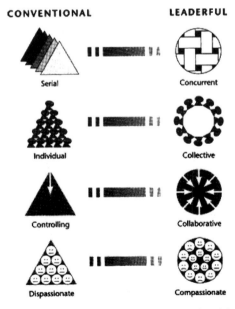

FIGURE 1-2. The Continua of Leadership

Leaderful leadership is not only concurrent, but is also *collective*. Since we have dispelled the assumption that a group can have only one leader, we can entertain the view that many people within the community might operate as leaders. The community does not solely depend on one individual to mobilize action or make decisions on behalf of others. I include in this assertion the role of the position leader. This "authority" may have formal power conferred on him or her by the organization, but formal authority is not necessarily the most valuable to the operation. Decisions are made by whoever has the relevant responsibility. Leadership may thus emerge from multiple members of the community, especially when important needs arise, whether preparing for a strategic mission, creating meaning for the group, or proposing a change in direction. Although someone may initiate an activity, others may become involved and share leadership with the initiator. Have you ever experienced being in a team that was temporarily stymied in its attempt to solve a problem? Feeling disconsolate, members wonder if they will ever find a solution. Then, all of sudden, someone offers an idea, perhaps not a mainstream idea but one that has an immediate appeal, one that engages the community's imagination. Soon, everyone begins throwing out additional thoughts and tactics to build on the original idea. For a time, an almost breathless quality descends on the team's functioning as it becomes absorbed in this all-encompassing solution process. The team is experiencing collective leadership; it is not dependent on any one member, not the position leader, not the idea initiator— everyone is participating in leadership.

Leaderful leadership is also *collaborative*. All members of the community, not just the position leader, are in control of and may speak for the entire community. They may advocate a point of view that they believe can contribute to the common good of the community. Although they might assert themselves at times, they remain equally sensitive to the views and feelings of others and consider their viewpoints as equally valid. They thus seek to engage in a public dialogue in which they willingly open their beliefs and values to the scrutiny of others. Their listening to others becomes rapt. They also understand the difference between collaborating as a pretense and becoming fully involved. In pretentious involvement, you quickly discover that all the critical decisions seem to get made without you. Collaborative leaders realize that everyone counts; every opinion and contribution sincerely matter.

Finally, leaderful managers are *compassionate.* By demonstrating compassion, one extends unadulterated commitment to preserving the dignity of others. Shareholders' views are considered before making a decision for the entire enterprise. Each member of the community is valued regardless of his or her background or social standing, and all viewpoints are considered regardless of whether they conform to current thought processes. In practicing compassion, leaders take the stance of a learner who sees the adaptability of the community as dependent upon the contribution of others. Members of the community, not necessarily the position leader, handle problems as they arise. Compassionate leaders recognize that values are intrinsically interconnected with leadership and that there is no higher value than democratic participation. When people who have a stake in a community venture are given every chance to participate in that venture—including its implementation—their commitment to the venture will be assured. The endowment of participation extends to the wider community affected by the actions of an organization. For example, if building a new corporate complex will affect the existing ecology or serenity of a neighboring property, the compassionate leader will include the neighbors in deliberations concerning the construction.

SECTION II

PERSONAL QUALITIES
OF LEADERS

Roots of the trait approach to leadership can be traced back to the mid 1800s and the work of Sir Francis Galton. Galton believed that leadership qualities, such as wisdom, courage, and honesty, were genetic characteristics, passed on from one generation to the next within families (Wren, 1995). In the nineteenth century, leaders and followers were thought to be distinct from one another.

Trait theorists continued their work into the twentieth century. Their lists usually included intelligence, strong values, and high levels of personal energy, not to mention certain personality traits and physical attributes that would differentiate the leader from his or her followers. Sifting through these studies, Stogdill (1948) concluded that these traits in leaders were not qualitatively different from those of followers. Certain qualities can be attributed to almost everyone. However, leaders possess these qualities to an exceptional degree. Because of these differing views of leadership traits, readings found in this section explore the qualities of some of the finest leaders. Interestingly, Sophocles' *Ajax* (found in this section) explores one of the extremely negative qualities that can cause a leader's downfall.

Sources:

Stogdill, R. M. (1948). Personal factors associated with leadership: A survey of the literature. *Journal of Psychology*, 25, 35-71.

Wren, T. (1995). *Leader's companion: Insights on leadership through the ages.* New York: The Free Press.

NEHEMIAH

ca. 431-430 B. C. E.

In this Old Testament book of the Bible, Nehemiah, the governor of the Persian province of Judah, felt called by God to leave Persia and to go to Jerusalem to rebuild its walls after the city had been destroyed in the Babylonian attack on Judah. Nehemiah, often credited with being a leader of vision in the rebuilding of Jerusalem, took over the responsibility, becoming the governor of this building project. Despite innumerable opposing forces, including conflicts with enemies, the city walls were built in fifty-two days (Nehemiah 6:15). The following excerpt illustrates how a leader can prevail despite formidable odds. Which characteristics of leadership are highlighted by Nehemiah's feat?

Source:

Merrill, E. H. A theology of Ezra-Nehemiah and Esther. In R. Zuck, E. Merrill & D. Bock (Eds.), *A biblical theology of the Old Testament,* (pp. 200-201). Chicago: Moody.

Selection from:

Nehemiah 1: 1-6, 11; 2:1-20; 5: 1-19; 6: 1-15. (Revised Standard Version).

The Book of Nehemiah
(Bible, Revised Standard Version)

Neh. 1

[1]The words of Nehemi'ah the son of Hacali'ah.

Now it happened in the month of Chislev, in the twentieth year, as I was in Susa the capital, [2]that Hana'ni, one of my brethren, came with certain men out of Judah; and I asked them concerning the Jews that survived, who had escaped exile, and concerning Jerusalem. [3]And they said to me, "The survivors there in the province who escaped exile are in great trouble and shame; the wall of Jerusalem is broken down, and its gates are destroyed by fire."

[4]When I heard these words I sat down and wept, and mourned for days; and I continued fasting and praying before the God of heaven. [5]And I said, "O LORD God of heaven, the great and terrible God who keeps covenant and steadfast love with those who love him and keep his commandments; [6] let thy ear be attentive, and thy eyes open, to hear the prayer of thy servant which I now pray before thee day and night for the people of Israel thy servants, confessing the sins of the people of Israel, which we have sinned against thee. Yea, I and my father's house have sinned. [11] O Lord, let thy ear be attentive to the prayer of thy servant, and to the prayer of thy servants who delight to fear thy name; and give success to thy servant today, and grant him mercy in the sight of this man."

Now I was cupbearer to the king.

Neh. 2

[1] In the month of Nisan, in the twentieth year of King Ar-ta-xerx'es, when wine was before him, I took up the wine and gave it to the king. Now I had not been sad in his presence.

² And the king said to me, "Why is your face sad, seeing you are not sick? This is nothing else but sadness of the heart." Then I was very much afraid.

³ I said to the king, "Let the king live for ever! Why should not my face be sad, when the city, the place of my fathers' sepulchres, lies waste, and its gates have been destroyed by fire?"

⁴ Then the king said to me, "For what do you make request?" So I prayed to the God of heaven.

⁵ And I said to the king, "If it pleases the king, and if your servant has found favor in your sight, that you send me to Judah, to the city of my fathers' sepulchres, that I may rebuild it."

⁶ And the king said to me (the queen sitting beside him), "How long will you be gone, and when will you return?" So it pleased the king to send me; and I set him a time.

⁷ And I said to the king, "If it pleases the king, let letters be given me to the governors of the province Beyond the River, that they may let me pass through until I come to Judah;

⁸ and a letter to Asaph, the keeper of the king's forest, that he may give me timber to make beams for the gates of the fortress of the temple, and for the wall of the city, and for the house which I shall occupy." And the king granted me what I asked, for the good hand of my God was upon me.

⁹ Then I came to the governors of the province Beyond the River, and gave them the king's letters. Now the king had sent with me officers of the army and horsemen.

¹⁰ But when Sanbal'lat the Hor'onite and Tobi'ah the servant, the Ammonite, heard this, it displeased them greatly that some one had come to seek the welfare of the children of Israel.

¹¹ So I came to Jerusalem and was there three days.

¹² Then I arose in the night, I and a few men with me; and I told no one what my God had put into my heart to do for Jerusalem. There was no beast with me but the beast on which I rode.

¹³ I went out by night by the Valley Gate to the Jackal's Well and to the Dung Gate, and I inspected the walls of

Jerusalem which were broken down and its gates which had been destroyed by fire.

¹⁴ Then I went on to the Fountain Gate and to the King's Pool; but there was no place for the beast that was under me to pass.

¹⁵ Then I went up in the night by the valley and inspected the wall; and I turned back and entered by the Valley Gate, and so returned.

¹⁶ And the officials did not know where I had gone or what I was doing; and I had not yet told the Jews, the priests, the nobles, the officials, and the rest that were to do the work.

¹⁷Then I said to them, "You see the trouble we are in, how Jerusalem lies in ruins with its gates burned. Come, let us build the wall of Jerusalem, that we may no longer suffer disgrace."

¹⁸And I told them of the hand of my God which had been upon me for good, and also of the words which the king had spoken to me. And they said, "Let us rise up and build." So they strengthened their hands for the good work.

¹⁹ But when Sanbal'lat the Hor'onite and Tobi'ah the servant, the Ammonite, and Geshem the Arab heard of it, they derided us and despised us and said, "What is this thing that you are doing? Are you rebelling against the king?"

²⁰ Then I replied to them, "The God of heaven will make us prosper, and we his servants will arise and build; but you have no portion or right or memorial in Jerusalem."

Neh. 5

¹Now there arose a great outcry of the people and of their wives against their Jewish brethren.

² For there were those who said, "With our sons and our daughters, we are many; let us get grain, that we may eat and keep alive."

³ There were also those who said, "We are mortgaging our fields, our vineyards, and our houses to get grain because of the famine."

[4] And there were those who said, "We have borrowed money for the king's tax upon our fields and our vineyards.

[5] Now our flesh is as the flesh of our brethren, our children are as their children; yet we are forcing our sons and our daughters to be slaves, and some of our daughters have already been enslaved; but it is not in our power to help it, for other men have our fields and our vineyards."

[6] I was very angry when I heard their outcry and these words.

[7] I took counsel with myself, and I brought charges against the nobles and the officials. I said to them, "You are exacting interest, each from his brother." And I held a great assembly against them, [8] and said to them, "We, as far as we are able, have bought back our Jewish brethren who have been sold to the nations; but you even sell your brethren that they may be sold to us!" They were silent, and could not find a word to say.

[9] So I said, "The thing that you are doing is not good. Ought you not to walk in the fear of our God to prevent the taunts of the nations our enemies?

[10] Moreover I and my brethren and my servants are lending them money and grain. Let us leave off this interest.

[11] Return to them this very day their fields, their vineyards, their olive orchards, and their houses, and the hundredth of money, grain, wine, and oil which you have been exacting of them."

[12] Then they said, "We will restore these and require nothing from them. We will do as you say." And I called the priests, and took an oath of them to do as they had promised.

[13] I also shook out my lap and said, "So may God shake out every man from his house and from his labor who does not perform this promise. So may he be shaken out and emptied." And all the assembly said "Amen" and praised the LORD. And the people did as they had promised.

[14] Moreover from the time that I was appointed to be their governor in the land of Judah, from the twentieth year to the thirty-second year of Ar-ta-xerx'es the king, twelve years, neither I nor my brethren ate the food allowance of the governor.

¹⁵ The former governors who were before me laid heavy burdens upon the people, and took from them food and wine, besides forty shekels of silver. Even their servants lorded it over the people. But I did not do so, because of the fear of God.

¹⁶ I also held to the work on this wall, and acquired no land; and all my servants were gathered there for the work.

¹⁷ Moreover there were at my table a hundred and fifty men, Jews and officials, besides those who came to us from the nations which were about us.

¹⁸ Now that which was prepared for one day was one ox and six choice sheep; fowls likewise were prepared for me, and every ten days skins of wine in abundance; yet with all this I did not demand the food allowance of the governor, because the servitude was heavy upon this people.

¹⁹ Remember for my good, O my God, all that I have done for this people.

Neh. 6

¹ Now when it was reported to Sanbal'lat and Tobi'ah and to Geshem the Arab and to the rest of our enemies that I had built the wall and that there was no breach left in it (although up to that time I had not set up the doors in the gates),

² Sanbal'lat and Geshem sent to me, saying, "Come and let us meet together in one of the villages in the plain of Ono." But they intended to do me harm.

³ And I sent messengers to them, saying, "I am doing a great work and I cannot come down. Why should the work stop while I leave it and come down to you?"

⁴ And they sent to me four times in this way and I answered them in the same manner.

⁵ In the same way Sanbal'lat for the fifth time sent his servant to me with an open letter in his hand.

⁶ In it was written, "It is reported among the nations, and Geshem also says it, that you and the Jews intend to rebel; that

is why you are building the wall; and you wish to become their king, according to this report.

⁷ And you have also set up prophets to proclaim concerning you in Jerusalem, `There is a king in Judah.' And now it will be reported to the king according to these words. So now come, and let us take counsel together."

⁸ Then I sent to him, saying, "No such things as you say have been done, for you are inventing them out of your own mind."

⁹ For they all wanted to frighten us, thinking, "Their hands will drop from the work, and it will not be done." But now, O God, strengthen thou my hands.

¹⁰ Now when I went into the house of Shemai'ah the son of Delai'ah, son of Mehet'abel, who was shut up, he said, "Let us meet together in the house of God, within the temple, and let us close the doors of the temple; for they are coming to kill you, at night they are coming to kill you."

¹¹ But I said, "Should such a man as I flee? And what man such as I could go into the temple and live? I will not go in."

¹² And I understood, and saw that God had not sent him, but he had pronounced the prophecy against me because Tobi'ah and Sanbal'lat had hired him.

¹³ For this purpose he was hired, that I should be afraid and act in this way and sin, and so they could give me an evil name, in order to taunt me.

¹⁴ Remember Tobi'ah and Sanbal'lat, O my God, according to these things that they did, and also the prophetess No-adi'ah and the rest of the prophets who wanted to make me afraid.

¹⁵ So the wall was finished on the twenty-fifth day of the month Elul, in fifty-two days.

SOPHOCLES

497-406 B.C.E.

Ajax

ca. 440 B.C.E.

The ancient Greeks' concept of leadership was best exemplified by their stories of heroes. The Athenian playwright Sophocles wrote over 120 plays, including *Ajax,* which depicts characters and their motives with great insight. In the play excerpted in this section, we see what can happen when an individual's pride overwhelms his sense of responsibility. Ajax is a controversial hero, who is depicted as unable or unwilling to change. At the beginning of the play, Ajax is angry because Odysseus was awarded Achilles' armor, which Ajax had expected to receive based on the belief that he is more deserving than Odysseus. Ajax avows revenge on Odysseus as the winner of the armor as well as on those who gave the armor to Odysseus.

The excerpt below reveals the leader as a fallible being and explores the possible consequences of destructive emotions, such as pride, which can overwhelm otherwise effective leaders.

Source:

Standford, W. B. (Ed.) (1963). Introduction. In *Sophocles: Ajax* (pp. ix-xii). London: Macmillan.

Selection from:

Sophocles. (1919). *Ajax*. (F. Storr, Trans.) (pp. 37-53). New
    York: G.P. Putnam's Sons.

[***]

List of characters:
Chorus—Mariners of Salamis
Ajax—Leader of the Men of Salamis
Tecmessa—his captive wife
Eurysaces, their infant son

CHORUS
O listen, I adjure thee, and be ruled.

AJAX
Wretch to let those fiends, my foes,
Slip, while on the flock my blows
And the goodly cattle rained,
Till with their dark blood all the house was stained.

CHORUS
Why vex thyself for what is past recall?
What's done is done and naught can alter it.

AJAX
Spy of the time, apt tool for any guile, *(Ant. 2)*
Of all the host the sublest knave, most vile,
Son of Laertes, loud and long, I trow,
Thou laughest in malignant triumph now.

CHORUS
Laughter or mourning comes as God ordains.

AJAX

Would I could see him; shattered though I be!
Ah me!

CHORUS

No boastful words; see'st not thy piteous case?

AJAX

O Zeus, my grand sire, would that I
Might slay that knave, my bane,
That arch-dissembler and the generals twain.
Then let me die!

TECMESSA

When thus thou prayest, pray that I with thee
May die; why should I live when thou art dead?

AJAX

O woe is me! *(Sir. 3)*
Darkness, my light!
O nether gloom to me more bright
Than midday, take, O take me to your care!
I am too vile to share
The kindly aid of mortals, and the gods
Have left me. Nay, the Warrior Maid, Zeus-born,
Laughs me to scorn;
I quail beneath her rods.
Whither to fly? What hope of rest is left,
If of my ancient fame bereft,
Dead as these slaughtered sheep around me slain,
A madman's crown I gain,
While all the host at my devoted head
Would strike, and smite me dead?

TECMESSA

Ah me that one so good should utter words

That hitherto he ne'er had deigned to breathe!

AJAX

Paths of the roaring waves, *(Ant. 3)*
Ye salt sea caves
And pastures by the shore,
Where long, too long I roam
In Troy-land, far from home;
Me shall ye see no more—
No more in life. Give ear
All who can hear.
Streams of Scamander, rills
That flow from Ida's hills,
Streams to the Greeks so dear,
Ne'er shall ye look on Ajax more;

AJAX

A paladin whose peer
(For I will utter a proud boast)
In all the Grecian host
That sailed from Hellas' shore
Troy ne'er beheld. But now
Low in the dust, o'erthrown, his head doth bow.

CHORUS

How to restrain or bow to let thee speak
I cannot tell, beset by endless woes.

AJAX

Ay me! Whoe'er had thought how well my name
Would fit my misery? Ay me! Ay me![1]
Yea, twice and thrice may I repeat the wail
That syllables my woe-begone estate.
My sire, a peerless warrior, home returned

---

[1]   Like Shakespeare's 'Gaunt' (*Richard II*, II. i) he plays on his name *Aias*.

Back from the land of Ida, crowned with fame,
Proclaimed as champion bravest of the brave.
And I, his son, in might not less than he,
Sailed after him to this same land of Troy,
And served the host by deeds of no less worth,
And for reward I perish by the Greeks
Dishonoured. Yet one thing I know full well:
If to Achilles living it had fallen
His arms as meed of valour to award,
No man had grasped the prize, preferred to me.
But now the Atridae, scouting my just claim,
Have yielded to a miscreant's base intrigue.
Had not mine eyes been dazed, my mind distraught
And wrested from its purpose, they had never
Procured false sentence 'gainst a second man.
Alas! the grim-eyed goddess, unsubdued
Daughter of Zeus—as I was at their heels,
Almost at grips with them, in act to strike—
Foiled me, abused me by a frenzy fit,
Imbrued my hands with blood of these poor beasts.
And thus my foes exult in their escape,
Albeit I willed it not, and mock at me.
But if some god or goddess intervene,
Even a knave may worst the better man.
And now what's left me? By the gods, 'tis clear,
I am detested, hated by the host
Of Greeks, abhorred by Troy and all the camp.
Shall I sail homeward o'er the Aegean, leave
The sons of Atreus to fight on alone,
This roadstead undefended? Then how face
My father Telamon? How will he endure
To look on me returning empty-handed
Without the meed of valour that he held
Himself, a crown of everlasting fame?
That were intolerable. Am I then
Alone to storm the Trojan battlements,

And facing single-handed a whole host,
Do some high deed of prowess—and so die?
Nay, that methinks would give the Atridae joy.
It may not be; some emprise must be found
That shall convince my aged sire his son
Is not degenerate from his father's breed.
Base were it that a man should want long life
When all he gets is long unchanging trouble.
To-morrow, and to-morrow, and to-morrow—
What pleasure comes of that? 'Tis but a move
Forward or backward and the end—is death!
I would not count that mortal worth a doigt
Who lives on, fed by visionary hopes.
Nobly to live—that is the true knight's choice,
Or nobly end his life. I have said my say.
No man will charge thee, Ajax, with feigned words,
'Twas thy heart spoke; yet pause and put aside
These dark thoughts; let thyself be ruled by friends.

TECMESSA

Ah, my lord Ajax, heavier lot is none
Than to lie helpless in the coils of fate.
I was the daughter of a high-born sire
Of Phrygians unsurpassed in wealth and might.
And now, I am a slave; 'twas so ordained
By Heaven, methinks, and by thy might of arm.
Since fate has willed, then, I should share thy bed,
Thy good is mine; and O by the god of the hearth,
O by the wedded bond that made us one,
Let me not fall into a stranger's hand,
A laughing-stock! For, surely, if thou die
And leave me widowed, on that very day
I shall be seized and haled away by force,
I and thy son, prey to the Argive host,
Our portion slavery. Then shall I hear
The flouts and gibes that my new lords let fly.

"Look on her," one will say, "the leman once
Of Ajax, mightiest of the Argive chiefs,
How has she fallen from her place of pride!"
Thus will they prate, and hard will be my lot,
But on thy race and thee how foul a slur.
Take pity and bethink thee of the sire
Thou leavest, an old man, disconsolate;
Bethink thee of thy mother bowed with years,
Think of her prayers and vows for thy return.
And, O my lord, take pity on thy son,
Orphaned, without a father's fostering care,
The ward of loveless guardians; if thou die,
What heritage of woe is his and mine!
For I have naught to look to anywhere
Save thee. By thee my country was laid waste,
My mother and my father too were snatched
To dwell with Hades by another fate.
What home is left me then, if thou art ta'en?
What weal? my welfare is bound up in thee.
Think of me also: gratitude is due
From man for favours that a woman gives.
Kindness return of kindness e'er begets.
Who lets the memory of service pass
Him will I ne'er with noble spirits rank.

CHORUS

Ajax, I would that thou wert moved as I
To pity; then wouldst thou approve her rede.

AJAX

Yea, and my full approval she shall win,
If only she take heart to do my hest.

TECMESSA

Aye, my dear lord, I will obey in all.

AJAX

Bring hither then my son, that I may see him.

TECMESSA

Oh, in alarm I sent him from my charge.

AJAX

When I was stricken? Or what meanest thou?

TECMESSA

Yea, lest the poor child meeting thee should die.

AJAX

That fate indeed had matched my fortunes well.

TECMESSA

Well, I averted that calamity.

AJAX

Thy forethought and the action I commend.

TECMESSA

As the case stands, how can I do thy hest?

AJAX

Let me speak to him—see him face to face.

TECMESSA

Good; he is in our servants' charge close by.

AJAX

Then wherefore is his coming thus delayed?

TECMESSA

My child, thy father calls thee.
(*To the* SERVANTS)

Bring him hither,
Whoever of you guides his infant steps.

AJAX

Comes he, or has he failed to hear thy call?

TECMESSA

I see one just approaching with the boy.
(EURYSACES *is led forward*.)

AJAX

Lift him, O lift him to my arms; no dread,
If he be mine, his father's true-born son,
He'll feel in gazing on this fresh spilt blood.
He must be early trained and broken in
To the stern rule of life his father held,
And moulded to the likeness of his sire.
My boy, mayst thou prove happier than thy sire,
But like him in all else, and thou wilt prove
No weakling; nay, e'en now, in this at least
I envy thee: of woes thou wottest naught,
For ignorance is life's extremest bliss—
The years when joy and sorrow are both unknown.
But when thou reachest manhood, then's the time
To prove the inbred virtue of thy race,
And shew thy father's foes whose son thou art.
Meanwhile let light airs feed thee; cherish thou
Thy tender years to glad thy mother's heart.
Thou need'st not fear that any of the Greeks
Will tease or vex thee, e'en when I am gone.
So stout a guardian will I leave in charge,
Whose watchful eye will slumber not, though now
A foray 'gainst his enemies keeps him hence.
And ye, my seamen, comrades in the fight,
(On you no less than him I lay this charge
Of love) to him convey my last behest.

Bid him from me take home this son of mine
To Eriboea and to Telamon,
That he may comfort their old age till death.
And for my arms, let no Greek arbiter
Of games (so bid him) nor my venomous foe
Set them as prize for the Achaean host.
But this, the shield from which thou took'st thy name,[2]
Take this, my son, this sevenfold, spear-proof targe,
Take it and wield it by the close-stitched thongs.
My other arms shall lie with me interred.
Quick, take the child, delay not; close the doors,
Nor at the tent side moan and make lament.
In sooth a woman is a tearful thing.
Quick, make all fast: 'tis not a skilful leech
Who mumbles charms o'er ills that need the knife.

CHORUS
I tremble as I mark this eager haste:
Thy words are sharp as swords and like me not.

TECMESSA
O my lord Ajax, what is in thy heart?

AJAX
Question not, ask not; be discreet and wise.

TECMESSA
Ah me, I quail, I faint. O by thy child,
By heaven I implore thee, fail us not.

AJAX
Thou art importunate; know'st not that I
Henceforward owe no duty to the gods?

---

[2]   Eurysaces means 'broad shield.'

TECMESSA
Oh hush, blaspheme not!

AJAX
Speak to ears that hear.

TECMESSA
Wilt thou not heed?

AJAX
I have heard from thee too much.

TECMESSA
Fear, my lord, makes me speak.

AJAX
Quick, close the doors.

TECMESSA
Yield, I implore thee.

AJAX
Fond simplicity
If at this hour thou think'st to mould my mood.
[*Exit* AJAX.

[Ajax kills himself because he ultimately loses face by not
receiving the armor, and therefore, he feels dishonored in the
eyes of his fellow men—loss of face and loss of pride.]

Miyamoto Musashi

1584-1645

The Book of Five Rings

1993 (Original work written *ca.* 1645)

Born in the Mimasaka province of Japan in 1584, Musashi was a samurai and son of a samurai. He was excellent in both martial and artistic endeavors and believed in living in disciplined balance. Balance of opposites is considered key to understanding Musashi's work. It is reputed that Musashi was such an accomplished swordsman that he could defeat other warriors who were considered to be unbeatable. Using a technique involving two swords, he is alleged to have single-handedly defeated over thirty samurai who attempted to simultaneously attack him with guns, arrows, and swords. (*The Book of Five Rings, Concerning the Life of Miyamoto Mushasi*).

Musashi wrote, "When you have attained the Way of strategy, there will be not one thing that you cannot understand" and "You will see the Way in everything." He wrote *Five Rings* in the form of a letter to a pupil after having studied men, such as artists, craftsmen, and priests, who helped improve and expand his knowledge of the samurai. The following passage explores the mental state of true vs. false mind as being foundational for the samurai. The challenge for the reader is to figure out why one's state of mind is fundamental to combat and life.

The reader is also challenged to reflect upon the trials brought upon the leader who is not based in true mind.

Source:

Fullerton, B. (1996) *Concerning the life of Miyamoto Musashi.* Retrieved from http://samuraiconsulting.ca/5rings/ transintro/life.html.

Selection from:

Miyamoto Musashi. (1993) *The book of five rings,* (T. Cleary, Trans.), (pp. 99-100). Boston: Shambhala,

The Life-Giving Sword

TRUE AND FALSE MIND

There is a poem that says,

> *It is the mind*
> *that is the mind*
> *confusing the mind.*
> *Do not leave the mind,*
> *O mind,*
> *to the mind.*

The mind in the first line refers to the false mind, which is bad because it is false and which confuses the original mind. The mind in the second line refers to the false mind. The mind in the third line refers to the original mind, which the false mind confuses. The mind in the fourth line refers to the original mind. The mind in the fifth line refers to the original mind. The mind in the sixth line refers to the false mind.

This poem expresses the true and the false. There are two minds, the original mind and the false mind. If you find the original mind and act in accord, all things are straightforward. When this original mind is warped and polluted by the obscurity of the false mind covering it up, all actions are therefore warped and polluted.

The original mind and the false mind are not two distinct entities. The original mind is the "original countenance," which is there before our parents give birth to us; having no form, it has no origination and no extinction. It is the physical body that is borne by our parents; since the mind is formless and immaterial, we cannot say our parents have given birth to it. It is inherently there in the body when people are born.

Zen is understood to be a teaching that communicates this mind. There is also imitation Zen. A lot of people say similar things that are not really the right path, so people who are supposedly Zennists are not all the same.

When we speak of the false mind, this refers to the energy of the blood, which is personal and subjective. Blood energy is the action of blood; when blood rises, the color of the face changes and one becomes angry.

Also, when people despise what we love, we become angry and resentful. But if others similarly despise what we despise, we enjoy this and twist wrong into right.

When people are given valuables, they receive them with delight; they break into smiles, and blood energy produces a glow in their faces. Then they take what is wrong to be right.

These are all states of mind that come from the energy in the blood in the body, from this physical body, when dealing with temporal situations. These states of mind are referred to as the false mind.

When this false mind is aroused, the original mind is concealed, becoming a false mind, so nothing but bad things emerge. Therefore enlightened people are honorable because they reduce the false mind by means of the original mind. In unenlightened people, the original mind is hidden, while the false mind is powerful; therefore they act wrongly and get a sullied reputation.

Although the poem quoted above is nothing special, it expresses the distinction between the false and true quite well. Whatever the false mind does is wrong. If this wrong mind emerges, you will lose at martial arts; you will miss the mark with bow and gun, and will not even be able to ride a horse. If you performed in a drama or a dance in this state, it would also be unpleasant to watch and listen. Mistakes will also show up in what you say. Everything will be off. If you accord with the original mind, however, everything you do will be good.

People contrive falsehoods, yet claim they are not false. That is the false mind acting, so its falsehood is immediately evident. If the heart is truthful, people who listen eventually realize it, without any need for explanations or rationalizations. The original mind needs no rationalizations or excuses.

The false mind is sickness of mind; getting rid of this false mind is called getting rid of sickness. Rid of this sickness, the mind is healthy. This sound mind is called the original mind. If you accord with the original mind, you will excel in martial arts. This principle is relevant to everything, without exception.

CARL VON CLAUSEWITZ

1780-1831

On War

1831

Carl Philip Gottfried von Clausewitz, the youngest son of a bourgeois family, was a Prussian soldier, military historian, and theorist. From the age of twelve, he served as a soldier in the Prussian army and was active in its reform after its early defeat by Napoleon. As a reformer, von Clausewitz sought to reconstitute the army during peacetime so that it would be professionally prepared in the event of a future war. In 1819, von Clausewitz began the book from which the passage below is excerpted. He died of cholera in 1831, not having fully finished the eight parts of his massive volume. The passage excerpted below explores qualities of the leader of a military establishment. Clausewitz prompts his readers to reflect upon the relationship between leadership and context.

Source:

Clausewitz, von C. (1994) *On war, Hartwick classic leadership cases.* New York: Hartwick Humanities in Management Institute.

Selection from:

Clausewitz, von C., (1976). *On war,* M. Howard & P. Paret
(Eds. & Trans). (Original work written 1819-1831). (pp.
186-193). New Jersey: Princeton University Press.

CHAPTER FOUR
The Principal Moral Elements

They are: *the skill of the commander, the experience and
courage of the troops, and their patriotic spirit.* The relative value
of each cannot be universally established; it is hard enough
to discuss their potential, and even more difficult to weigh
them against each other. The wisest course is not to underrate
any of them—a temptation to which human judgment, being
fickle, often succumbs. It is far preferable to muster historical
evidence of the unmistakable effectiveness of all three.

Nevertheless it is true that at this time the armies of
practically all European states have reached a common level
of discipline and training. To use a philosophic expression: the
conduct of war was developed in accordance with its natural
laws. It has evolved methods that are common to most armies,
and that no longer even allow the commander scope to employ
special artifices (in the sense, for example, of Frederick the
Great's oblique order of battle). It cannot be denied, therefore,
that as things stand at present proportionately greater scope
is given to the troops' patriotic spirit and combat experience.
A long period of peace may change this again.

The troops' national feeling (enthusiasm, fanatical zeal,
faith, and general temper) is most apparent in mountain
warfare where every man, down to the individual soldier, is on
his own. For this reason alone mountainous areas constitute
the terrain best suited for action by an armed populace.

Efficiency, skill, and the tempered courage that welds the
body of troops into a single mold will have their greatest scope
in operations in open country.

The commander's talents are given greatest scope in rough hilly country. Mountains allow him too little real command over his scattered units and he is unable to control them all; in open country, control is a simple matter and does not test his ability to the fullest.

These obvious affinities should guide our planning.

CHAPTER FIVE
Military Virtues of the Army

Military virtues should not be confused with simple bravery, and still less with enthusiasm for a cause. Bravery is obviously a necessary component. But just as bravery, which is part of the natural make-up of a man's character, can be developed in a soldier—a member of an organization—it must develop differently in him than in other men. In the soldier the natural tendency for unbridled action and outbursts of violence must be subordinated to demands of a higher kind: obedience, order, rule, and method. An army's efficiency gains life and spirit from enthusiasm for the cause for which it fights, but such enthusiasm is not indispensable.

War is a special activity, different and separate from any other pursued by man. This would still be true no matter how wide its scope, and though every able-bodied man in the nation were under arms. An army's military qualities are based on the individual who is steeped in the spirit and essence of this activity; who trains the capacities it demands, rouses them, and makes them his own; who applies his intelligence to every detail; who gains ease and confidence through practice, and who completely immerses his personality in the appointed task.

No matter how clearly we see the citizen and the soldier in the same man, how strongly we conceive of war as the business of the entire nation, opposed diametrically to the pattern set by the *condottieri* of former times, the business of war will always remain individual and distinct. Consequently for as long as they practice this activity, soldiers will think of themselves as members of a kind of guild, in whose regulations, laws, and customs the spirit of war is given pride of place. And that does seem to be the case. No matter how much one may be inclined to take the most sophisticated view of war, it would be a serious mistake to underrate professional pride (*esprit de corps*) as something that may and must be present in an army to greater or lesser degree. Professional pride is the bond between the various natural forces that activate the military virtues; in the context of this professional pride they crystallize more readily.

An army that maintains its cohesion under the most murderous fire; that cannot be shaken by imaginary fears and resists well-founded ones with all its might; that, proud of its victories, will not lose the strength to obey orders and its respect and trust for its officers even in defeat; whose physical power, like the muscles of an athlete, has been steeled by training privation and effort as a means to victory rather than a curse on its cause; that is mindful of all these duties and qualities by virtue of the single powerful idea of the honor of its arms—such an army is imbued with the true military spirit.

It is possible to fight superbly, like the men of the Vendée, and to achieve great results, like the Swiss, the Americans, and the Spaniards without developing the kind of virtues discussed here; it is even possible to be the victorious commander of a regular army, like Prince Eugene and Marlborough, without drawing substantially on their help. No one can maintain that it is impossible to fight a successful war without these qualities. We stress this to clarify the concept, and not lose sight of the idea in a fog of generalities and give the impression that military spirit is all that counts in the end. That is not the case. The spirit of an army may be envisioned as a definite moral factor that can be mentally subtracted, whose influence may therefore be estimated—in other words, it is a tool whose power is measurable.

Having thus characterized it, we shall attempt to describe its influence and the various ways of developing it.

Military spirit always stands in the same relation to the parts of any army as does a general's ability to the whole. The general can command only the overall situation and not the separate parts. At the point where the separate parts need guidance, the military spirit must take command. Generals are chosen for their outstanding qualities, and other high-ranking officers are carefully tested; but the testing process becomes less thorough the further we descend on the scale of command, and we must be prepared for a proportionate diminution of personal talent. What is missing here must be made up by military virtues. The same role is played by the natural qualities of a people mobilized for war: *bravery, adaptability, stamina,* and *enthusiasm.* These, then, are the qualities that can act as substitutes for the military spirit and vice-versa, leading us to the following conclusions:

1. Military virtues are found only in regular armies, and they are the one that need them most. In national uprisings and peoples' wars their place is taken by natural warlike qualities, which develop faster under such conditions.

2. A regular army fighting another regular army can get along without military virtues more easily that when it is opposed by a people in arms; for in the latter case, the forces have to be split up, and the separate units will more frequently have to fend for themselves. Where the troops can remain concentrated, however, the talents of the commander are given greater scope, and can make up for any lack of spirit among the troops. Generally speaking, the need for military virtues becomes greater the more the theater of operations and other factors tend to complicate the war and disperse the forces.

If there is a lesson to be drawn from these facts, it is that when an army lacks military virtues, every effort should be made to keep operations as simple as possible, or else twice as much attention should be paid to other aspects of the military system. The mere fact that soldiers belong to a "regular army" does not automatically mean they are equal to their tasks.

Military spirit, then, is one of the most important moral elements in war. Where this element is absent, it must either be replaced by one of the others, such as the commander's superior ability or popular enthusiasm, or else the results will fall short of the efforts expended. How much has been accomplished by this spirit, this sterling quality, this refinement of base ore into precious metal, is demonstrated by the Macedonians under Alexander, the Roman legions under Caesar, the Spanish infantry under Alexander Farnese, the Swedes under Gustavus Adolphus and Charles XII, the Prussian under Frederick the Great, and the French under Bonaparte. One would have to be blind to all the evidence of history if one refused to admit that the outstanding successes of these commanders and their greatness in adversity were feasible only with the aid of an army possessing these virtues.

There are only two sources for this spirit, and they must interact in order to create it. The first is a series of victorious wars; the second, frequent exertions of the army to the utmost limits of its strength. Nothing else will show a soldier the full extent of his capacities. The more a general is accustomed to place heavy demands on his soldiers, the more he can depend on their response. A soldier is just as proud of the hardships he has overcome as of the dangers he has faced. In short, the seed will grow only in the soil of constant activity and exertion, warmed by the sun of victory. Once it has grown into a tree, it will survive the wildest storms of misfortune and defeat, and even the indolent inertia of peace, at least for a while. Thus, this spirit can be *created* only in war and by great generals, though admittedly it may endure, for several generations at least, even under generals of average ability and through long periods of peace.

One should be careful not to compare this expended and refined solidarity of a brotherhood of tempered, battle-scarred veterans with the self-esteem and vanity of regular armies which are patched together only by service-regulations and drill. Grim severity and iron discipline may be able to preserve the military virtues of a unit, but it cannot create them. These factors are valuable, but they should not be overrated. Discipline, skill, goodwill, a certain pride, and high morale, are the attributes of an army trained in times of peace. They command respect, but they have no strength of their own. They stand or fall together. One crack and the whole thing goes, like a glass too quickly cooled. Even the highest morale in the world can, at the first upset, change all too easily into despondency, an almost boastful fear; the French would call it *sauve qui peut*[1]. An army like this will be able to prevail only by virtue of its commander, never on its own. It must be led with more than normal caution until, after a series of victories and exertions, its inner strength will grow to fill its external panoply. We should take care never to confuse the real spirit of an army with its mood.

Chapter Six
Boldness

In the chapter dealing with the certainty of success, we discussed the place that boldness occupies in the dynamic system of forces, and the part it plays when opposed to prudence and discretion. We tried to show that the theorist has no right to restrict boldness on doctrinal grounds.

But this noble capacity to rise above the most menacing dangers should also be considered as a principle in itself, separate and active. Indeed, in what field of human activity is boldness more at home than in war?

---

[1]   Every man for himself

A soldier, whether drummer boy or general, can possess no nobler quality; it is the very metal that gives edge and luster to the sword.

Let us admit that boldness in war even has its own prerogatives. It must be granted a certain power over and above successful calculations involving space, time, and magnitude of forces, for wherever it is superior, it will take advantage of its opponent's weakness. In other words, it is a genuinely creative force. This fact is not difficult to prove even scientifically. Whenever boldness encounters timidity, it is likely to be the winner, because timidity in itself implies a loss of equilibrium. Boldness will be at a disadvantage only in an encounter with deliberate caution, which may be considered bold in its own right, and is certainly just as powerful and effective; but such cases are rare. Timidity is the root of prudence in the majority of men.

In most soldiers, the development of boldness can never be detrimental to other qualities, because the rank and file is bound by duty and the conditions of the service to a higher authority, and thus is led by external intelligence. With them boldness acts like a coiled spring, ready at any time to be released.

The higher up the chain of command, the greater is the need for boldness to be supported by a reflective mind, so that boldness does not degenerate into purposeless bursts of blind passion. Command becomes progressively less a matter of personal sacrifice and increasingly concerned for the safety of others and for the common purpose. The quality that in most soldiers is disciplined by service regulations that have become second nature to them, must in the commanding officer, be disciplined by reflection. In a commander a bold act may prove to be a blunder. Nevertheless, it is a laudable error, not to be regarded on the same footing as others. Happy the army where ill-timed boldness occurs frequently; it is a luxuriant weed, but indicates the richness of the soil. Even foolhardiness—that is, boldness without any object—is not to be despised; basically it stems from daring, which in this case has erupted with a passion unrestrained by thought. Only when boldness rebels against obedience, when it defiantly ignores an expressed command, must it be treated as a dangerous offense; then it must be prevented, not for its innate qualities, but because an order has been disobeyed, and in war obedience is of cardinal importance.

Given the same amount of intelligence, timidity will do a thousand times more damage in war than audacity. The truth of this observation will be self-evident to our readers.

In fact, the supervention of a rational purpose ought to make it easier to be bold, and therefore less meritorious. Yet the opposite is true.

The power of the various emotions is sharply reduced by the intervention of lucid thought and, more, by self control. Consequently, boldness grows *less common in the higher ranks.* Even if the growth of an officer's perception and intelligence does not keep pace with his rise in rank, the realities of war will impose their conditions and concerns on him. Indeed their influence on him will be greater the less he really understands them. In war, this is the main basis for the experience expressed in the French proverb, "Tel brille au second qui s'éclipse au premier."[2] Nearly every general known to us in history as mediocre, even vacillating, was noted for dash and determination as a junior officer.

A distinction should be made among acts of boldness that result from sheer necessity. Necessity comes in varying degrees. If it is pressing, a man in pursuit of his aim may be driven to incur one set of risks in order to avoid others just as serious. In that event one can admire only his powers of resolution, which, however, are also of value. The young man who leaps across a deep chasm to show off his horsemanship displays boldness; if he takes the same leap to escape a band of savage janissaries all he shows is resolution. The greater the distance between necessity and

---

[2] The same man who shines at the second level is eclipsed at the top. Eds.

action, the more numerous the possibilities that have to be identified and analyzed before action is taken, the less is the factor of boldness reduced. When Frederick the Great perceived in 1756 that war was unavoidable and that he was lost unless he could forestall his enemies, it became a necessity for him to initiate hostilities; but at the same time it was an act of boldness, because few men in his position would have dared to act in this way.

While strategy is exclusively the province of generals and other senior officers, boldness in the rest of the army is as important a factor in planning as any other military virtue. More can be achieved with an army drawn from people known for their boldness, an army in which a daring spirit has always been nurtured, than with an army that lacks this quality. For that reason, boldness in general has been mentioned here, even though our actual subject is the boldness of the commander. After having given a broad description of this military virtue, however, there is not much left to say. The higher the military rank, the greater is the degree to which activity is governed by the mind, by the intellect, by insight. Consequently boldness, which is a quality of temperament, will tend to be held in check. This explains why it is so rare in the higher ranks, and why it is all the more admirable when found there. Boldness governed by superior intellect is the mark of a hero. This kind of boldness does not consist in defying the natural order of things and in crudely offending the laws of probability; it is rather a matter of energetically supporting that higher form of analysis by which genius arrives at a decision: rapid, only partly conscious weighing of the possibilities. Boldness can lend wings to intellect and insight; the stronger the wings then, the greater the heights, the wider the view, and the better the results; though a greater prize, of course, involves greater risks. The average man, not to speak of a hesitant or weak one, may in an imaginary situation, in the peace of his room far removed from danger and responsibility, arrive at the right answer—that is, insofar as this is possible without exposure to reality. But beset on every side with danger and responsibility he will lose perspective. Even if this is provided by others, he will lose his powers of decision, for here no one else can help him.

In other words a distinguished commander without boldness is unthinkable. No man who is not born bold can play such a role, and therefore we consider this quality the first prerequisite of the great military leader. How much of this quality remains by the time he reaches senior rank, after training and experience have affected and modified it, is another question. The greater the extent to which it is retained, the greater the range of his genius. The magnitude of the risks increases, but so does that of the goal. To the critical student there is not much difference between actions governed by some compelling long-range aim and those that are dictated by pure ambition—between the policies of a Frederick and an Alexander. The actions of the latter may fascinate the imagination because of their supreme boldness, while those of the former may be more satisfying to the intellect because they are dictated by an inner necessity.

We must mention one more factor of importance.

An army may be imbued with boldness for two reasons: it may come naturally to the people from which the troops are recruited, or it may be the result of a victorious war fought under bold leadership. If the latter is the case, boldness will at the outset be lacking.

Today practically no means other than war will educate a people in this spirit of boldness; and it has to be a war waged under daring leadership. Nothing else will counteract the softness and the desire for ease which debase the people in times of growing prosperity and increasing trade.

A people and nation can hope for a strong position in the world only if national character and familiarity with war fortify each other by continual interaction.

CHAPTER SEVEN
Perseverance

The reader expects to hear of strategic theory, of lines and angles, and instead of these denizens of the scientific world he finds himself encountering only creatures of everyday life. But the author cannot bring himself to be in the slightest degree more scientific than he considers his subject to warrant—strange as this attitude may appear.

In war more than anywhere else things do not turn out as we expect. Nearby they do not appear as they did from a distance. With what assurance an architect watches the progress of his work and sees his plans gradually take shape! A doctor, though much more exposed to chance and to inexplicable results, knows his medicines and the effects they produce. By contrast, a general in time of war is constantly bombarded by reports both true and false: by errors arising from fear or negligence or hastiness: by disobedience born of right or wrong interpretations, of ill will, of a proper or mistaken sense of duty, of laziness, or of exhaustion; and by accidents that nobody could have foreseen. In short, he is exposed to countless impressions, most of them disturbing, few of them encouraging. Long experience of war creates a knack of rapidly assessing these phenomena; courage and strength of character are as impervious to them as a rock to the rippling waves. If a man were to yield to these pressures, he would never complete an operation. *Perseverance* in the chosen course is the essential counterweight, provided that no compelling reasons intervene to the contrary. Moreover, there is hardly a worthwhile enterprise in war whose execution does not call for infinite effort, trouble, and privation; and as man under pressure tends to give in to physical and intellectual weakness, only great strength of will can lead to the objective. It is steadfastness that will earn the admiration of the world and of posterity.

ROBERT E. LEE

1807-1870

Recollections and Letters of General Robert E. Lee

1924

Robert E. Lee is revered in many quarters as one of the most, if not the most, celebrated generals of the Confederate forces during the American Civil War. His name is both synonymous with the Confederacy and with helping to re-unite the country with his surrender to General Ulysses S. Grant at Appomattox Court House. Despite Lee's being on the losing side, Grant accorded him respect and dignity. Lee went on to become president of Washington College, now Washington and Lee University. The following passage was prepared by Lee's son, also called Robert E. Lee, whose book pulled from his father's many letters of correspondence. What qualities did Lee exhibit that made his soldiers love and admire him?

Selection from:

Lee, R. E. (1924). *Recollections and letters of General Robert E. Lee.* (pp.144-160). Garden City, N. Y.: Garden City.

Chapter VIII
THE SURRENDER

FORT FISHER CAPTURED—LEE MADE COMMANDER-IN-
CHIEF-BATTLE OF FIVE FORKS—RETREAT OF THE
ARMY OF NORTHERN VIRGINIA—FAREWELL TO HIS
MEN—THE GENERAL'S RECEPTION IN RICHMOND
AFTER THE SURRENDER—PRESIDENT DAVIS HEARS
THE NEWS—LEE'S VISITORS—HIS SON ROBERT
TURNS FARMER

THE year 1865 had now commenced. The strength of that
thin gray line, drawn out to less than one thousand men to
the mile, which had repulsed every attempt of the enemy to
break through it, was daily becoming less. The capture of Fort
Fisher, our last open port, January 15th, cut off all supplies
and munitions from the outside world. Sherman had reached
Savannah in December, from which point he was ready to unite
with Grant at any time. From General Lee's letters, official
and private, one gets a clear view of the desperateness of his
position. He had been made commander-in-chief of all the
military forces in the Confederate States on February 6th. In
his order issued on accepting this command he says:

> " . . . Deeply impressed with the difficulties and
> responsibilities of the position, and humbly
> invoking the guidance of Almighty God, I rely
> for success upon the courage and fortitude of the
> army, sustained by the patriotism and firmness
> of the people, confident that their united efforts
> under the blessing of Heaven will secure peace and
> independence . . ."

General Beauregard, who had so ably defended Petersburg
when it was first attacked, and who had assisted so materially
in its subsequent defense, had been sent to gather troops to

try to check Sherman's advance through the Carolinas. But Beauregard's health was now very bad, and it was feared he would have to abandon the field. In a letter to the Secretary of War, dated February 21, 1865, my father says:

" . . . In the event of the necessity of abandoning our position on James River, I shall endeavour to unite the corps of the army about Burkeville[1], so as to retain communication with the North and South as long as practicable, and also with the West. I should think Lynchburg, or some point west, the most advantageous place to which to remove stores from Richmond. This, however, is a most difficult point at this time to decide, and the place may have to be changed by circumstances. It was my intention in my former letter to apply for General Joseph E. Johnston, that I might assign him to duty, should circumstances permit. I have had no official report of the condition of General Beauregard's health. It is stated from many sources to be bad. If he should break down entirely, it might be fatal. In that event, I should have no one with whom to supply his place. I therefore respectfully request General Johnston may be ordered to report to me, and that I may be informed where he is."

In a letter to the Secretary of War, written the next day:

" . . . But you may expect Sheridan to move up the Valley, and Stoneman from Knoxville, as Sherman draws near Roanoke. What then will become of those sections of the country? I know of no other troops that could be given to Beauregard. Bragg will be forced back by Schofield, I fear, and, until

---

[1]   Junction of Southside and Danville Railroad

I abandon James River, nothing can be sent from this army. Grant, I think, is now preparing to draw out by his left with the intent of enveloping me. He may wait till his other columns approach nearer, or he may be preparing to anticipate my withdrawal. I cannot tell yet . . . Everything of value should be removed from Richmond. It is of the first importance to save all powder. The cavalry and artillery of the army are still scattered for want of provender, and our supply and ammunition trains, which ought to be with the army in case of a sudden movement, are absent collecting provisions and forage—some in western Virginia and some in North Carolina. You will see to what straits we are reduced; but I trust to work out."

On the same day, in a letter to my mother, he writes:

" . . . After sending my note this morning, I received from the express office a bag of socks. You will have to send down your offerings as soon as you can, and bring your work to a close, for I think General Grant will move against us soon—within a week, if nothing prevents —and no man can tell what may be the result; but trusting to a merciful God, who does not always give the battle to the strong, I pray we may not be overwhelmed. I shall, however, endeavour to do my duty and fight to the last. Should it be necessary to abandon our position to prevent being surrounded, what will you do? You must consider the question, and make up your mind. It is a fearful condition, and we must rely for guidance and protection upon a kind Providence . . ."

About this time, I saw my father for the last time until after the surrender. We had been ordered up to the army from our camp nearly forty miles away, reaching the vicinity of Petersburg the morning of the attack of General Gordon on Fort Stedman, on March 25th. My brother and I had ridden ahead of the division to report its presence, when we met the General riding Traveller, almost alone, back from that part of the lines opposite the fort. Since then I have often recalled the sadness of his face, its careworn expression. When he caught sight of his two sons, a bright smile at once lit up his countenance, and he showed very plainly his pleasure at seeing us. He thanked my brother for responding so promptly to his call upon him, and regretted that events had so shaped themselves that the division would not then be needed, as he had hoped it would be.

No good results followed Gordon's gallant attack. His supports did not come up at the proper time, and our losses were very heavy, mostly prisoners. Two days after this, Sheridan, with ten thousand mounted men, joined Grant, having marched from the Valley of Virginia *via* Staunton and Charlottesville. On the 28th, everything being ready, General Grant commenced to turn our right, and having more than three men to our one, he had no difficult task. On that very day my father wrote to my mother:

> " . . . I have received your note with a bag of socks. I return the bag and receipt. The count is all right this time. I have put in the bag General Scott's autobiography, which I thought you might like to read. The General, of course, stands out prominently, and does not hide his light under a bushel, but he appears the bold, sagacious, truthful man that he is. I inclose a note from little Agnes. I shall be very glad to see her to-morrow, but cannot recommend pleasure trips now . . ."

On April 1st the Battle of Five Forks was fought, where about fifty thousand infantry and cavalry—more men than were in our entire army—attacked our extreme right and turned it, so that, to save our communications, we had to abandon our lines at Petersburg, giving up that city and Richmond. From that time to April 9th the Army of Northern Virginia struggled to get back to some position where it could concentrate its forces and make a stand; but the whole world knows of that six-days' retreat. I shall not attempt to describe it in detail—indeed, I could not if I would, for I was not present all the time—but will quote from those who have made it a study and who are far better fitted to record it than I am. General Early, in his address at Lexington, Virginia, January 19, 1872—General Lee's birthday—eloquently and briefly describes these six days as follows:

> "... The retreat from the lines of Richmond and Petersburg began in the early days of April, and the remnant of the Army of Northern Virginia fell back, more than one hundred miles, before its overpowering antagonist, repeatedly presenting front to the latter and giving battle so as to check his progress. Finally, from mere exhaustion, less than eight thousand men with arms in their hands, of the noblest army that ever fought 'in the tide of time,' were surrendered at Appomattox to an army of 150,000 men; the sword of Robert E. Lee, without a blemish on it, was sheathed forever; and the flag, to which he had added such luster, was furled, to be, henceforth, embalmed in the affectionate remembrance of those who remained faithful during all our trials, and will do so to the end."

Colonel Archer Anderson, in his address at the unveiling of the Lee monument in Richmond, Virginia, May 29, 1890, speaking of the siege of Petersburg and of the surrender, utters these noble words:

" . . . Of the siege of Petersburg, I have only time
to say that in it for nine months the Confederate
commander displayed every art by which genius
and courage can make good the lack of numbers
and resources. But the increasing misfortunes of
the Confederate arms on other theatres of the war
gradually cut off the supply of men and means. The
Army of Northern Virginia ceased to be recruited,
it ceased to be adequately fed. It lived for months
on less than one-third rations. It was demoralized,
not by the enemy in its front, but by the enemy in
Georgia and the Carolinas. It dwindled to 35,000
men, holding a front of thirty-five miles; but over
the enemy it still cast the shadow of its great name.
Again and again, by a bold offensive, it arrested the
Federal movement to fasten on its communications.
At last, an irresistible concentration of forces broke
through its long thin line of battle. Petersburg had
to be abandoned. Richmond was evacuated. Trains
bearing supplies were intercepted, and a starving
army, harassed for seven days by incessant attacks
on rear and flank, found itself completely hemmed
in by overwhelming masses. Nothing remained to
it but its stainless honour, its unbroken courage.
In those last solemn scenes, when strong men,
losing all self-control, broke down and sobbed like
children, Lee stood forth as great as in the days of
victory and triumph. No disaster crushed his spirit,
no extremity of danger ruffled his bearing. In the
agony of dissolution now invading that proud army,
which for years had wrested victory from every peril,
in that blackness of utter darkness, he preserved the
serene lucidity of his mind. He looked the stubborn
facts calmly in the face, and when no military
resource remained, when he recognised the
impossibility of making another march or fighting

another battle, he bowed his head in submission to that Power which makes and unmakes nations. The surrender of the fragments of the Army of Northern Virginia closed the imperishable record of his military life . . ."

From the London *Standard,* at a time of his last illness, I quote these words relating to this retreat:

"When the Army of Northern Virginia marched out of the lines around Petersburg and Richmond, it still numbered some twenty-six thousand men. After a retreat of six days, in the face of an overwhelming enemy, with a crushing artillery—a retreat impeded by constant fighting and harassed by countless hordes of cavalry—eight thousand were given up by the capitulation at Appomattox Court House. Brilliant as were General Lee's earlier triumphs, we believe that he gave higher proofs of genius in his last campaign, and that hardly any of his victories were so honourable to himself and his army as that of his six-days' retreat."

Swinton, in his "History of the Army of the Potomac," after justly praising its deeds, thus speaks of its great opponent, the Army of Northern Virginia:

"Nor can there fail to arise the image of that other army that was the adversary of the Army of the Potomac, and—who that once looked upon it can ever forget it? —that array of tattered uniforms and bright muskets—that body of incomparable infantry, the Army of Northern Virginia, which, for four years, carried the revolt on its bayonets, opposing a constant front to the mighty concentration of power brought against it; which, receiving terrible blows, did not fail to give the like, and which, vital in all its parts, died only with its annihilation."

General Long, in speaking of its hardships and struggles during the retreat, thus describes how the army looked up to their commander and trusted him to bring them through all their troubles:

"General Lee had never appeared more grandly heroic than on this occasion. All eyes were raised to him for a deliverance which no human power seemed able to give. He alone was expected to provide food for the starving army and rescue it from the attacks of a powerful and eager enemy. Under the accumulation of difficulties, his courage seemed to expand, and wherever he appeared his presence inspired the weak and weary with renewed energy to continue the toilsome march. During these trying scenes his countenance wore its habitual calm, grave expression. Those who watched his face to catch a glimpse of what was passing in his mind could gather thence no trace of his inner sentiments."

No one can tell what he suffered. He did in all things what he considered right. Self he absolutely abandoned. As he said, so he believed, that "human virtue should equal human calamity." A day or two before the surrender, he said to General Pendleton:

" . . . I have never believed we could, against the gigantic combination for our subjugation, make good in the long run our independence unless foreign powers should, directly or indirectly, assist us . . . But such considerations really made with me no difference. We had, I was satisfied, sacred principles to maintain and rights to defend, for which we were in duty bound to do our best, even if we perished in the endeavour."

After his last attempt was made with Gordon and Fitz Lee to break through the lines of the enemy in the early morning of the 9th, and Colonel Venable informed him that it was not possible, he said:

> "Then there is nothing left me but to go and see General Grant." When some one near him, hearing this, said:
>
> "Oh, General, what will history say of the surrender of the army in the field?" he replied:
>
> "Yes, I know they will say hard things of us; they will not understand how we were overwhelmed by numbers; but that is not the question, Colonel; the question is, is it right to surrender this army? If it is right, then I will take all the responsibility."

There had been some correspondence with Grant, just before the conversation with General Pendleton. After Gordon's attack failed, a flag of truce was sent out, and, about eleven o'clock, General Lee went to meet General Grant. The terms of surrender were agreed upon, and then General Lee called attention to the pressing needs of his men. He said:

> "I have a thousand or more of your men and officers, whom we have required to march along with us for several days. I shall be glad to send them to your lines as soon as it can be arranged, for I have no provisions for them. My own men have been living for the last few days principally upon parched corn, and we are badly in need of both rations and forage."

Grant said he would at once send him 25,000 rations. General Lee told him that amount would be ample and would be a great relief. He then rode back to his troops. The rations issued then to our army were the supplies destined for us but captured at Amelia Court House. Had they reached us in time, they would have given the half-starved troops that were left strength enough to make a further struggle. General Long graphically pictures the last scenes:

> "It is impossible to describe the anguish of the troops when it was known that the surrender of the army was inevitable. Of all their trials, this was the greatest and hardest to endure. There was no consciousness of shame; each heart could boast with honest pride that its duty had been done to the end, and that still unsullied remained its honour. When, after his interview with General Grant, General Lee again appeared, a shout of welcome instinctively went up from the army. But instantly recollecting the sad occasion that brought him before them, their shouts sank into silence, every hat was raised, and the bronzed faces of thousands of grim warriors were bathed in tears. As he rode slowly along the lines, hundreds of his devoted veterans pressed around the noble chief, trying to take his hand, touch his person, or even lay their hands upon his horse, thus exhibiting for him their great affection. The General then with head bare, and tears flowing freely down his manly cheeks, bade adieu to the army."

In a few words: "Men, we have fought through the war together; I have done my best for you; my heart is too full to say more," he bade them good-bye and told them to return to their homes and become good citizens. The next day he issued his farewell address, the last order published to the army:

HEADQUARTERS, ARMY OF
NORTHERN VIRGINIA,
April 10, 1865.

"After four years' of arduous service, marked by unsurpassed courage and fortitude, the Army of Northern Virginia has been compelled to yield to overwhelming numbers and resources. I need not tell the survivors of so many hard-fought battles, who have remained steadfast to the last, that I have consented to this result from no distrust of them; but, feeling that valour and devotion could accomplish nothing that could compensate for the loss that would have attended the continuation of the contest, I have determined to avoid the useless sacrifice of those whose past services have endeared them to their countrymen. By the terms of the agreement, officers and men can return to their homes and remain there until exchanged. You will take with you the satisfaction that proceeds from the consciousness of duty faithfully performed; and I earnestly pray that a merciful God will extend to you His blessing and protection. With an increasing admiration of your constancy and devotion to your country, and a grateful remembrance of your kind and generous consideration of myself, I bid you an affectionate farewell.

"R. E. LEE, General."

General Long says that General Meade called on General Lee on the 10th, and in the course of conversation remarked:

"Now that the war may be considered over, I hope you will not deem it improper for me to ask, for my personal information, the strength of your army during the operations about Richmond and Petersburg." General Lee replied:

"At no time did my force exceed 35,000 men; often it was less." With a look of surprise, Meade answered:

"General, you amaze me; we always estimated your force at about seventy thousand men."

General de Chanal, a French officer, who was present, states that General Lee, who had been an associate of Meade's in the engineers in the "old army," said to him pleasantly:

"Meade, years are telling on you; your hair is getting quite gray."

"Ah, General Lee," was Meade's prompt reply, "it is not the work of years; you are responsible for my gray hairs!"

"Three days after the surrender," says Long, "the Army of Northern Virginia had dispersed in every direction, and three weeks later the veterans of a hundred battles had exchanged the musket and the sword for the implements of husbandry. It is worthy of remark that never before was there an army disbanded with less disorder. Thousands of soldiers were set adrift on the world without a penny in their pockets to enable them to reach their homes. Yet none of the scenes of riot that often follow the disbanding of armies marked their course."

A day or two after the surrender, General Lee started for Richmond, riding Traveller, who had carried him so well all through the war. He was accompanied by some of his staff. On the way, he stopped at the house of his eldest brother, Charles Carter Lee, who lived on the Upper James in Powhatan County. He spent the evening in talking with his brother, but when bedtime came, though begged by his host to take the room and bed prepared for him, he insisted on going to his old tent, pitched by the roadside, and passed the night in the quarters that he was accustomed to. On April 15th he arrived in Richmond. The people there soon recognised him; men, women, and children crowded around him, cheering and waving hats and handkerchiefs. It was more like the welcome to a conqueror than to a defeated prisoner on parole. He raised his hat in response to their greetings, and rode quietly to his home on Franklin Street, where my mother and sisters were anxiously awaiting him. Thus he returned to that private family life for which he had always longed, and became what he always desired to be—a peaceful citizen in a peaceful land.

In attempting to describe these last days of the Army of Northern Virginia, I have quoted largely from Long, Jones, Taylor, and Fitz Lee, all of whom have given more or less full accounts of the movements of both armies.

It so happened that shortly after we left our lines, April 2d or 3d, in one of the innumerable contests, my horse was shot, and in getting him and myself off the field, having no choice of routes, the pursuing Federal cavalry intervened between me and the rest of our command, so I had to make my way around the head of Sheridan's advance squadrons before I could rejoin our forces. This I did not succeed in accomplishing until April 9th, the day of the surrender, for my wounded horse had to be left with a farmer, who kindly gave me one of his own in exchange, saying I could send him back when I was able, or, if I was prevented, that I could keep him and he would replace him with mine when he got well.

As I was riding toward Appomattox on the 9th, I met a body of our cavalry with General T. H. Rosser at the head. He told me that General Lee and his army had surrendered, and that this force had made its way out, and was marching back to Lynchburg, expecting thence to reach General Johnston's army. To say that I was surprised does not express my feelings. I had never heard the word "surrender" mentioned, nor even suggested, in connection with our general or our army. I could not believe it, and did not until I was positively assured by all my friends who were with Rosser's column that it was absolutely so. Very sadly I turned back and went to Lynchburg along with them. There I found some wagons from our headquarters which had been sent back, and with them the horses and servants of the staff. These I got together, not believing for an instant that our struggle was over, and, with several officers from our command and others, we made our way to Greensboro, North Carolina. There I found Mr. Davis and his cabinet and representatives of the Confederate departments from Richmond. There was a great diversity of opinion amongst all present as to what we should do. After waiting a couple of days, looking over the situation from every point of view, consulting with my uncle, Commodore S. S. Lee, of the Confederate Navy, and with many others, old friends of my father and staunch adherents of the Southern cause, it was determined to go back to Virginia to get our paroles, go home, and go to work.

While at Greensboro I went to see President Davis, just before he proceeded on his way farther south. He was calm and dignified, and, in his conversation with several officers of rank who were there, seemed to think, and so expressed himself, that our cause was not lost, though sorely stricken, and that we could rally our forces west of the Mississippi and make good our fight. While I was in the room, Mr. Davis received the first official communication from General Lee of his surrender. Colonel John Taylor Wood, his aide-de-camp, had taken me in to see the President, and he and I were standing by him when the despatch from General Lee was brought to him. After reading it, he handed it without comment to us; then, turning away, he silently wept bitter tears. He seemed quite broken at the moment by this tangible evidence of the loss of his army and the misfortune of its general. All of us, respecting his great grief, silently withdrew, leaving him with Colonel Wood. I never saw him again.

I started for Richmond, accompanied by several companions, with the servants and horses belonging to our headquarters. These I had brought down with me from Lynchburg, where I had found them after the surrender. After two weeks of marching and resting, I arrived in Richmond and found my father there, in the house on Franklin Street, now the rooms of the "Virginia Historical Society," and also my mother, brother, and sisters. They were all much relieved at my reappearance.

As well as I can recall my father at this time, he appeared to be very well physically, though he looked older, grayer, more quiet and reserved. He seemed very tired, and was always glad to talk of any other subject than that of the war or anything pertaining thereto. We all tried to cheer and help him. And the people of Richmond and of the entire South were as kind and considerate as it was possible to be. Indeed, I think their great kindness tired him. He appreciated it all, was courteous, grateful, and polite, but he had been under such a terrible strain for several years that he needed the time and quiet to get back his strength of heart and mind. All sorts and conditions of people came to see him: officers and soldiers from both armies, statesmen, politicians, ministers of the Gospel, mothers and wives to ask about husbands and sons of whom they had heard nothing. To keep him from being overtaxed by this incessant stream of visitors, we formed a sort of guard of the young men in the house, some of whom took it by turns to keep the door and, if possible, turn strangers away. My father was gentle, kind, and polite to all, and never willingly, so far as I know, refused to see any one.

Dan Lee, late of the Confederate States Navy, my first cousin, and myself, one day had charge of the front door, when at it appeared a Federal soldier, accompanied by a darkey carrying a large willow basket filled to the brim with provisions of every kind. The man was Irish all over, and showed by his uniform and carriage that he was a "regular," and not a volunteer. On our asking him what he wanted, he replied that he wanted to see General Lee, that he had heard down the street the General and his family were suffering for lack of something to eat, that he had been with "the Colonel" when he commanded the Second Cavalry, and, as long as he had a cent, his old colonel should not suffer. My father, who had stepped into another room as he heard the bell ring, hearing something of the conversation, came out into the hall. The old Irishman, as soon as he saw him, drew himself up and saluted, and repeated to the General, with tears streaming down his cheeks, what he had just said to us. My father was very much touched, thanked him heartily for his kindness and generosity, but told him that he did not need the things he had brought and could not take them. This seemed to disappoint the old soldier greatly, and he pleaded so hard to be allowed to present the supplies to his old colonel, whom he believed to be in want of them, that at last my father said that he would accept the basket and send it to the hospital, for the sick and wounded, who were really in great need. Though he was not satisfied, he submitted to this compromise, and then to our surprise and dismay, in bidding the General good-bye, threw his arms around him and was attempting to kiss him, when "Dan" and I interfered. As he was leaving, he said:

"Good-bye, Colonel! God bless ye! If I could have got over in time I would have been with ye!"

A day or two after that, when "Dan" was doorkeeper, three Federal officers, a colonel, a major, and a doctor, called and asked to see General Lee. They were shown into the parlour, presented their cards, and said they desired to pay their respects as officers of the United States Army. When Dan went out with the three cards, he was told by some one that my father was up stairs engaged with some other visitor, so he returned and told them this and they departed. When my father came down, was shown the cards and told of the three visitors, he was quite put out at Dan's not having brought him the cards at the time, and that afternoon mounted him on one of his horses and sent him over to Manchester, where they were camped, to look up the three officers and to tell them he would be glad to see them at any time they might be pleased to call. However, Dan failed to find them.

He had another visit at this time which affected him deeply. Two Confederate soldiers in very dilapidated clothing, worn and emaciated in body, came to see him. They said they had been selected from about sixty other fellows, too ragged to come themselves, to offer him a home in the mountains of Virginia. The home was a good house and farm, and near by was a defile, in some rugged hills, from which they could defy the entire Federal Army. They made this offer of a home and their protection because there was a report that he was about to be indicted for treason. The General had to decline to go with them, but the tears came into his eyes at this hearty exhibition of loyalty.

After being in Richmond a few days, and by the advice of my father getting my parole from the United States Provost Marshal there, the question as to what I should do came up. My father told me that I could go back to college if I desired and prepare myself for some profession—that he had a little money which he would be willing and glad to devote to the completion of my education. I think he was strongly in favour of my going back to college. At the same time he told me that, if I preferred it, I could take possession of my farm land in King William County, which I had inherited from my grandfather, Mr. Custis, and make my home there. As there was little left of the farm but the land, he thought he could arrange to help me build a house and purchase stock and machinery.

My brother, General W. H. F. Lee, had already gone down to his place, "The White House" in New Kent County, with Major John Lee, our first cousin, had erected a shanty, and gone to work, breaking up land for a corn crop, putting their cavalry horses to the plow. As I thought my father had use for any means he might have in caring for my mother and sisters, and as I had this property, I determined to become a farmer. However, I did not decide positively, and in the meantime it was thought best that I should join my brother and cousin at the White House and help them make their crop of corn. In returning to Richmond, I had left at "Hickory Hill," General Wickham's place in Hanover County, our horses and servants, taken with me from Lynchburg to Greensboro and back. So bidding all my friends and family good-bye, I went by rail to "Hickory Hill" and started the next day with three servants and about eight horses for New Kent, stopping the first night at "Pampatike." The next day I reached the White House, where the reinforcements I brought with me were hailed with delight. Though I have been a farmer from that day to this, I will say that the crop of corn which we planted that summer, with ourselves and army servants as laborers and our old cavalry horses as teams, and which we did not finish planting until the 9th of June, was the best I ever made.

CHESTER I. BARNARD

1886-1961

The Functions of the Executive

1968

For most of Barnard's working life, he was an executive of AT&T. Following this career, he engaged in public service, working for the Rockefeller Foundation as chairman of the National Science Foundation and as a fellow of the American Association for the Advancement of Science and the American Academy of Arts and Sciences.

Having almost forty years of experience as an executive in organizational settings, Barnard observed that people were much more complex and their motives much more varied than the then current literature suggested. His views, at the time, were considered revolutionary for their focus upon the individual as a person rather than as a cog in a machine. Barnard's book, *The Function of the Executive*, launched the contemporary fields of leadership studies and organizational behavior. In this book Barnard defined many organizational core concepts, including the preconditions of a willingness to cooperate, to communicate, and to be both efficient and effective. In the following excerpt, Barnard details particular qualities of the leader who operates at the executive level.

Source:

Kellerman, B. (2005). Required reading, *Harvard Business Review: General Management Articles*. (pp. 5-11). New York: McGraw-Hill.

Selection from:

Barnard, C. I. (1968). *The functions of the executive*. (pp. 220-223). Cambridge, MA: Harvard University Press.

II. Personnel

The scheme of organization is dependent not only upon the general factors of the organization as a whole, but likewise, as we have indicated, on the availability of various kinds of services for the executive positions. This becomes in its turn the strategic factor. In general, the principles of the economy of incentives apply here as well as to other more general personnel problems. The balance of factors and the technical problems of this special class, however, are not only different from those generally to be found in other spheres of organization economy but are highly special in different types of organizations.

The most important single contribution required of the executive, certainly the most universal qualification, is loyalty, domination by the organization personality. This is the first necessity because the lines of communication cannot function at all unless the personal contributions of executives will be present at the required positions, at the times necessary, without default for ordinary personal reasons. This, as a personal qualification, is known in secular organizations as the quality of "responsibility"; in political organizations as "regularity"; in governmental organizations as fealty or loyalty; in religious organizations as "complete submission" to the faith and to the hierarchy of objective religious authority.

The contribution of personal loyalty and submission is least susceptible to tangible inducements. It cannot be bought either by material inducements or by other positive incentives, except all other things be equal. This is as true of industrial organizations, I believe, as of any others. It is rather generally understood that although money or other material inducements must usually be paid to responsible persons, responsibility itself does not arise from such inducements.

However, love of prestige is, in general, a much more important inducement in the case of executives than with the rest of the personnel. Interest in work and pride in organization are other incentives that usually must be present. These facts are much obscured as respects commercial organizations, where material inducements appear to be the effective factors partly because such inducements are more readily offered in such organizations and partly because, since the other incentives are often equal as between such organizations, material inducements are the only available differential factor. It also becomes an important secondary factor to individuals in many cases, because prestige and official responsibilities impose heavy material burdens on them. Hence neither churches nor socialistic states have been able to escape the necessity of direct or indirect material inducements for high dignitaries or officials. But this is probably incidental and superficial in all organizations. It appears to be true that in all of them adequate incentives to executive services are difficult to offer. Those most available in the present age are tangible, materialistic; but on the whole they are both insufficient and often abortive.[1]

---

[1] After much experience, I am convinced that the most ineffective services in a continuing effort are in one sense those of volunteers, or of semi-volunteers; for example, half-pay workers. What appears to be inexpensive is in fact very expensive, because non-material incentives—such as prestige, toleration of too great personal interest in the work with its accompanying fads and "pet" projects, the yielding to exaggerated conceptions of individual importance—are causes of internal friction and many other

Following loyalty, responsibility, and capacity to be dominated by organization personality, come the more specific personal abilities. They are roughly divided into two classes: relatively general abilities, involving general alertness, comprehensiveness of interest, flexibility, faculty of adjustment, poise, courage, etc.; and specialized abilities based on particular aptitudes and acquired techniques. The first kind is relatively difficult to appraise because it depends upon innate characteristics developed through general experience. It is not greatly susceptible of immediate inculcation. The second kind may be less rare because the division of labor, that is, organization itself, fosters it automatically, and because it is susceptible to development (at a cost) by training and education. We deliberately and more and more turn out specialists; but we do not develop general executives well by specific efforts, and we know very little about how to do it.

The higher the positions in the line of authority, the more general the abilities required. The scarcity of such abilities, together with the necessity for keeping the lines of authority as short as feasible, controls the organization of executive work. It leads to the reduction of the number of formally executive positions to the minimum, a measure made possible by creating about the executives in many cases staffs of specialists who supplement them in time, energy, and technical capacities. This is made feasible by elaborate and often delicate arrangements to correct error resulting from the faults of over-specialization and the paucity of line executives.

The operation of such systems of complex executive organization requires the highest development of the executive arts. Its various forms and techniques are most definitely exemplified in the armies and navies of the major powers, the Postal Administrations of several European countries, the Bell

---

undesirable consequences. Yet in many emergency situations, and in a large part of political, charitable, civic, educational, and religious organization work, often indispensable services cannot be obtained by material incentives.

Telephone System, some of the great railway systems, and the Catholic Church; and perhaps in the political organization of the British Empire.[2] One of the first limitations of world-wide or even a much more restricted international organization is the necessity for the development of these forms and techniques far beyond their present status.

Thus, jointly with the development of the scheme of organization, the selection, promotion, demotion, and dismissal of men becomes the essence of maintaining the system of communication without which no organization can exist. The selection in part, but especially the promotion, demotion, and dismissal of men, depend upon the exercise of supervision or what is often called "control."

Control relates directly, and in conscious application chiefly, to the work of the organization as a whole rather than to the work of executives as such. But so heavily dependent is the success of cooperation upon the functioning of the executive organization that practically the control is over executives for the most part. If the work of an organization is not successful, if it is inefficient, if it cannot maintain the services of its personnel, the conclusion is that its "management" is wrong; that is, that the scheme of communication or the associated personnel or both, that is, the executive department directly related, are at fault. This is, sometimes at least, not true, but often it is. Moreover, for the correction of such faults the first reliance is upon executive organization. The methods by which control is exercised are, of course, numerous and largely technical to each organization, and need not be further discussed here.

---

[2] From a structural point of view the organization of the United States of America is especially noteworthy, but from the viewpoint of the executive functions it is intended to be defective; that is, the system of States Rights or dual sovereignty and the separation of legislative, judicial, and executive departments precludes a common center of authoritative communication in American government as a formal organization. It is intended or expected that the requirements will be met by informal organization.

SECTION III

WHAT LEADERS DO

The leader's behavior is a manifestation of his or her interior life. Thus, the qualities of leaders explored in Section II become the leader-like behaviors explored in Section III. The leader's behavior, explored by the works in Section III, is focused on the followers—bringing out their self-leadership, nurturing their inner giants, and gaining their trust.

Leadership behaviors are not always simple to execute. In the first reading, Lao-tzu writes, "If you don't trust the people, you make them untrustworthy." [17] People respond in kind to a leader's behaviors and underlying expectations. Thus, the leader's reflection on his or her own behavior is important. In general, many of the fundamental leader behaviors, such as leadership by example, coaching, gaining a confidence, and giving effective feedback, are far more difficult to execute than might be imagined. The readings in this section are intended to ease the reader into deeper levels of reflection on what leaders actually need to do.

LAO-TZU

ca. 604-517 B.C.E.

Tao Te Ching

ca. 509 B.C.E.

It is reputed that Lao-tzu, originally named Li-erh, was born in central China fifty years before the birth of Confucius. His work is mainly a system of ethics, and he is recognized as the founder of Taoism. Following a lifetime of meditation and careful observation, he wrote the *Tao Te Ching* ("How Things Work" or "Book of the Way and Virtue") in two sections comprised of five thousand characters.

Lao-tzu has been a major influence on Chinese thinking for two-and-a-half millennia and remains widely read in China today. His work has important things to say about leadership and management. Core principles of the book include the achievement of ends through peace and harmony rather than through conflict and the belief that true achievement comes not through action but rather through its opposite, *wu wei* or non-action.

Selection from:

Lao-tzu. (1988). *Tao Te Ching.* (S. Mitchell, Trans). (Sections 10, 15, 17, 19, 30, 33, 38, 57, 68). New York: HarperCollins Publishers.

10

Can you coax your mind from its wandering
and keep to the original oneness?
Can you let your body become
supple as a newborn child's?
Can you cleanse your inner vision
until you see nothing but the light?
Can you love people and lead them
without imposing your will?
Can you deal with the most vital matters
by letting events take their course?
Can you step back from your own mind
and thus understand all things?

Giving birth and nourishing,
having without possessing,
acting with no expectations,
leading and not trying to control:
this is the supreme virtue.

15

The ancient Masters were profound and subtle.
Their wisdom was unfathomable.
There is no way to describe it;
all we can describe is their appearance.

They were careful
as someone crossing an iced-over stream.
Alert as a warrior in enemy territory.
Courteous as a guest.
Fluid as melting ice.
Shapable as a block of wood.
Receptive as a valley.
Clear as a glass of water.

Do you have the patience to wait
till your mud settles and the water is clear?
Can you remain unmoving
till the right action arises by itself?

The Master doesn't seek fulfillment.
Not seeking, not expecting,
she is present, and can welcome all things.

17

When the Master governs, the people
are hardly aware that he exists.
Next best is a leader who is loved.
Next, one who is feared.
The worst is one who is despised.

If you don't trust the people,
you make them untrustworthy.

The Master doesn't talk, he acts.
When his work is done,
the people say, "Amazing:
we did it, all by ourselves!"

19

Throw away holiness and wisdom,
and people will be a hundred times happier.
Throw away morality and justice,
and people will do the right thing.
Throw away industry and profit,
and there won't be any thieves.

If these three aren't enough,

just stay at the center of the circle
and let all things take their course.

30

Whoever relies on the Tao in governing men
doesn't try to force issues
or defeat enemies by force of arms.
For every force there is a counterforce.
Violence, even well intentioned,
always rebounds upon oneself.

The Master does his job
and then stops.
He understands that the universe
is forever out of control,
and that trying to dominate events
goes against the current of the Tao.
Because he believes in himself,
he doesn't try to convince others.
Because he is content with himself,
he doesn't need others' approval.
Because he accepts himself,
the whole world accepts him.

33

Knowing others is intelligence;
knowing yourself is true wisdom.
Mastering others is strength;
mastering yourself is true power.

If you realize that you have enough,
you are truly rich.
If you stay in the center

and embrace death with your whole heart,
you will endure forever.

38

The Master doesn't try to be powerful;
thus he is truly powerful.
The ordinary man keeps reaching for power;
thus he never has enough.

The Master does nothing,
yet he leaves nothing undone.
The ordinary man is always doing things,
yet many more are left to be done.

The kind man does something,
yet something remains undone.
The just man does something,
and leaves many things to be done.
The moral man does something,
and when no one responds
he rolls up his sleeves and uses force.

When the Tao is lost, there is goodness.
When goodness is lost, there is morality.
When morality is lost, there is ritual.
Ritual is the husk of true faith,
the beginning of chaos.

Therefore the Master concerns himself
with the depths and not the surface,
with the fruit and not the flower.
He has no will of his own.
He dwells in reality,
and lets all illusions go.

57

If you want to be a great leader,
you must learn to follow the Tao.
Stop trying to control.
Let go of fixed plans and concepts,
and the world will govern itself.

The more prohibitions you have,
the less virtuous people will be.
The more weapons you have,
the less secure people will be.
The more subsidies you have,
the less self-reliant people will be.

Therefore the Master says:
I let go of the law,
and people become honest.
I let go of economics,
and people become prosperous.
I let go of religion,
and people become serene.
I let go of all desire for the common good,
and the good becomes common as grass.

68

The best athlete
wants his opponent at his best.
The best general
enters the mind of his enemy.
The best businessman
serves the communal good.
The best leader
follows the will of the people.

All of them embody
the virtue of non-competition.
Not that they don't love to compete,
but they do it in the spirit of play.
In this they are like children
and in harmony with the Tao.

CAROLINE ALEXANDER

1874-1922

The Endurance:
Shackleton's Legendary Antarctic Expedition

1999

Ernest Shackleton was an Anglo-Irish explorer who was knighted for his success commanding the 1907-1909 British Antarctic Expedition. However, during the 1914-1916 return expedition in the ship, *The Endurance,* Shackleton and his crew of twenty-seven men were stranded off Antarctica when massive blocks of ice crushed their ship. After seven months of staggering through the Antarctic, Shackleton and his crew reached civilization on South Georgia Island. Shackleton completed one of the most celebrated feats in maritime history; he managed to bring each one of his men home alive.

The following excerpt includes some details of the end of the expedition when the men wandered into Stromness Station to safety and what happened to some of the men afterwards. The reader is challenged to consider what fundamentals of leadership would be essential to accomplishing such a death-defying feat.

Selection from:

Alexander, C. (1999). *The Endurance: Shackleton's legendary Antarctic expedition.* (pp.164-169). New York: Alfred A. Knopf.

[***]

An hour later they stood on the last ridge, looking down into Stromness Bay.

A whaling boat came in sight, and after it a sailing ship; tiny figures could be seen moving about the sheds of the station. For the last time on the journey, they turned and shook each other's hands.

Marching mechanically now, too tired for thought, they moved through the last stages of their trek. Searching for a way down the ridge to the harbor, they followed the course of a small stream, up to their ankles in its icy water. The stream ended in a waterfall with a twenty-five-foot drop, and without a second thought, they determined to follow it over. There was no time left, their strength and wits were failing; they could no longer calculate or strategize, but only keep moving forward. Securing one end of their worn rope to a boulder, they first lowered Crean over the edge, and he vanished entirely into the waterfall. Then Shackleton, and then Worsley, who was, as Shackleton wrote, "the lightest and most nimble of the party." Leaving the rope dangling, they staggered ahead.

At three in the afternoon, they arrived at the outskirts of Stromness Station. They had traveled for thirty-six hours without rest. Their bearded faces were black with blubber smoke, and their matted hair, clotted with salt, hung almost to their shoulders. Their filthy clothes were in tatters; in vain Worsley had tried to pin together the seat of his trousers, shredded in their glissade down the mountain. Close to the station they encountered the first humans outside their own party they had set eyes on in nearly eighteen months—two small children, who ran from them in fright. As in a dream the men kept moving, through the outskirts of the station, through the dark digesting house, out towards the wharf, each banal fixture of the grimy station now fraught with significance. A man saw them, started, and hurriedly passed on, probably thinking the ragged trio were drunken, derelict sailors—it would not have occurred to anyone that there could be castaways on South Georgia Island.

The station foreman, Matthias Andersen, was on the wharf. Speaking English, Shackleton asked to be taken to Captain Anton Andersen, who had been winter manager when the *Endurance* sailed. Looking them over, the foreman replied that Captain Andersen was no longer there, but he would take them to the new manager, Thoralf Sørlle. Shackleton nodded; he knew Sørlle. Sørlle had entertained them two years previously, when the expedition had touched in at Stromness.

Tactfully unquestioning, the foreman led the three to the station manager's home. "Mr. Smile came out to the door and said, 'Well?'" Shackleton recorded.

"'Don't you know me?' I said.

"'I know your voice,' he replied doubtfully. 'You're the mate of the *Daisy*.'"

An old Norwegian whaler who was also present gave an account, in his broken

English, of the meeting.

"Manager say: 'Who the *hell* are you?' and terrible bearded man in the centre of the three say very quietly: 'My name is Shackleton.' Me—I turn away and weep."

They had done it all; and now long-held dreams came true. Hot baths, the first in two years; a shave, clean new clothes, and all the cakes and starch they could eat. The hospitality of the whalers was boundless. After an enormous meal, Worsley was dispatched with a relief ship, the *Samson*, to collect the rest of the party at King Haakon Bay, while Shackleton and Sørlle urgently talked over plans to rescue the men on Elephant Island.

That night, the weather took a turn for the worse. Lying in his bunk on the *Samson*, Worsley listened to the rising gale.

"Had we been crossing that night," he wrote, "nothing could have saved us." McNish, McCarthy, and Vincent were sheltered under the upturned *Caird* when Worsley came ashore in a whaler to greet them the following morning. Thrilled to be rescued, they nonetheless grumbled that none of their own party had come and that collecting them had been left to the Norwegians.

"'Well, I'm here,'" Worsley reported himself as saying, clearly delighted by the turn of events.

"[T]hey stared," he continued. "Clean and shaved, they had taken me for a Norwegian!"

Taking up their meager possessions, the last of the *James Caird* crew boarded the *Samson*, McNish holding his diary. Worsley had also determined to bring the *James Caird* along. The men had none of the depth of feeling for her they had held for the *Endurance*, which had sheltered and protected them as long as she was able; nonetheless, though the *Caird* had provided them little comfort, they and she had battled for their lives together and had won.

A great gale and snowstorm descended on the *Samson* as she approached Stromness, keeping her at sea for two extra days. But mindless of the weather, the men on board ate and rested to their hearts' content.

In Sørlle's home, Shackleton and Crean lay in bed, listening to the snow drive against the windows. They now knew how slim had been their margin of safety. On Sunday, May 21, Shackleton sailed round to Husvik Station, also in Stromness Bay, to arrange a loan of a likely rescue ship, the English-owned *Southern Sky*, for immediate departure to Elephant Island. Another old friend from *Endurance* days, Captain Thom, was in the harbor and immediately signed on as captain; the whalers eagerly volunteered as crew.

When the *Samson* arrived in the harbor, the men from the whaling station came to greet her, and congregated around the *James Caird*, carrying the boat ashore on their shoulders. "The Norwegians would not let us put a hand to her," wrote Worsley. That same night, Monday evening, Sørlle held a reception at the station clubhouse for Shackleton, and invited the captains and officers of his whaling fleet.

"They were 'old stagers'," Shackleton recorded, "with faces lined and seamed by the storms of half a century."

The club room was "blue and hazy with tobacco smoke," according to Worsley. "Three or four white-haired veterans of the sea came forward. One spoke in Norse, and the Manager translated. He said he had been at sea over 40 years; that he knew this stormy Southern Ocean intimately, from South Georgia to Cape Horn, from Elephant Island to the South Orkneys, and that never had he heard of such a wonderful feat of daring seamanship as bringing the 22-foot open boat from Elephant Island to South Georgia . . . All the seamen present then came forward and solemnly shook hands with us in turn. Coming from brother seamen, men of our own cloth and members of a great seafaring race like the Norwegians, this was a wonderful tribute."

Passages back to England were arranged for McNish, Vincent, and McCarthy; tensions between McNish and Vincent and the rest of the party seem to have persisted until the very end. McNish's description of Worsley doing "the Nimrod," a facetious reference to the great biblical hunter, shows that he had lost none of his fine sardonic touch in the course of the journey. Likewise, his dry observation that Vincent remained in his bag smoking while others did work suggests that Vincent's performance in the boats had not changed the carpenter's opinion of this young cub of a trawler. The attitude of Shackleton and Worsley to these two men would be made manifest much later. Together, the six had performed a prodigy of seamanship and courage; but they parted as they had entered the expedition—tough, independent-minded, unsentimental old salts. None of the three returning to England would see one another, or any member of the *James Caird* crew, ever again.

On May 23, only three days after their arrival in Stromness, Shackleton, Worsley, and Crean left in the *Southern Sky* for Elephant Island. This was the moment for which Shackleton had lived through all the difficult days. Driving steadily against the familiar westerly gales, the *Southern Sky* was within 100 miles of Elephant Island when she ran into ice. Forty miles farther, she was brought to a complete stop.

"To attempt to force the unprotected steel whaler through the masses of pack-ice that now confronted us would have been suicidal," wrote Worsley. Skirting the pack for many miles, they began to run dangerously low of coal, and were at last forced to turn back. The *Southern Sky* now made for the Falkland Islands in order to seek another vessel; from here Shackleton was able to cable to England.

News of Shackleton's survival created a sensation. Newspaper headlines heralded the story, and the king cabled the Falklands with a congratulatory message:

"Rejoice to hear of your safe arrival in the Falkland Islands and trust your companions on Elephant Island may soon be rescued.—George, R.I."

Even Robert E. Scott's widow, Kathleen Scott, ever watchful of her husband's reputation, conceded, "Shackleton or no Shackleton, I think it is one of the most wonderful adventures I ever read of, magnificent."

But for all the excitement, the British government was not able to provide for the final rescue. Britain was still at war and had no spare ships for non-military efforts, let alone any fitted for the ice. The only suitable vessel was the *Discovery*, Scott's old ship—but she could not be ready to sail before October.

This was not good enough. The Foreign Office approached the governments of

Uruguay, Argentina, and Chile for assistance as Shackleton desperately scoured the southern ports for an appropriate wooden vessel. More than anyone alive, he knew how difficult it would be to find one—the stout little *Endurance* had been unique. On June 10, the Uruguayan government came forward with a small survey ship, the *Instituto de Pesca No I,* and crew, for no charge. After three days, she came in sight of Elephant Island, but the ice allowed her no closer. Six days after setting out, she limped back to port.

In Punta Arenas, a subscription from the British Association chartered the *Emma,* a forty-year-old schooner built of oak, and a multinational scratch crew. Setting out on July 12, they too came to within 100 miles of Elephant Island before ice and tempestuous weather turned them back.

"Some members of the scratch crew were played out by the cold and violent tossing," wrote Shackleton, with the restrained irony of a veteran of the *James Caird.* The ferocious weather kept the *Emma* three weeks at sea, and it was August 3 before she reached harbor. Back in Punta Arenas, Shackleton waged another desperate search. The unthinkable was happening: Weeks of waiting were passing into months.

"The wear and tear of this period was dreadful," wrote Worsley. "To Shackleton it was little less than maddening. Lines scored themselves on his face more deeply day by day; his thick, dark, wavy hair was becoming silver. He had not had a grey hair when we had started out to rescue our men the first time. Now, on the third journey, he was grey-haired."

He had also begun, uncharacteristically, to drink. In a photograph taken by Hurley at Ocean Camp, Shackleton sits on the ice preoccupied, but strangely debonair. But in a photograph taken of him during this period of searching for a ship, he is utterly unrecognizable. Pinched with tension, his face is that of an old man. It was now mid-August—*four months* since the departure of the *James Caird.*

From Chile, Shackleton sent yet another cable to the Admiralty, pleading for any wooden vessel. The reply stated that the *Discovery* would arrive sometime around September 20;

but it also cryptically implied that the captain of the *Discovery* would be in charge of the rescue operation—Shackleton would essentially go along as a passenger and answer to him.

Incredulous, Shackleton cabled both the Admiralty and his friend and agent Ernest Perris seeking clarification.

"Impossible to reply to your question except to say unsympathetic attitude to your material welfare," Perris replied, "and customary attitude of Navy to Mercantile Marine which it seems resulted from desire of Admiralty to boom its own relief Expedition."

Among Norwegians and South Americans Shackleton had met with nothing but open-handed and open-hearted support; only in England did the concern to put him in his place exceed that for the plight of his men. Galvanized into frenetic action by this response, Shackleton begged the Chilean government to come forward once again. Knowing perhaps that honor as well as life was now at stake, they lent him the *Telcho*, a small, steel-built tug steamer entirely unsuitable for the purpose, and on August 25, Shackleton, Crean, and Worsley set out with a Chilean crew for Elephant Island.

In a moment of introspective summing up, Shackleton at the end of his account of crossing South Georgia had written:

> When I look back at those days I have no doubt that Providence guided us, not only across those snowfields, but across the storm-white sea that separated Elephant Island from our landing-place on South Georgia. I know that during that long and racking march of thirty-six hours over the unnamed mountains and glaciers of South Georgia it seemed to me often that we were four, not three. I said nothing to my companions on the point, but afterwards Worsley said to me, "Boss, I had a curious feeling on the march that there was another person with us." Crean confessed to the same idea.

Now that they were back in the world of men, this guiding presence seemed to have fled; and the grace and strength that had brought them so far would count for nothing if, when they eventually arrived, they found even one man dead on Elephant Island.

MARSHALL SASHKIN

1944–

The Visionary Leader

1988

Marshall Sashkin is a professor *emeritus* of human resource development at George Washington University. Previously, he served as a senior associate with the U.S. Department of Educational Research and Improvement. He has authored or co-authored more than fifty research reports and over a dozen books, including *Leadership that Matters* (2003). The following reading has been chosen because it masterfully explains how an abstract vision may be made behavioral.

Source:

The George Washington University, Executive Leadership Doctoral Program in Human and Organizational Learning. (n.d.) Faculty: Dr. Marshall Sashkin, *Professor Emeritus*. Retrieved from http://www.gwu.edu/elp/sashkin.html

Selection from:

Sashkin, M. (1988). The visionary leader. In J. A. Conger, R. N. Kanungo, and associates. *Charismatic leadership: The elusive factor in organizational effectiveness.* (pp.142-148). San Francisco: Jossey-Bass.

[***]

Personal Behavior of the Visionary Leader

An organizational philosophy to support the vision is necessary and critical but not enough to make a vision real. A third and often deciding factor concerns the personal actions of the leader. Leaders must communicate their visions in ways that reach out to organization members, gripping them and making them want to get involved in carrying out the vision.

Leaders who are especially effective in getting across their visions are often said to be "charismatic." Bennis and Nanus (1985) observe that "charisma is the result of effective leadership, not the other way around" (p. 224). Charisma is a consequence of effective behavior expressed by leaders to communicate their visions.

Drawing on the work of Bennis (1984) and Bennis and Nanus (1985), one can identify five types of behavior used by effective leaders (Sashkin, 1984a; Sashkin and Fulmer, 1985):

Focusing Attention. The first type of behavior concerns getting others' attention focused clearly on specific key issues. In this way, leaders help others understand and become committed to the leader's visions. This may involve odd, unusual, and creative actions on the part of the leader, all designed to capture and concentrate attention on an important aspect of the leader's vision. For instance, in Chrysler's television commercials, Lee Iacocca physically demonstrated his closeness to employees, emphasized the quality of the product, and referred repeatedly to the "*New* Chrysler Corporation." His aim was to concentrate viewers' attention on the three critical themes: people, goals, and change. Taking a more dramatic, perhaps even odd approach, Frank Perdue grabs television viewers' attention by holding up a chunk of chicken in each hand, one his own and the other a competitor's. Observing that a yellower color indicates health and quality of the chicken (the competitor's a sickly white), he says, "I wonder where the yellow went!"

Communicating Personally. The second set of leader behaviors centers on effective interpersonal communication of the vision. This means listening for understanding ("active listening" [Rogers, 1952]), rephrasing what the other person says to show understanding and to help clarify the message while at the same time identifying and making explicit the feelings expressed (whether implicit or overt). Personal communication skills also include giving feedback effectively (for example, being descriptive rather than evaluative, being specific rather than general), questioning and probing skillfully, and summarizing appropriately. Effective leaders understand that their visions are more likely to be heard, understood, and accepted if they hear and understand the other person. Effective personal communication skills are easy to describe but rare in practice, despite being part of the curriculum of most business schools. These skills are common to all types of effective leaders, from the CEO of a small company to the leader of a nation. In a television interview, Henry Kissinger was asked if Mao Tse-tung actually had two-way conversations when holding the sort of rare private meetings that Kissinger had experienced. Or, he was asked, did Mao simply lecture and more or less ignore the views of the other party? Kissinger responded that Mao insisted on hearing out the other person in detail and made sure he understood before presenting his own views. According to Kissinger, when in a one-to-one situation, Mao never spoke as though he was delivering a position statement; he would first show that he had listened and understood what the other person had said and then explain his own views concisely and clearly. Effective communication on the part of visionary leaders is not just a matter of good media presence, but it is achieved through one-to-one communication skills.

Demonstrating Trustworthiness. The third type of behavior involves consistency and trustworthiness. Bennis (1984) found that outstanding CEOs are very consistent in their actions. They do not "flip-flop" on positions but stand firm, having once taken a position. Thus, it is easy to be sure where they stand. Though one might not always agree with leaders, they are trusted because they say what they mean and mean what they say.

Consider again the example of Jack Welch, CEO of General Electric Corporation. As noted earlier, a key aspect of Welch's vision and of the philosophy he has created for GE is the need for technological innovation and risk taking. To encourage such internal entrepreneurship, Welch insists that no one should be punished for taking a worthwhile risk, even if the risk does not "pan out." If such a failure situation led to sanctions against the risk taker, Welch's credibility would be lost and his vision could fail. Thus, Welch looks for risks that did not work out and has been known to make what would under other circumstances be seen as management awards. For example, it became clear that a long-term effort to produce a very long-lasting, energy-efficient light bulb had failed; after an investment of several million dollars, the project was technically successful, but the product cost far more than customers were willing to spend. Welch closed out the project with a major ceremony and full-scale party. Senior employees involved in the project were given tangible awards, such as VCRs, and some were even promoted—including the person in charge of the project. An executive vice-president observed that this was all part of an effort to get organization members "to understand that you could take a run at something with the management's blessing, give it your best shot, and, if the market wasn't there or we couldn't crack the technology, the individual didn't end up losing" (Potts, 1984, p. G10). But in addition to firmly establishing the reality of a key element of the culture Welch was trying to build, this symbolic rewarding of a failure also reinforced Welch's credibility and trustworthiness, strengthening his position as a visionary leader and increasing the likelihood of attaining that vision.

Displaying Respect. Shows of respect toward ones self, as well as toward others, comprise the fourth set of behaviors exhibited by effective visionary leaders. Rogers (1959) sees positive regard as a critical aspect of both human development and psychotherapeutic treatment. Through "unconditional positive regard" from significant others, one develops positive *self*-regard. This is critical, because without self-respect one cannot really care about others.

Visionary leaders are self-assured, certain of their own abilities. They express this not through arrogance or postures of superiority but in simple self-confidence. Bennis (1984) gives a good example: Dr. Franklin Murphy, former chancellor of the University of California, Los Angeles, and now chairman of the Times-Mirror Company, has been offered several cabinet-level appointments in recent years. He has repeatedly declined what many—and most who feel pressured to prove their personal worth—would find difficult or impossible to refuse. His reason? "I just don't think I'd be good at that sort of thing," Bennis quotes him as saying. This sense of self-respect, of confidence in themselves and their abilities, is apparent also in how visionary leaders treat others.

Organization members feel good around effective visionary leaders. Such leaders boost the sense of self-worth of those around them by expressing unconditional positive regard: paying attention, showing trust, sharing ideas, and making clear how important and valued organization members are. Visionary leaders not only tell organization members they are important but, consistent with Holdstock and Rogers (1977), they also communicate this message through behavioral acts, such as supporting certain policies and programs or providing symbolic and material rewards.

Taking Risks. The fifth type of behavior used by effective visionary leaders involves creating and taking calculated risks and making clear and strong commitments to risks once they are decided on. Bennis (1984) has called this "the Wallenda Factor," after the great tightrope walker, Karl Wallenda. Wallenda failed and fell to his death, Bennis suggests, because he invested all his thought and energy in ways of avoiding failure rather than focusing on succeeding at the risk he was taking. Effective visionary leaders have no energy to spare for covering their rear ends; all of their efforts go toward achieving their goals. This does not mean taking foolish or thoughtless risks; any important risk is carefully evaluated and entered into only after a thoughtful calculation of the chances of success. But, once taken, the focus is on making the risk work, not on avoiding, minimizing, or recovering from failure.

Visionary leaders build opportunities for others into their risks, chances for others to buy in, to take the risk with the leader and share in both the effort and the reward. Visionary leaders motivate by "pulling" people along with them, as Bennis (1984) puts it, rather than by trying to push people in the direction desired by the leader.

On a smaller scale, visionary organizational leaders often involve employees in ownership of the organization through stock awards, purchase plans, or formal employee stock ownership plans. Rosen, Klein, and Young (1986) observe that employee ownership is strongly associated with corporate performance; they have found that publicly held companies that are at least 10 percent employee-owned outperform from 62 to 75 percent of comparable competitor firms. They go on to say that visionary leaders "who are committed to employee ownership see it as a critical part of the company's corporate culture and identity." They recognize employee ownership as an important part of their "managerial philosophy and they translate this . . . into action in concrete ways," such as stock-voting rights or opportunities for participation in decisions. With regard to employee ownership programs, Rosen,

Klein, and Young found that the strength of management's philosophical commitment made a difference. Employees were more satisfied with their jobs and more committed to the organization. The stronger the managerial philosophy toward employee ownership and involvement, the less likely employees were to say they planned to leave the organization. Again, this illustrates how visionary leaders can create risks with opportunities for others to join in.

Interactions Among Types of Behavior. I have described the five types of behavior as though they are quite separate and distinct, but this is a conceptual convenience; one must recognize that visionary leaders often display specific behaviors that reflect several of the behavior types at the same time. For example, having part of one's pay committed to stock purchases entails certain risks, but Rosen, Klein, and Young note that another important aspect of employee stock ownership plans is that "employees are treated like owners—with respect, trust, and consideration."

Other Behavior. It would be foolish to suggest that the types of behaviors defined and described above represent all of the important personal behaviors of visionary leaders. There are doubtless other specific behaviors and behavior categories that are used by visionary leaders to get across their visions. However, the behaviors initially identified by Bennis (1984) and discussed above are among the more important of such personal expressions used by visionary leaders, as shown by evidence now being accumulated.

Consequences of Personal Behaviors. I have developed a questionnaire based on the five sets of personal leader behaviors just described (Sashkin, 1984a). Subsequent studies using revised versions of the Leader Behavior Questionnaire (LBQ) have shown that the scales are internally reliable, with alphas no less than .78 (Valley, 1986). The LBQ contains a scale to measure each of the five types of personal leader behavior and a sixth scale to assess the degree to which the leader is seen as charismatic by others.

Leaders' self-reports of frequency of behavior were summed across the first five scales and correlated with subordinates' reports of leaders' charismatic affect (scale six), obtained independently (Sashkin and Fulmer, 1985). The correlation is .26 (p < .05). When subordinates' reports of leaders' behaviors are correlated with subordinates' reports of charismatic feelings toward the leaders, the correlation increases substantially, with r = .59 (p < .01). Thus, there is some evidence that the more leaders engage in these behaviors, the more strongly they are seen as charismatic by their subordinates. It remains to be seen, of course, whether engaging in these behaviors leads to the implementation of leaders' visions.

In summary, this section has dealt with how visionary leaders go about making their visions real through three types of action. The first action takes place at the organizational level, involving top managers in designing an organizational philosophy that clearly expresses the leader's vision and is understood by members of the organization. The second action, although initiated at the top, really involves middle managers in designing and implementing specific programs that promote policies derived from the organizational philosophy. The third action of visionary leaders to implement their visions consists of the personal behaviors they use to communicate their visions in specific, explicit detail and to engage individual organization members in concrete actions that will help make the leaders' visions real.

References:

Bennis, W. G. "The Four Competences of Leadership." *Training & Development Journal,* 1984, *38* (8), 14-19.

Bennis, W. G., and Nanus, B. *Leaders.* New York: Harper & Row, 1985.

Holdstock, T. L., and Rogers, C. R. "Person-Centered Theory." In R. J. Corsini (ed.), *Current Personality Theories.* Itasca, Ill: Peacock, 1977.

Potts, M. "GE: Changing a Corporate Culture." Part I. *Washington Post,* Sept. 23, 1984, pp. G1, G10-G11.

Rogers, C. R., "Barriers and Gateways to Communication." *Harvard Business Review,* 1952, *30* (4), 46-49.

Rogers, C. R. "A Theory of Therapy, Personality, and Interpersonal Relations, as Developed in the Client-Centered Framework." In S. Koch (ed.), *Psychology: A Study of a Science.* Vol. 3. *Formulations of the Person and the Social Context.* New York: McGraw-Hill, 1959.

Rosen, C., Klein, K. J., and Yang K. M. *Employee Ownership in America.* Boston: Lexington, 1986.

Saskin, M. *The Leader Behavior Questionnaire.* Bryn Mawr, Pa.: Organization Design and Development, 1984a.

Sashkin, M., and Fulmer, R. M. "A New Framework for Leadership: Vision, Charisma, and Culture Creation." Paper presented at the Biennial International Leadership Symposium, Texas Tech University, Lubbock, July 1985.

Valley, C. A. "The Relationship Between the Leader Behavior of Pastors and Church Growth." Unpublished doctoral dissertation, Department of Educational Leadership, Western Michigan University, 1986.

CHARLES MANZ

1952-

HENRY P. SIMS JR.

1939-

The New SuperLeadership

2001

Dr. Manz is the Nirenberg Professor of Business Leadership at the University of Massachusetts. An established author of over two hundred articles and scholarly papers and more than twenty books, Manz focuses on the self as leader and self-managed work teams. He has held teaching positions at the Harvard Business School, the University of Minnesota, Auburn University, Arizona State University, and Pennsylvania State University.

Dr. Henry P. Sims, Jr. is currently a professor of management and organization at the University of Maryland's Smith School of Business. He is also a former director of that School's doctoral program. A recent Fulbright Fellow and Visiting Professor at Hong Kong Baptist University, Sims has held teaching positions at Pennsylvania State University; Indiana University; University of California, Irvine; Stanford University;

and George Mason University. In 1989, he received the Styble-Peabody Award for the best book in human resources, The New SuperLeadership: Leading Others to Lead Themselves.

SuperLeadership involves teaching others to lead themselves. Manz and Sims imply that followers must take charge of and, in fact, learn to lead themselves.

Sources:

University of Massachusetts Amherst. (2008). Charles C. Manz, *Nirenberg Professor of Leadership.* Retrieved from http://people.umass.edu/cmanz/

University of Maryland, Robert H. Smith School of Business (n.d). *Faculty Profile, Dr. Henry P Sims.* Retrieved from http://www.rhsmith.umd.edu/ management/faculty/sims.aspx

Selection from:

Manz, C. & Sims, H., (2001). *The new superleadership: Leading others to lead themselves.* (pp.77-86). San Francisco: Berrett-Koehler.

4
Self-Leadership in Action

YOU ARE DEEPLY SETTLED into the conference room chair as you listen to Bart, the new division general manager (and your boss). This is the first meeting between Bart and his staff, and he is outlining some of his philosophy and ideas about how he expects the division to be managed. You are new yourself, having assumed the position of department manager only two weeks ago.

Both you and Bart have been brought into the division as part of an attempt to salvage an organization that has been in the red for the last three years. You haven't worked for Bart before, but you hear through the grapevine that he has a record as a top-notch performer.

"One of the most important attributes by which I judge managers," says Bart, "is how good they are at self-leadership. Are they able to lead themselves?"

As you sit, you wonder what he really means by "self-leadership."

How about you? Do you believe the most important leadership you exercise is over the person staring back at you when you look in the mirror? Are you an effective self-leader? What *is* self-leadership?

The idea of self-leadership provides a new definition of followership

The core of SuperLeadership—leading others to lead themselves—is self-leadership. Self-leadership is the influence we exert over ourselves in order to perform better. A SuperLeader inspires and facilitates self-leadership in others. And a core of our philosophy is that in order to lead others, you must first learn to lead yourself. In this chapter and the next two, we address the topic of self-leadership in detail, to lay the foundation for addressing Super-Leadership throughout the remainder of the book.

Based on our years of studying and advising employees and executives in many work settings, at many organizational levels, three basic assumptions underlie our ideas on self-leadership. First, everyone practices self-leadership to some degree, but not everyone is an effective self-leader. Second, *effective* self-leadership can be learned and thus is not restricted to people we intuitively describe as being "born" self-starters, self-directed, or self-motivated. And third, self-leadership is relevant to executives, managers, and nonmanagers alike—that is, to anyone who works.

There are different categories of self-leadership strategies. The first, discussed in this chapter, focuses on effective action. In the next two chapters we focus on strategies that use natural rewards, and promote effective thinking and feeling.

S *SuperLeadership inspires and facilitates self-leadership in others.*

SELF-LEADERSHIP STRATEGIES FOR
EFFECTIVE ACTION

The majority stockholder and manager of a small commuter airline found himself in a profit squeeze. Many of his competitors had already gone out of business. In addition to the countless duties involved in managing the firm on a daily basis, including personally flying some of the routes, he was convinced he needed a new, larger plane to operate more profitably. Somehow he managed to juggle the details of his job while putting together a creative financing plan for acquiring the plane he needed. This plan, along with adoption of several other changes, including rerouting his flight patterns, kept his firm on a growth trend in the face of pressures toward decline.

How does he do it? How does he put out the daily fires and still manage to introduce new, innovative ways of doing business? Much of the answer lies in his action-oriented self-leadership practices.

First, he uses the strategy of self-observation by keeping a detailed log or record of how he spends his time. In his pocket he carries a small portable computer "organizer" to do this. A few times a day, he uses a wireless connection to interface with his main business computer to exchange data and bring his records up to date. He also keeps a record of what he says to others over the phone regarding business matters, to help him be consistent in his future dealings with these people. In addition, he has adopted various cueing strategies to help him manage his performance. Once a week, being still a bit old-fashioned, he prints out in large type the notes that will serve as a reminder and a guide for his work efforts. He posts this printout right above his desk. He keeps a separate "follow up" file. He frequently rehearses what he will say during important phone calls before dialing. And he makes use of self-rewards. He enjoys reviewing his accomplishments against his goals and mentally rewarding himself for his achievements. As he puts it, "Self-gratification—that's what it's all about."

We have seen variations of these same strategies in use in many different work settings. Following are some details about using additional self-leadership strategies including self-set goals, management of cues, rehearsal, self-observation, self-rewards, and self-correcting feedback.

Self-Set Goals

Goals are an important part of successful self-leadership. Setting goals, for both immediate work tasks and longer-term career achievements, establishes the basis for self-direction and establishing priorities. Limiting informal e-mail communications to forty-five minutes of a normal workday might be a reasonable self-set goal for someone who has a problem with excessive electronic chatting. Similarly, making six sales calls a day or increasing sales by eight percent for the fiscal quarter might be a self-set goal for someone in sales. Earning an MBA degree (by taking evening on-line classes) or becoming a vice president are examples of longer-term career goals. Much of the research on goal setting suggests that goals should be challenging but achievable and specific in order to have an optimal effect.

> *"If a man constantly aspires, is he not elevated?"*
> **—Henry David Thoreau**

Management of Cues

Managing cues in our immediate work environment can help trigger constructive activities and reduce or eliminate destructive ones. Resigning from those annoying and distracting unnecessary electronic mailing lists, having phone calls held during specific times of the workday, eliminating distracting noises by closing the door, or even surrounding ourselves with talented people who bring out our best, all reflect different cueing strategies. An office, for example, can be decorated and equipped with things that stimulate performance. Simple devices such as installing an inspiring screensaver on our computer, or placing motivating plaques or pictures on the walls, can be helpful to some people. Posting the message "Are you using your time effectively right now?" in full view is a cue for effective time management. In fact, the time-management movement over the last few decades is largely based on cueing strategies.

David Packard, co-founder of Hewlett-Packard, described how, as a young man, he used a daily schedule as a cueing strategy to organize his own efforts. "I was resolved that I was going to have everything organized, so as a freshman I had a schedule set for every day . . . what I was going to do every hour of the day . . . and times set up in the morning to study certain things . . . You did have to allocate your time, because as you know, there are a lot of things to do: Packard was a man before his time, a customer-in-waiting for the invention of the Palm Pilot!

As we go deeper into the electronic age, technology seems to be making us more isolated. More and more people work out of their homes or at remote work sites and much communication takes place electronically. This can rob us of the important cues we receive from one another through face-to-face interaction. Of course one solution is video conferencing, or to equip our computers with software and devices such as digital cameras that enable us to electronically relate on a more personal level. Nevertheless, there is no substitute for physical, face-to-face interaction. To facilitate this valuable component of working with others requires more personal strategies, such as scheduling an informal monthly breakfast with other employees.

This is an age-old strategy that was used by former 3M CEO William McKnight during the early foundational years that led to that company's rise to prominence. On Saturday mornings he would join 3M employees in the employee cafeteria for an elbow-to-elbow breakfast that allowed him the kind of direct personal contact that provided encouragement for him and his workforce. Similarly, Bill Hewlett, co-founder of Hewlett-Packard, was noted for his extensive interaction with others at HP as part of his daily management style. Both of these examples reveal cueing strategies that provide opportunities to enhance an executive's informal information network.

Rehearsal

Rehearsal or practice is another useful self-leadership strategy. Practice is natural for improvement in golf or tennis—it should be just as natural in other parts of life, including work. Thinking through and practicing important tasks before they are done "for keeps" can contribute significantly to performance. Rehearsing a crucial formal presentation about a new Internet business to be made to a venture capitalist is an obvious example of this strategy. But many less formal activities are potential occasions for practice. A few minutes of mental rehearsal before calling on clients, practicing sensitive parts of an employee's performance review, going over the key steps required to safely and efficiently start up a machine, are all appropriate ways of using a rehearsal strategy. Role playing, for example, is commonly used in performance-appraisal training.

Self-Observation

Self-observation provides the necessary information—the lifeblood—for effective self-leadership. By observing our behavior we can discover some clues about what needs to change and how to go about it. A simple record of what leads to a targeted behavior, its frequency, how long it lasts, and when it does or does not occur, can provide a wealth of information.

For example, if an employee is dissatisfied with her level of productivity she can observe, and briefly record on a personal organizer, notes about nonproductive behaviors. These behaviors might include informal conversations, unnecessary busywork, time spent surfing the Web, and so on. Also she could keep a record of the frequency and duration of these behaviors and the events that distracted more productive efforts. If these observations eventually disclose that an average of 17 hours a week are spent on informal conversations, an obvious problem has been identified. Also, if the records indicate that most of this chatting is triggered by trips to the department coffee machine, steps can be taken to limit this behavior, such as keeping a small coffee maker in her office. (However, she should be careful: coffee-machine conversations can provide rich interpersonal exchanges of information and knowledge.)

Self-observation also provides information for self-evaluation. By analyzing the information that she has collected, she sets the stage for personally assessing the effectiveness of her work efforts.

Self-Rewards

Whatever we receive for our efforts has a major impact on our motivation and choices of future activities. Typically, the rewards received from the organization and others become the focus of attention, but self-rewards (and criticisms) can be just as important.

Using self-rewards can be an especially powerful strategy for creating motivation to do tasks we find difficult or unappealing.

These self-rewards can be concrete and physical, like a nice dinner out or a lazy afternoon sailing on the bay after completing an especially challenging task. Taking a weekend at the beach as a reward for finally working the bugs out of the new office computer system, or after making a big sale, can help motivate future successes. Sometimes we can deliberately put aside a self-reward until a particular task has been accomplished. The rewards can also be private, mental creations such as imagining a favorite vacation spot or the future success and benefits resulting from successful work efforts. Intentionally providing ourselves with both physical and mental rewards for high performance can help sustain motivation and effort.

Self-Correcting Feedback (Not Self-Punishment)

Self-correcting feedback can also be part of the process, although the related practice of self-punishment generally is not very effective. Actually, most self-punishment is mental or cognitive in nature. A mild degree of guilt can sometimes be useful, but when it becomes excessive or habitual it can undermine motivation and effort. Habitual guilt and self-criticism can seriously damage self-confidence and self-esteem, and even lead to depression. The key is to study patterns of self-criticism by asking, for example, "Do I focus on destructive self-punishment or constructive corrective feedback? Does my self-criticism help or hinder my performance?" An introspective self-examination of a failure, trying to learn from it, providing constructive self-corrective feedback and refocusing energy on feeling good about accomplishments, represents a better alternative.

Self-rewards and corrective feedback are important ingredients of self-leadership, and are as important as rewards and criticisms received from others.

Of course, ignoring our negative choices when we are obviously behaving and performing in undesirable ways can be a problem as well. There are times when a good self-scolding is appropriate. Generally, however, focusing on learning and providing ourselves with corrective feedback and then concentrating on self-rewards for our desirable behavior will be more effective.

AN EXAMPLE OF SELF-LEADERSHIP IN ACTION

We have observed action-oriented self-leadership strategies being used in a variety of work settings. Knowledge-based work settings that rely heavily on information technology involve a number of substantial challenges for self-leadership. People can find themselves spending much time on their own staring at computer screens and trying to find motivation within themselves. The days when people called "bosses" closely monitored and directed other people referred to as "subordinates" are quickly fading into the past (we even titled one of our previous books *Business Without Bosses*).

Many self-managing work systems found in today's organizations originally emerged from manufacturing settings rather than electronic-based offices. For example, in one particularly impressive high-performing plant organized according to a self-managed team concept (the system is structured around teams of workers who are largely responsible for managing themselves), we observed countless scribbled notes pasted to machines to serve as self-established cues for guiding workers. (For more details, see the chapter on leading teams.) And workers used other strategies such as self-observation, rehearsal, self-praise, and self-criticism readily within their teams. The following examples illustrate what we observed:

"Hey Frank, you did a hell of a job in cleaning up our work area," Tom shouted with obvious sincerity over the hum of the machines. After giving Frank a quick pat on the back, Tom returned to his work location. He glanced at a note he had stuck to the front of his machine that described the new, more efficient welding procedure that he had helped to develop. After a moment of reflection, he began working again. A couple of hours later, as his team left for lunch, they noticed that the previous month's efficiency ratings were posted on the bulletin board outside the cafeteria. "All right" shrieked Elizabeth, one of Tom's energetic peers, "we did it! We improved by ten percent!" The group stopped to give one another hearty handshakes, backslaps, and hugs before going in for lunch with their pride apparent in their strides.

Two o'clock that afternoon the team held a special meeting. "You know Bill didn't show up for work again today after being out twice last week," Tom started. "We agreed if it happened one more time we'd have to counsel him. That's why I invited Smitty [Smitty was the team's external leader, though he served more as a coach and counselor than supervisor] to help us practice what we would say to him." Frank played the role of Bill while the rest of the team practiced what it planned to say. Smitty provided feedback and suggestions while the team worked out its plan.

CONCLUSION

In this chapter we focused on action-oriented self-leadership strategies and examples. These strategies are especially useful for enhancing work performance on difficult and often unattractive tasks. Later, we discuss how SuperLeaders can promote employee self-leadership by modeling, encouraging, guiding, and reinforcing use of these kinds of tools. Before we turn to the details of how a SuperLeader might accomplish this, we need to explore additional self-leadership strategies. These additional strategies provide the potential for helping people discover natural motivation in their feelings about their work, and to establish constructive patterns of thinking. More specifically, in the next two chapters we turn to the role of natural rewards that produce self-motivation, and self-leadership of the mind.

PETER M. SENGE

1947-

The Fifth Discipline:
The Art and Practice of the Learning Organization

2006

Peter Senge is world renowned as one of the most innovative thinkers about management and leadership. He teaches at the MIT Sloan School of Management and is a founder of the Society for Organizational Learning (SoL). Other books that he has co-authored include The *Dance of Change* (1999), *Schools that Learn The Fifth Discipline* (2000), and *Presence* (2004).

Senge's book, *The Fifth Discipline* (2006), is known as a best-selling classic. Fundamentally, the only long-term way to maintain a competitive advantage is for the organization's leadership to consistently learn faster than the competition. In *The Fifth Discipline,* an organization's learning disabilities are counter-acted with the strategies of the learning organization. In the passage that follows, the leader is advised to work on self-growth and development before attempting to work on others' growth.

Source:

Senge, P. M. (2006). *The fifth discipline: The art and practice of the learning organization.* New York: Currency, Random House.

Selection from:

Senge, P. M. (2006). *The fifth discipline: The art and practice of the learning organization.* (pp.262-266). New York: Currency, Random House.

12
FOUNDATIONS

[***]

GROWING PEOPLE

As I look back now, perhaps the most radical of the five disciplines was personal mastery, the idea that an organizational environment could be created in which people could truly grow as human beings. Most companies today espouse some variation on the philosophy that "people are our most important asset" and invest considerable sums in work force development, largely through training programs. But truly committing to helping people grow requires much more than this. I've listened to people like Vivienne Cox and Roger Saillant share their experiences for many years, and the emotional center of their stories is always the same. Through diverse life experiences they have formed an unshakable conviction of the power inherent in releasing and aligning human spirit—and they are on a lifelong journey to discover what this means and how to do it.

In 2005, a group of business leaders in Worcester, Massachusetts, initiated the first William J. O'Brien Memorial

Lecture Series. The aim was to honor and extend Bill O'Brien's legacy through an annual speech given by a business leader who exemplified O'Brien's conviction that "the best way to grow financial capital is through growing human capital." The first speaker in this series was Rich Teerlink, former CEO of Harley-Davidson and one of the founders of the SoL network. "Being truly committed to growing people is an act of faith," says Teerlink. "You have to believe in your heart that people want to pursue a vision that matters, that they want to contribute and be responsible for results, and that they are willing to look at shortfalls in their own behavior and correct problems whenever they are able. These beliefs are not easy for control-oriented managers, and that is why there remains a big gap between the 'talk' and the 'walk' regarding developing people."

A PURPOSE WORTHY OF COMMITMENT

Creating an environment where people can grow starts with "having a purpose worthy of people's commitment," says Goran Carstedt, former president of Volvo Sweden and IKEA North America (and SoL's first managing director). "Business leaders often ask their people to be committed to the organization's goals," says Carstedt. "But the real question is what is the organization committed to, and is that worth my time?" Despite much literature on organizational purpose, and ubiquitous vision and values statements, "there is a lot of cynicism," says Saillant, among employees about where their company's real commitment lies. And a lot of confusion—starting with the idea that the purpose of a company is, by definition, to maximize return on invested capital. Years ago, Peter Drucker said that "making money for a company is like oxygen for a person; if you don't have enough of it you're out of the game." In other words, profitability is a performance requirement for all businesses, but it is not a purpose. Extending Drucker's metaphor, companies who take profit as their purpose are like people who think life is about breathing. They're missing something.

Ironically, equating a business's purpose with the economic bottom line also dooms the enterprise to financial mediocrity, as countless studies of long-term business performance have shown.[1] In a world where more people have more choices about where and how they work, it matters that an organization stand for something. A company that lacks a purpose worthy of commitment fails to foster commitment. It forces people to lead fragmented lives that can never tap the passion, imagination, willingness to take risks, patience, persistence, and desire for meaning that are the cornerstones of long-term financial success.

"I just wanted my work life and personal life to be one life," says Brigitte Tantawy-Monsou of Unilever. After a career in supply chain management, R&D, and business excellence, Tantawy-Monsou says her introduction to organizational learning, personal mastery, and mental models in 2002 "helped me to make sense of my past experiences. Because I am very analytical and scientific, it also gave me a new dimension, a 'soft' dimension. It helped me see that you can understand an organization or team as a social system, and that there is a more integrated way of looking at problems." She found that the systems view also applied to her personally. "I was especially interested in the idea of alignment between a person and [his or her] company's goals and values. This was a new management concept, and it spoke to my personal desire for alignment."

Gradually, Tantawy-Monsou found herself drawn into projects truly worthy of her commitment, applying organizational learning tools to Unilever's sustainability agenda. Eventually she was even able to redefine her job so that she could work full-time on sustain-ability. "I wanted to contribute more, both inside the organization and beyond,

[1] Jay Bragdon, *Living Asset Management* (Cambridge, Mass:SoL), 2006 (forthcoming); Jim Collins, *Built to Last* (New York: HarperCollins), 1997.

to issues that really mattered, and organizational learning helped me build my capabilities to have more influence. It's coincided with a step in my career, and in my life as a whole." But this would not have been possible had not Unilever's top management, several years earlier, begun to recognize that historic environmental changes threatened the future of their businesses. As one of the largest sellers of fish products (food products made with fish) in the world, they realized by the mid-1990s that, in the words of one top executive, "We won't have a fish business worth being in if there aren't fundamental changes toward sustainable fishing."[2] Today, in addition to working on business-related sustainability initiatives within Unilever, Tantawy-Monsou is an organizer of the European SoL Sustainability Consortium, an extension of the U.S.-based SoL Sustainability Consortium. "I've almost always enjoyed my work, but for the first time I feel now that I am able to work on what really matters to me as a person," she says.

TRANSFORMATIVE RELATIONSHIPS

As Tantawy-Monsou's story illustrates, growing as a human being starts with a commitment to something that truly matters. It unfolds within what the people at Roca call networks of "transformative relationships."

Roca (Spanish for "rock") is an organization whose purpose is to build a safe and healthy community for young people. Chelsea, Massachusetts, where Roca is based, is less than two miles from Boston's financial center, but it is a world away culturally. It is inhabited mostly by Latino, Southeast Asian, and Central African immigrants. "As an immigrant, you have lost your friends, your job, your standards, and your standing in

---

2   Unilever recruited other businesses, governmental, and nongovernmental organizations to establish a global certification process for sustainable fisheries, the Marine Stewardship Council. The company has also started related initiatives focused on sustainable agriculture and water conservation. See the Web site www.unilever.com.

your community," says Seroem Phong, former director of the Roca street workers. "Families become dysfunctional. Typically, the father cannot speak the language, so he cannot hold a job. Because he no longer can be a provider, he becomes an abuser. Usually the second generation has even more difficulty, because they grow up without any family stability. They have no drive to advance because they have no hope that advancing is possible. So they, as I did, join gangs."

Recruiting former teenage gang members, young parents, and community members to work on the streets to help others and to rebuild community, Roca has become an interface between police, courts, schools, and a host of social service agencies. In the eighteen years since Roca's founding, Chelsea has seen dramatic decreases in crime rates and violence, and increases in graduation rates. Many young people who probably would not have survived their teens have ended up in community and four-year colleges and are holding jobs and living productive lives. "What Roca has accomplished is nothing short of amazing," says Harry Spence, director of the Department of Social Services (DSS) for the Commonwealth of Massachusetts. "If we had a half-dozen Rocas, it would make a huge impact on our work across the state."

I've spent a fair amount of time with the youth leaders of Roca, and I continue to learn from their deep understanding of how to help people grow. "Creating transformative relationships is the basis of our work," Tun Krouch told me during one of my visits with a group of street workers. "The young people we're dealing with need a relationship that can help them to live," says founder Molly Baldwin. "Our first job is simply to show up for them. Many have never had someone they could count on to be consistent, to be with them in a relationship of complete support for who they really are as human beings. Over time, they then start to do that for one another."

Roca's core method and continual training ground for this "showing up for one another" is what the group calls "peacekeeping circles," a type of collective reflective practice based on Native American traditions of learning and healing. "We learn to truly listen to each other in circles," says Omar Ortez.

Marina Rodriguez tells a typical circle story: "Recently, we had a young woman who had gotten pregnant, and she didn't know how to tell her mom. She was afraid. In a more typical situation, the girl might have run away, or some family friend might have intervened but instead we decided that the best way to support her was to create a circle. The street worker had a good relationship with her, and formed a small circle with a few people the girl and the mother trusted. We dealt with the situation together, which is wholly different than the girl and the mom just yelling at each other. The key was to create a conversation that would let the mother listen to her daughter, and let them accept one another. The whole idea is to enlarge your circle to build the support that you need."

"It becomes about cooperative learning," Susan Ulrich adds. "A circle conversation is where you can all sit together and figure out what is going on and how we're going to deal with it. You see that a problem is not just one person's problem, it is [everyone's] problem. In circle, we are equals, we all have problems and we learn by helping one another."

"We have a saying we learned from a chief justice of a Navajo tribal court," adds Baldwin. "He says, 'You can't get to a good place in a bad way.' Circles keep us grounded in our connectedness and create community day by day as we confront whatever we have to confront together."[3]

IT STARTS WITH ME

The commitment to personal growth is important—and it is most important for those in positions of leadership. "I always have to be willing to work on my own stuff," says Baldwin. "If

---

[3] Sayra Pinto, Jasson Guevera, and Molly Baldwin, "Living the Change You Seek: Roca's Core Curriculum for Human Development," *Reflections, the SoL Journal*, vol. 5, no. 4. For more on Roca, see the Web site www.roca.org.

we are in a disagreement with the cops, I have to look at what I have invested in maintaining that battle—there are so many times that I would just rather go out and yell at somebody than remain calm and look at my part in perpetuating whatever is going on."

"It all starts with personal mastery," says Saillant. "It all starts with my willingness to see the shortcomings that are all too evident to those around me. I can never expect the people around me in an organization to be more open and willing to learn and improve than I am."

MARGARET J. WHEATLEY

1944-

Leadership and the New Science: Learning about Organization from an Orderly Universe

1992

Margaret J. Wheatley is a professor of management at Brigham Young University and a consultant to a variety of organizations. She specializes in participative techniques that involve the whole system of an organization in planning desired organizational futures. Dr. Wheatley received her doctorate from Harvard University in the Program for Administration, Planning, and Social Policy, with a primary focus on organizational diagnosis and interventions.

In her book, *Leadership and the New Science*, Wheatley suggests that applications based on quantum physics, chaos theory, and molecular biology can inform our understanding of organizational behaviors. She believes that our organizational assumptions have come from seventeenth-century physics and that we need to update our thinking to include current scientific understanding. Her work applies these three areas of new scientific knowledge to analyze how people and organizations interact. In the following passage, Wheatley suggests a new, natural, elegant, and simple way to lead organizations.

Source:

Wheatley, M. J. (1992). *Leadership and the new science: Learning about organization from and orderly universe.* San Francisco: Berrett-Koehler.

Selection from:

Wheatley, M. J. (1992). *Leadership and the new science: Learning about organization from an orderly universe.* (pp.1-13). San Francisco: Berrett-Koehler.

Searching for A Simpler Way to Lead Organizations

I am not alone in wondering why organizations aren't working well. Many of us are troubled by questions that haunt our work. Why do so many organizations feel dead? Why do projects take so long, develop ever-greater complexity, yet so often fail to achieve any truly significant results? Why does progress, when it appears, so often come from unexpected places, or as a result of surprises or serendipitous events that our planning had not considered? Why does change itself, that event we're all supposed to be "managing," keep drowning us, relentlessly reducing any sense of mastery we might possess? And why have our expectations for success diminished to the point that often the best we hope for is staying power and patience to endure the disruptive forces that appear unpredictably in the organizations where we work?

These questions had been growing within me for several years, gnawing away at my work and diminishing my sense of competency. The busier I became with work and the more projects I took on, the greater my questions grew. Until I began a journey.

Like most important journeys, mine began in a mundane place—a Boeing 757, flying soundlessly above America. High in the air as a weekly commuter between Boston and Salt

Lake City, with long stretches of reading time broken only by occasional offers of soda and peanuts, I opened my first book on the new science—Fritj of Capra's *The Turning Point*, which described the new world view emerging from quantum physics. This provided my first glimpse of a new way of perceiving the world, one that comprehended its processes of change and patterns of connections.

I don't think it accidental that I was introduced to a new way of seeing at 37,000 feet. The altitude only reinforced the message that what was needed was a larger perspective, one that took in more of the whole of things. From that first book, I took off, seeking out as many new science books as I could find in biology, evolution, chaos theory, and quantum physics. Discoveries and theories of new science called me away from the details of my own field of management inquiry and up to a vision of the inherent orderliness of the universe, of creative processes and dynamic, continuous change that still maintained order. This was a world where order and change, autonomy and control were not the great opposites that we had thought them to be. It was a world where change and constant creation signalled new ways of maintaining order and structure.

I don't believe I could have grasped these ideas if I had stayed on the ground.

During the past fifteen to twenty years, books that translate new science findings for lay readers have proliferated, some more reputable and scientific than others. Of the many I read, some were too challenging, some were too bizarre, but others contained images and information that were breathtaking. I became aware that I was wandering in a realm that created new visions of freedom and possibility, giving me new ways to think about my work. I couldn't always draw immediate corollaries between science and my dilemmas, but I noticed myself developing a new serenity in response to the questions that surrounded me. I was reading of chaos that contained order; of information as the primal, creative force; of systems that by design fell apart so they could renew themselves; and of invisible forces that structured space and held complex things together. These were compelling, evocative ideas, and they gave me hope, even if they did not reveal immediate solutions.

Somewhere—I knew then and believe even more firmly now—there is a simpler way to lead organizations, one that requires less effort and produces less stress than the current practices. For me, this new knowledge is only beginning to crystallize into applications, but I no longer believe that organizations are inherently unmanageable in our world of constant flux and unpredictability. Rather, I believe our present ways of understanding organizations are skewed, and that the longer we remain entrenched in our ways, the farther we move from those wonderful breakthroughs in understanding that the world of science calls "elegant." The layers of complexity, the sense of things being beyond our control and out of control, are but signals of our failure to understand a deeper reality of organizational life, and of life in general.

We are all searching for this simplicity. In many different disciplines, we live today with questions for which our expertise provides no answers. At the turn of the century, physicists faced the same unnerving confusion. There is a frequently told story about Niels Bohr and Werner Heisenberg, two founders of quantum theory. This version is from *The Turning Point:*

In the twentieth century, physicists faced, for the first time, a serious challenge to their ability to understand the universe. Every time they asked nature a question in an atomic experiment, nature answered with a paradox, and the more they tried to clarify the situation, the sharper the paradoxes became. In their struggle to grasp this new reality, scientists became painfully aware that their basic concepts, their language, and their whole way of thinking were inadequate to describe atomic phenomena. Their problem was not only intellectual but involved an intense emotional and existential experience, as vividly described by Werner Heisenberg: "I remember discussions with Bohr which went through many hours till very late at night and ended almost in despair; and when at the end of the discussion I went alone for a walk in the neighboring park I repeated to myself again and again the question: Can nature possibly be so absurd as it seemed to us in these atomic experiments?"

It took these physicists a long time to accept the fact that the paradoxes they encountered are an essential aspect of atomic physics . . . Once this was perceived, the physicists began to learn to ask the right questions and to avoid contradictions . . . and finally they found the precise and consistent mathematical formulation of [quantum] theory.

. . . Even after the mathematical formulation of quantum theory was completed, its conceptual framework was by no means easy to accept. Its effect on the physicists' view of reality was truly shattering. The new physics necessitated profound changes in concepts of space, time, matter, object, and cause and effect; and because these concepts are so fundamental to our way of experiencing the world, their transformation came as a great shock. To quote Heisenberg again: "The violent reaction to the recent development of modern physics can only be understood when one realizes that here the foundations of physics have started moving; and that this motion has caused the feeling that the ground would be cut from science." (In Capra 1983, 76-77. Used with permission)

For the past several years, I have found myself often relating this story to groups of managers involved in organizational change. The story speaks with a chilling authority. Each of us recognizes the feelings this tale describes, of being mired in the habit of solutions that once worked yet that are now totally inappropriate, of having rug after rug pulled from beneath us, whether by a corporate merger, reorganizations, downsizing, or a level of personal disorientation. But the story also gives great hope as a parable teaching us to embrace our despair as a step on the road to wisdom, encouraging us to sit in the unfamiliar seat of not knowing and open ourselves to radically new ideas. If we bear the confusion, then one day, the story promises, we will begin to see a whole new landscape, one of bright illumination that will dispel the oppressive shadows of our current ignorance. I still tell Heisenberg's story. It never fails to speak to me from this deep place of reassurance.

I believe that we have only just begun the process of discovering and inventing the new organizational forms that will inhabit the twenty-first century. To be responsible inventors and discoverers, though, we need the courage to let go of the old world, to relinquish most of what we have cherished, to abandon our interpretations about what does and doesn't work. As Einstein is often quoted as saying: No problem can be solved from the same consciousness that created it. We must learn to see the world anew.

There are many places to search for new answers in a time of paradigm shifts. For me, it was appropriate that my inquiry led back to the natural sciences, reconnecting me to an earlier vision of myself. At fourteen, I aspired to be a space biologist and carried thick astronomy texts on the New York subway to weekly classes at the Hayden Planetarium. These texts were far too dense for me to understand, but I carried them anyway because they looked so impressive. My abilities in biology were better founded, and I began college with full intent to major in biology, but my initial encounters with advanced chemistry ended that career, and I turned to the greater ambiguity of the social sciences. Like many social scientists, I am at heart a lapsed scientist, still hoping that the world will yield up its secrets to me in predictable formulations.

But my focus on science is more than a personal interest. Each of us lives and works in organizations designed from Newtonian images of the universe. We manage by separating things into parts, we believe that influence occurs as a direct result of force exerted from one person to another, we engage in complex planning for a world that we keep expecting to be predictable, and we search continually for better methods of objectively perceiving the world. These assumptions, as I explain in chapter 2, come to us from seventeenth-century physics, from Newtonian mechanics. They are the base from which we design and manage organizations, and from which we do research in all of the social sciences. Intentionally or not, we work from a world view that has been derived from the natural sciences.

But the science has changed. If we are to continue to draw from the sciences to create and manage organizations, to design research, and to formulate hypotheses about organizational design, planning, economics, human nature, and change processes (the list can be much longer), then we need to at least ground our work in the science of our times. We need to stop seeking after the universe of the seventeenth century and begin to explore what has become known to us in the twentieth century. We need to expand our search for the principles of organization to include what is presently known about the universe.

The search for the lessons of new science is still in progress, really in its infancy, but what I hope to convey in these pages is the pleasure of sensing those first glimmers of a new way of thinking about the world and its organizations. The light may be dim, but its potency grows as the door cracks wider and wider. Here there are scientists who write about natural phenomena with a poetry and a lucidity that speak to dilemmas we find in organizations. Here there are new images and metaphors for thinking about our own organizational experiences. This is a world of wonder and not knowing, where scientists are as awestruck by what they see as were the early explorers who marvelled at new continents. In this realm, there is a new kind of freedom, where it is more rewarding to explore than to reach conclusions, more satisfying to wonder than to know, and more exciting to search than to stay put.

This is not a book of conclusions, cases, or exemplary practices of excellent companies. It is deliberately *not* that kind of book, for two reasons. First, I no longer believe that organizations can be changed by imposing a model developed elsewhere. So little transfers to, or even inspires, those trying to work at change in their own organizations. Second, and much more important, the new physics cogently explains that there is no objective reality out there waiting to reveal its secrets. There are no recipes or formulae, no checklists or advice that describe "reality." There is only what we create through our engagement with others and with events. Nothing really transfers; everything is always new and different and unique to each of us.

This book attempts to be true to that new vision of reality, where ideas and information are but half of what is required to evoke reality. The creative possibilities of the ideas represented here depend on your engagement with them. I have interpreted my task as presenting material to provoke and engage you, knowing that your experience with these pages will produce different ideas, different hopes, and different experiments than did mine. It is not important that we agree on one expert interpretation or one sure-fire application. That is not the nature of the universe in which we live. We inhabit a world that is always subjective and shaped by our interactions with it. Our world is impossible to pin down, constantly changing and infinitely more interesting than we ever imagined.

Though the outcomes to be gained from reading this book are unique to each reader, the ideas I have chosen to think about focus on the meta-issues that concern those of us who work in large organizations: What are the sources of order? How do we create organizational coherence, where activities correspond to purpose? How do we create structures that move with change, that are flexible and adaptive, even boundaryless, that enable rather than constrain? How do we simplify things without losing both control and differentiation? How do we resolve personal needs for freedom and autonomy with organizational needs for prediction and control?

The new science research referred to comes from the disciplines of physics, biology, and chemistry, and from theories of evolution and chaos that span several disciplines. Each chapter inquires into metaphorical links between certain scientific perspectives and organizational phenomena, but it may be useful first to say something in general about the directions of new science research.

Scientists in many different disciplines are questioning whether we can adequately explain how the world works by using the machine imagery created in the seventeenth century, most notably by Sir Isaac Newton. In the machine model, one must understand parts. Things can be taken apart, dissected literally or representationally (as we have done with business functions and academic disciplines) and then put back together without any significant loss. The assumption is that by comprehending the workings of each piece, the whole can be understood. The Newtonian model of the world is characterized by materialism and reductionism—a focus on things rather than relationships and a search, in physics, for the basic building blocks of matter.

In new science, the underlying currents are a movement toward holism, toward understanding the system as a system and giving primary value to the relationships that exist among seemingly discrete parts. Donella Meadows, a systems thinker, quotes an ancient Sufi teaching that captures this shift in focus: "You think because you understand *one* you must understand *two*, because one and one makes two. But you must also understand *and*" (1982, 23). When we view systems from this perspective, we enter an entirely new landscape of connections, of phenomena that cannot be reduced to simple cause and effect, and of the constant flux of dynamic processes.

Explorations into the subatomic world began early in this century, creating the dissonance described in Heisenberg's story. In physics, therefore, the search for radically new models now has a long and somewhat strange tradition. The strangeness lies in the pattern of discovery that characterized many of the major discoveries in quantum mechanics. "A lucky guess based on shaky arguments and absurd ad hoc assumptions gives a formula that turns out to be right, though at first no one can see why on earth it should be" (March 1978, 3). I delight in that statement of scientific process. It gives me hope for an approach to discovery that can influence the methodical, incremental, linear work that leads to the plodding character of most social science research.

The quantum mechanical view of reality strikes against most of our notions of reality. Even to scientists, it is admittedly bizarre. But it is a world where *relationship* is the key determiner of what is observed and of how particles manifest themselves. Particles come into being and are observed only in relationship to something else. They do not exist as independent "things." Quantum physics paints a strange yet enticing view of a world that, as Heisenberg characterized it, "appears as a complicated tissue of events, in which connections of different kinds alternate or overlap or combine and thereby determine the texture of the whole" (1958, 107). These unseen *connections* between what were previously thought to be separate entities are the fundamental elements of all creation.

In other disciplines, especially biology, the use of nonmechanistic models is much more recent. At the outer edges of accepted practice (although gaining slowly in credibility) are theories like the Gaia hypothesis, which sees the earth as a living organism actively engaged in creating the conditions which support life, or Rupert Sheldrake's morphogenic fields, which describe species memory as contained in invisible structures that help shape behavior. Some of what we know how to do, Sheldrake argues, comes not from our own acquired learning, but from knowledge that has been accumulated in the human species field, to which we have access. Whole populations of a species can shift their behavior because the content of their field has changed, not because they individually have taken the time to learn the new behavior.

So many fundamental reformulations of prevailing theories in evolution, animal behavior, ecology, and neurobiology are underway that, in 1982, Ernst Mayr, a noted chronicler of biological thought, stated: "It is now clear that a new philosophy of biology is needed" (1982, 73).

In chemistry, Ilya Prigogine won the Noble Prize in 1977 for his work demonstrating the capacity of certain chemical systems (dissipative structures) to regenerate to higher levels of self-organization in response to environmental demands. In the older, mechanistic models of natural phenomena, fluctuations and disturbances had always been viewed as signs of trouble. Disruptions would only more quickly bring on the decay that was the inevitable future of all systems. But the dissipative structures that Prigogine studied demonstrated the capacity of living systems to respond to disorder (non-equilibrium) with renewed life. Disorder can play a critical role in giving birth to new, higher forms of order. As we leave behind our machine models and look more deeply into the dynamics of living systems, we begin to glimpse an entirely new way of understanding fluctuations, disorder, and change.

New understandings of change and disorder are also emerging from chaos theory. Work in this field, which keeps expanding to take in more areas of inquiry, has led to a new appreciation of the relationship between order and chaos. These two forces are now understood as mirror images, one containing the other, a continual process where a system can leap into chaos and unpredictability, yet within that state be held within parameters that are well-ordered and predictable.

New science is also making us more aware that our yearning for simplicity is one we share with natural systems. In many systems, scientists now understand that order and conformity and shape are created not by complex controls, but by the presence of a few guiding formulae or principles. The survival and growth of systems that range in size from large ecosystems down to tiny leaves are made possible by the combination of key patterns or principles that express the system's overall identity and great levels of autonomy for individual system members.

The world described by new science is changing our beliefs and perceptions in many areas, not just in the natural sciences. I see new science ideas beginning to percolate in my own field of management theory. One way to see their effect is to look at the problems that plague us most in organizations these days or, more accurately, what we *define* as the problems. Leadership, an amorphous phenomenon that has intrigued us since people began studying organizations, is being examined now for its relational aspects. More and more studies focus on followership, empowerment, and leader accessibility. And ethical and moral questions are no longer fuzzy religious concepts but key elements in our relationships with staff, suppliers, and stakeholders. If the physics of our universe is revealing the primacy of relationships, is it any wonder that we are beginning to reconfigure our ideas about management in relational terms?

In motivation theory, our attention is shifting from the enticement of external rewards to the intrinsic motivators that spring from the work itself. We are refocusing on the deep longings we have for community, meaning, dignity, and love in our organizational lives. We are beginning to look at the strong emotions that are part of being human, rather than segmenting ourselves (love is for home, discipline is for work) or believing that we can confine workers into narrow roles, as though they were cogs in the machinery of production. As we let go of the machine models of work, we begin to step back and see ourselves in new ways, to appreciate our wholeness, and to design organizations that honor and make use of the totality of who we are.

The impact of vision, values, and culture occupies a great deal of organizational attention. We see their effects on organizational vitality, even if we can't quite define why they are such potent forces. We now sense that some of the best ways to create continuity of behavior are through the use of forces that we can't really see. Many scientists now work with the concept of fields—invisible forces that structure space or behavior. I have come to understand organizational vision as a field—a force of unseen connections that influences employees' behavior—rather than as an evocative message about some desired future state. Because of field theory, I believe I can better explain why vision is so necessary, and this leads me to new activities to strengthen its influence.

Our concept of organizations is moving away from the mechanistic creations that flourished in the age of bureaucracy. We have begun to speak in earnest of more fluid, organic structures, even of boundaryless organizations. We are beginning to recognize organizations as systems, construing them as "learning organizations" and crediting them with some type of self-renewing capacity. These are our first, tentative forays into a new appreciation for organizations. My own experience suggests that we can forego the despair created by such common organizational events as change, chaos, information overload, and cyclical behaviors if we recognize that organizations are conscious entities, possessing many of the properties of living systems.

Some believe that there is a danger in playing with science and abstracting its metaphors because, after a certain amount of stretch, the metaphors lose their relationship to the tight scientific theories that gave rise to them. But others would argue that all of science is metaphor—a hopeful description of how to think of a reality we can never fully know. I share the sentiments of physicist Frank Oppenheimer who says: "If one has a new way of thinking, why not apply it wherever one's thought leads to? It is certainly entertaining to let oneself do so, but it is also often very illuminating and capable of leading to new and deep insights" (in Cole 1985, 2).

Section IV

Leading Change

Niccolo Machiavelli (1950), an advisor to the Medici prince in sixteenth century Italy, said, "There is nothing more difficult to take in hand, more perilous to conduct, or more uncertain in its success, than to take the lead in the introduction of a new order of things" (p. 21). While change is a constant in life, leading change is perhaps one of the most difficult challenges. The leader may experience pressures for change from external forces, such as mandate or market; from internal forces, such as growth initiatives, power, and political moves; or from both types of forces. Another difficulty for the leader who tries to implement change is that followers or other community members might resist the change. Once the change has been initiated, additional concerns include establishing the means to ensure that the change is more than a transitory flame.

Several passages from inspired lives of change masters—Betty Friedan, Martin Luther King Jr. and Nelson Mandela—are in this volume or in other volumes of the Lynchburg College Symposium Readings.

Source:

Machiavelli, N. (1950) *The prince and the discourses.* New York: The Modern Library. (Original work written 1513.)

MARTIN LUTHER KING Jr.
1929-1968

Perhaps one of the best known leaders of change in the twentieth century was Martin Luther King Jr. (1929-1968). Included among Martin Luther King's many awards are the J.F.K. Award, the Nobel Peace Prize, and the John Dewey Award. He received his Nobel Peace Prize for his efforts to end racial discrimination and desegregation through civil disobedience and other nonviolent means.

A Baptist minister, King was one of the main leaders of the American civil rights movement. His efforts led to the 1963 March on Washington, where King delivered his famous "I Have a Dream" speech. His classic work, "Letter from Birmingham Jail," was written in 1963 while he was incarcerated in Birmingham Jail. It is a passionate statement on nonviolent direct action and on strategies for overcoming resistance to change. Both of these readings, which are so appropriate for this leadership volume in the Lynchburg College Symposium Readings, can be found in Freeman J. (Ed.) (2005). *Freedom, authority, and resistance,* (3rd ed.) Vol. II (pp. 54-59 & 392-415). Philadelphia: Xlibris. (Original works written 1963.)

BETTY FRIEDAN

1921-2006

The Feminine Mystique

1963

An American feminist, political activist, and writer, Betty Friedan founded the National Organization for Women, convened the National Women's Political Caucus, and even though it failed to be ratified, she was instrumental in the struggle for passage of the Equal Rights Amendment.

In *The Feminine Mystique* (1963), Betty Friedan broke new ground when she supplied her readers with tactics and strategies to understand gender bias and to rouse them to action. Friedan explained the "feminine mystique" as the frustrated and worthless feelings women experience when they are financially, intellectually, and emotionally dependent upon their husbands. According to Friedan (1963), the feminine mystique arose as a consequence of the baby boom and the growth of suburbia that occurred in the decades after World War II. Her observations and research led her to hypothesize that many women succumb to the false belief that the only way to find identity and meaning in their lives is in their roles as wives and mothers. Friedan (1963) offered a hopeful alternative when she suggested that "the only way for a woman, as for a man, to find herself, to know herself as a person, is by creative work of her own. There is no other way" (p. 320).

Sources:

Friedan, B. (1963). *The feminine mystique*. New York: W. W. Norton.

National Women's Hall of Fame. (n.d.). Retrieved from www. greatwomen.org

Selection from:

Friedan, B. (1963). *The feminine mystique*. (pp. 117-138) New York: W.W. Norton.

THE FUNCTIONAL FREEZE, THE FEMININE PROTEST, AND MARGARET MEAD

Instead of destroying the old prejudices that restricted women's lives, social science in America merely gave them new authority. By a curious circular process, the insights of psychology and anthropology and sociology, which should have been powerful weapons to free women, somehow canceled each other out, trapping women in dead center.

During the last twenty years, under the catalytic impact of Freudian thought, psychoanalysts, anthropologists, sociologists, social psychologists, and other workers in the behavioral sciences have met in professional seminars and foundation-financed conferences in many university centers. Cross-fertilization seemed to make them all bloom, but some strange hybrids were produced. As psychoanalysts began to reinterpret Freudian concepts like "oral" and "anal" personality in the light of an awareness, borrowed from anthropology, that cultural processes must have been at work in Freud's Vienna, anthropologists set out for the South Sea islands to chart tribal personality according to literal "oral" and "anal" tables. Armed with "psychological hints for ethnological field workers," the anthropologists often found what they were looking for. Instead of translating, sifting, the cultural bias *out* of Freudian theories, Margaret Mead, and the others who pioneered in the fields of culture and personality, compounded the error by fitting their own anthropological observations into Freudian rubric. But none of this might have had the same freezing effect on women if it had not been for a simultaneous aberration of American social scientists called functionalism.

Centering primarily on cultural anthropology and sociology and reaching its extremes in the applied field of family-life education, functionalism began as an attempt to make social science more "scientific" by borrowing from biology the idea of studying institutions as if they were muscles or bones, in terms of their "structure" and "function" in the social body. By studying an institution only in terms of its function within its own society, the social scientists intended to avert unscientific value judgments. In practice, functionalism was less a scientific movement than a scientific word-game. "The function is" was often translated "the function should be"; the social scientists did not recognize their own prejudices in functional disguise any more than the analysts recognized theirs in Freudian disguise. By giving an absolute meaning and a sanctimonious value to the generic term "woman's role," functionalism put American women into a kind of deep freeze—like Sleeping Beauties, waiting for a Prince Charming to waken them, while all around the magic circle the world moved on.

The social scientists, male and female, who, in the name of functionalism, drew this torturously tight circle around American women, also seemed to share a certain attitude which I will call "the feminine protest." If there is such a thing as a masculine protest—the psychoanalytic concept taken over by the functionalists to describe women who envied men and wanted to be men and therefore denied that they were women and became more manly than any man—its counterpart can be seen today in a feminine protest, made by men and women alike, who deny what women really are and make more of "being a woman" than it could ever be. The feminine protest, at its most straightforward, is simply a means of protecting women from the dangers inherent in assuming true equality with men. But why should any social scientist, with godlike manipulative superiority, take it upon himself—or herself—to protect women from the pains of growing up?

Protectiveness has often muffled the sound of doors closing against women; it has often cloaked a very real prejudice, even when it is offered in the name of science. If an old-fashioned grandfather frowned at Nora, who is studying calculus because she wants to be a physicist, and muttered, "Woman's place is in the home," Nora would laugh impatiently, "Grandpa, this is 1963." But she does not laugh at the urbane pipe-smoking professor of sociology, or the book by Margaret Mead, or the definitive two-volume reference on female sexuality, when they tell her the same thing. The complex, mysterious language of functionalism, Freudian psychology, and cultural anthropology hides from her the fact that they say this with not much more basis than grandpa.

So our Nora would smile at Queen Victoria's letter, written in 1870: "The Queen is most anxious to enlist everyone who can speak or write to join in checking this mad, wicked folly of 'Woman's Rights' with all its attendant horrors, on which her poor feeble sex is bent, forgetting every sense of womanly feeling and propriety . . . It is a subject which makes the Queen so furious that she cannot contain herself. God created men and women different—then let them remain each in their own position."

But she does not smile when she reads in *Marriage for Moderns*:

The sexes are complementary. It is the works of my watch that move the hands and enable me to tell time. Are the works, therefore, more important than the case? . . . Neither is superior, neither inferior. Each must be judged in terms of its own functions. Together they form a functioning unit. So it is with men and women—together they form a functioning unit. Either alone is in a sense incomplete. They are complementary . . . When men and women engage in the same occupations or perform common functions, the complementary relationship may break down.[1]

This book was published in 1942. Girls have studied it as a college text for the past twenty years. Under the guise of sociology, or "Marriage and Family Life," or "Life Adjustment," they are offered advice of this sort:

The fact remains, however, that we live in a world of reality, a world of the present and the immediate future, on which there rests the heavy hand of the past, a world in which tradition still holds sway and the mores exert a stronger influence than does the theorist . . . a world in which most men and women do marry and in which most married women are homemakers. To talk about what might be done if tradition and the mores were radically changed or what may come about by the year 2000 may be interesting mental gymnastics, but it does not help the young people of today to adjust to the inevitables of life or raise their marriages to a higher plane of satisfaction.[2]

Of course, this "adjustment to the inevitables of life" denies the speed with which the conditions of life are now changing—and the fact that many girls who so adjust at twenty will still be alive in the year 2000. This functionalist specifically warns against any and all approaches to the "differences between men and women" except "adjustment" to those differences as they now stand. And if, like our Nora, a woman is contemplating a career, he shakes a warning finger.

For the first time in history, American young women in great numbers are being faced with these questions: Shall

---

[1]   Henry A. Bowman, *Marriage for Moderns*, New York, 1942, p. 21.

[2]   *Ibid.*, pp. 22 ff.

I voluntarily prepare myself for a lifelong celibate career? Or shall I prepare for a temporary vocation, which I shall give up when I marry and assume the responsibilities of homemaking and motherhood? Or should I attempt to combine homemaking and a career? . . . The great majority of married women are homemakers . . .

If a woman can find adequate self-expression through a career rather than through marriage, well and good. Many young women, however, overlook the fact that there are numerous careers that do not furnish any medium or offer any opportunity for self-expression. Besides they do not realize that only the minority of women, as the minority of men, have anything particularly worthwhile to express.[3]

And so Nora is left with the cheerful impression that if she chooses a career, she is also choosing celibacy. If she has any illusions about combining marriage and career, the functionalist admonishes her:

How many individuals . . . can successfully pursue two careers simultaneously? Not many. The exceptional person can do it, but the ordinary person cannot. The problem of combining marriage and homemaking with another career is especially difficult, since it is likely that the two pursuits will demand qualities of different types. The former, to be successful, requires self-negation; the latter, self-enhancement. The former demands cooperation; the latter competition . . . There is greater opportunity for happiness if husband and wife supplement each other than there is when there is duplication of function . . . [4]

And just in case Nora has any doubts about giving up her career ambitions, she is offered this comforting rationalization:

A woman who is an effective homemaker must know something about teaching, interior decoration, cooking, dietetics, consumption, psychology, physiology, social relations,

---

[3]   *Ibid.*, pp. 62 ff.

[4]   *Ibid.*, pp. 74-76.

community resources, clothing, household equipment, housing, hygiene and a host of other things . . . She is a general practitioner rather than a specialist . . .

The young woman who decides upon homemaking as her career need have no feeling of inferiority . . . One may say, as some do, "Men can have careers because women make homes." One may say that women are released from the necessity for wage earning and are free to devote their time to the extremely important matter of homemaking because men specialize in breadwinning. Or one may say that together the breadwinner and the homemaker form a complementary combination second to none.[5]

This marriage textbook is not the most subtle of its school. It is almost too easy to see that its functional argument is based on no real chain of scientific fact. (It is hardly scientific to say "this is what is, therefore this is what should be.") But this is the essence of functionalism as it came to pervade all of American sociology in this period, whether or not the sociologist called himself a "functionalist." In colleges which would never stoop to the "role-playing lessons" of the so-called functional family course, young women were assigned Talcott Parsons' authoritative "analysis of sex-roles in the social structure of the United States," which contemplates no alternative for a woman other than the role of "housewife," patterned with varying emphasis on "domesticity," "glamour," and "good companionship."

It is perhaps not too much to say that only in very exceptional cases can an adult man be genuinely self-respecting and enjoy a respected status in the eyes of others if he does not "earn a living" in an approved occupational role . . . In the case of the feminine role the situation is radically different . . . The woman's fundamental status is that of her husband's wife, the mother of his children . . . [6]

---

5   *Ibid.*, pp. 66 ff.

6   Talcott Parsons, "Age and Sex in the Social Structure of the United States," in *Essays in Sociological Theory,* Glencoe, Ill., 1949, pp. 223 ff.

Parsons, a highly respected sociologist and the leading functional theoretician, describes with insight and accuracy the sources of strain in this "segregation of sex roles." He points out that the "domestic" aspect of the housewife role "has declined in importance to the point where it scarcely approaches a full-time occupation for a vigorous person": that the "glamour pattern" is "inevitably associated with a rather early age level" and thus "serious strains result from the problem of adaptation to increasing age," that the "good companion" pattern—which includes "humanistic" cultivation of the arts and community welfare— "suffers from a lack of fully institutionalized status . . . It is only those with the strongest initiative and intelligence who achieve fully satisfying adaptations in this direction." He states that "it is quite clear that in the adult feminine role there is quite sufficient strain and insecurity so that widespread manifestations are to be expected in the form of neurotic behavior." But Parsons warns:

It is, of course, possible for the adult woman to follow the masculine pattern and seek a career in fields of occupational achievement in direct competition with men of her own class. It is, however, notable that in spite of the very great progress of the emancipation of women from the traditional domestic pattern only a very small fraction have gone very far in this direction. It is also clear that its generalization would only be possible with profound alterations in the structure of the family.

True equality between men and women would not be "functional"; the status quo can be maintained only if the wife and mother is exclusively a homemaker or, at most, has a "job" rather than a "career" which might give her status equal to that of her husband. Thus Parsons finds sexual segregation "functional" in terms of keeping the social structure as it is, which seems to be the functionalist's primary concern.

Absolute equality of opportunity is clearly incompatible with any positive solidarity of the family . . . Where married women are employed outside the home, it is, for the great majority, in occupations which are not in direct competition for status with those of men of their own class. Women's interests, and the standard of judgment applied to them, run, in our society, far more in the direction of personal adornment . . . It is suggested that this difference is functionally related to maintaining family solidarity in our class structure.[7]

Even the eminent woman sociologist Mirra Komarovsky, whose functional analysis of how girls learn to "play the role of woman" in our society is brilliant indeed, cannot quite escape the rigid mold functionalism imposes: adjustment to the status quo. For to limit one's field of inquiry to the function of an institution in a given social system, with no alternatives considered, provides an infinite number of rationalizations for all the inequalities and inequities of that system. It is not surprising that social scientists began to mistake their own function as one of helping the individual "adjust" to his "role," in that system.

A social order can function only because the vast majority have somehow adjusted themselves to their place in society and perform the functions expected of them . . . The differences in the upbringing of the sexes . . . are obviously related to their respective roles in adult life. The future homemaker trains for her role within the home, but the boy prepares for his by being given more independence outside the home, by his taking a "paper route" or a summer job. A provider will profit by independence, dominance, aggressiveness, competitiveness.[8]

The risk of the "traditional upbringing" of girls, as this sociologist sees it, is its possible "failure to develop in the girl the independence, inner resources, and that degree of self-assertion which life will demand of her"—in her role as wife. The functional warning follows:

Even if a parent correctly [sic] considers certain conventional attributes of the feminine role to be worthless, he creates risks

---

7   Talcott Parsons, "An Analytical Approach to the Theory of Social Stratification," *op. cit.,* pp. 174 ff.

8   Mirra Komarovsky, "*Women in the Modern World, Their Education and Their Dilemmas,* Boston, 1953, pp. 52-61.

for the girl in forcing her to stray too far from the accepted mores of her time . . . The steps which parents must take to prepare their daughters to meet economic exigencies and familial responsibilities of modern life—these very steps may awaken aspirations and develop habits which conflict with certain features of their feminine roles, as these are defined today. The very education which is to make the college housewife a cultural leaven of her family and her community may develop in her interests which are frustrated by other phases of housewifery . . . We run the risk of awakening interests and abilities which, again, run counter to the present definition of femininity.[9]

She goes on to cite the recent case of a girl who wanted to be a sociologist. She was engaged to a GI who didn't want his wife to work. The girl herself hoped she wouldn't find a good job in sociology.

An unsatisfactory job would, she felt, make it easier for her to comply eventually with her future husband's wishes. The needs of the country for trained workers, the uncertainty of her own future, her current interests notwithstanding, she took a routine job. Only the future will tell whether her decision was prudent. If her fiancé returns from the front, if the marriage takes place, if he is able to provide for the family without her assistance, if her frustrated wishes do not boomerang, then she will not regret her decision . . .

At the present historical moment, the best adjusted girl is probably one who is intelligent enough to do well in school but not so brilliant as to get all A's . . . capable but not in areas relatively new to women; able to stand on her own two feet and to earn a living, but not so good a living as to compete with men; capable of doing some job well (in case she doesn't marry, or otherwise has to work) but not so identified with a profession as to need it for her happiness.[10]

---

[9]   *Ibid.*, p. 66
[10]   *Ibid.*, pp. 72-74

So, in the name of adjustment to the cultural definition of femininity—in which this brilliant sociologist obviously does not herself believe (that word "correctly" betrays her)—she ends up virtually endorsing the continued *infantilizing* of American woman, except insofar as it has the unintended consequence of making "the transition from the role of daughter to that of the spouse more difficult for her than for the son."

Essentially, it is assumed that the extent that the woman remains more "infantile," less able to make her own decisions, more dependent upon one or both parents for initiating and channeling behavior and attitudes, more closely attached to them so as to find it difficult to part from them or to face their disapproval . . . or shows any other indices of lack of emotional emancipation—to that extent she may find it more difficult than the man to conform to the cultural norm of primary loyalty to the family she establishes later. It is possible, of course, that the only effect of the greater sheltering is to create in women a generalized dependency which will then be transferred to the husband and which will enable her all the more readily to accept the role of wife in a family which still has many patriarchal features.[11]

She finds evidence in a number of studies that college girls, in fact, are more infantile, dependent and tied to parents than boys, and do not mature, as boys do, by learning to stand alone. But she can find no evidence—in twenty psychiatric texts—that there are, accordingly, more in-law problems with the wife's parents than the husband's. Evidently, only with such evidence could a functionalist comfortably question the deliberate infantilization of American girls!

Functionalism was an easy out for American sociologists. There can be no doubt that they were describing things, "as they were," but in so doing, they were relieved of the responsibility

---

[11] Mirra Komarovsky, "Functional Analysis of Sex Roles," *American Sociological Review,* August, 1950. See also "Cultural Contradictions and Sex Roles," *American Journal of Sociology,* November, 1946.

of building theory from facts, of probing for deeper truth. They were also relieved of the need to formulate questions and answers that would be inevitably controversial (at a time in academic circles, as in America as a whole, when controversy was not welcome). They assumed an endless present, and based their reasoning on denying the possibility of a future different from the past. Of course, their reasoning would hold up only as long as the future did not change. As C. P. Snow has pointed out, science and scientists are future-minded. Social scientists under the functional banner were so rigidly present-minded that they denied the future; their theories enforced the prejudices of the past, and actually prevented change.

Sociologists themselves have recently come to the conclusion that functionalism was rather "embarrassing" because it really said nothing at all. As Kingsley Davis pointed out in his presidential address on "The Myth of Functional Analysis as a Special Method in Sociology and Anthropology" at the American Sociological Association in 1959:

For more than thirty years now "functional analysis" has been debated among sociologists and anthropologists . . . However strategic it may have been in the past, it has now become an impediment rather than a prop to scientific progress . . . The claim that functionalism cannot handle social change because it posits an integrated static society is true by definition . . . [12]

---

[12] Kingsley Davis, "The Myth of Functional Analysis as a Special Method in Sociology and Anthropology," *American Sociological Review*, Vol. 24, No. 6, December, 1959, pp. 757-772. Davis points out that functionalism became more or less identical with sociology itself. There is provocative evidence that the very study of sociology, in recent years, has persuaded college women to limit themselves to their "functional" traditional sexual role. A report on "The Status of Women in Professional Sociology" (Sylvia Fleis Fava, *American Sociological Review*, Vol. 25, No. 2, April, 1960) shows that while most of the students in sociology undergraduate classes are women, from 1949 to 1958 there was a sharp decline in both the number and proportion of degrees in sociology awarded to women. (4,143 B.A.'s in 1949 down to a low of 3,200 in 1955,

Unfortunately, the female objects of functional analysis were profoundly affected by it. At a time of great change for women, at a time when education, science, and social science should have helped women bridge the change, functionalism transformed "what is" for women, or "what was," to "what should be." Those who perpetrated the feminine protest, and made more of being a woman than it can ever be, in the name of functionalism or for whatever complex of personal or intellectual reasons, closed the door of the future on women. In all the concern for adjustment, one truth was forgotten: women were being adjusted to a state inferior to their full capabilities. The functionalists did not wholly accept the Freudian argument that "anatomy is destiny," but they accepted wholeheartedly an equally restrictive definition of woman: woman is what society says she is. And most of the functional anthropologists studied societies in which woman's destiny was defined by anatomy.

The most powerful influence on modern women, in terms both of functionalism and the feminine protest, was Margaret Mead. Her work on culture and personality—book after book, study after study—has had a profound effect on the women in my generation, the one before it, and the generation now growing up. She was, and still is, the symbol of the woman thinker in America. She has written millions of words in the thirty-odd years between *Coming of Age in Samoa* in 1928 and her latest article on American women in the *New York Times Magazine* or *Redbook*. She is studied in college classrooms by girls taking courses in anthropology, sociology, psychology, education, and marriage and family life; in graduate schools

---

3,606 in 1958). And while one-half to two-thirds of the undergraduate degrees in sociology were awarded to women, women received only 25 to 43 per cent of the masters' degrees, and only 8 to 19 per cent of the Ph.D.'s. While the number of women earning graduate degrees in all fields has declined sharply during the era of the feminine mystique, the field of sociology showed, in comparison to other fields, an unusually high "mortality" rate.

by those who will one day teach girls and counsel women; in medical schools by future pediatricians and psychiatrists; even in theological schools by progressive young ministers. And she is read in the women's magazines and the Sunday supplements, where she publishes as readily as in the learned journals, by girls and women of all ages. Margaret Mead is her own best popularizer—and her influence has been felt in almost every layer of American thought.

But her influence, for women, has been a paradox. A mystique takes what it needs from any thinker of the time. The feminine mystique might have taken from Margaret Mead her vision of the infinite variety of sexual patterns and the enormous plasticity of human nature, a vision based on the differences of sex and temperament she found in three primitive societies: the Arapesh, where both men and women were "feminine" and "maternal" in personality and passively sexual, because both were trained to be cooperative, unaggressive, responsive to the needs and demands of others; the Mundugumor, where both husband and wife were violent, aggressive, positively sexed, "masculine"; and the Tchambuli, where the woman was the dominant, impersonal managing partner, and the man the less responsible and emotionally dependent person.

If those temperamental attitudes which we have traditionally regarded as feminine—such as passivity, responsiveness, and a willingness to cherish children—can so easily be set up as the masculine pattern in one tribe, and in another be outlawed for the majority of women as well as for the majority of men, we no longer have any basis for regarding such aspects of behavior as sex-linked . . . The material suggests that we may say that many, if not all, of the personality traits which we have called masculine or feminine are as lightly linked to sex, as are the clothing, the manners, and the form of head-dress that a society at a given period assigns to either sex.[13]

---

[13] Margaret Mead, *Sex and Temperament in Three Primitive Societies*, New York, 1935, pp. 279 f.

From such anthropological observations, she might have passed on to the popular culture a truly revolutionary vision of women finally free to realize their full capabilities in a society which replaced arbitrary sexual definitions with a recognition of genuine individual gifts as they occur in either sex. She had such a vision, more than once:

Where writing is accepted as a profession that may be pursued by either sex with perfect suitability, individuals who have the ability to write need not be debarred from it by their sex, nor need they, if they do write, doubt their essential masculinity or femininity . . . and it is here that we can find a ground-plan for building a society that would substitute real differences for arbitrary ones. We must recognize that beneath the superficial classifications of sex and race the same potentialities exist, recurring generation after generation, only to perish because society has no place for them.

Just as society now permits the practice of an art to members of either sex, so it might also permit the development of many contrasting temperamental gifts in each sex. It would abandon its various attempts to make boys fight and to make girls remain passive, or to make all children fight . . . No child would be relentlessly shaped to one pattern of behavior, but instead there should be many patterns, in a world that had learned to allow to each individual the pattern which was most congenial to his gifts.[14]

But this is not the vision the mystique took from Margaret Mead; nor is it the vision that she continues to offer. Increasingly, in her own pages, her interpretation blurs, is subtly transformed, into a glorification of women in the female role—as defined by their sexual biological function. At times she seems to lose her own anthropological awareness of the malleability of human personality, and to look at anthropological data from the Freudian point of view—sexual biology determines all, anatomy is destiny. At times she seems

---

[14]   Margaret Mead, *From the South Seas,* New York, 1939, p. 321.

to be arguing in functional terms, that while woman's potential is as great and various as the unlimited human potential, it is better to preserve the sexual biological limitations established by a culture. At times she says both things in the same page, and even sounds a note of caution, warning of the dangers a woman faces in trying to realize a human potential which her society has defined as masculine.

The difference between the two sexes is one of the important conditions upon which we have built the many varieties of human culture that give human beings dignity and stature . . . Sometimes one quality has been assigned to one sex, sometimes to the other. Now it is boys who are thought of as infinitely vulnerable and in need of special cherishing care, now it is girls . . . Some people think of women as too weak to work out of doors, others regard women as the appropriate bearers of heavy burdens "because their heads are stronger than men's." . . . Some religions, including our European traditional religions, have assigned women an inferior role in the religious hierarchy, others have built their whole symbolic relationship with the supernatural world upon male imitations of the natural functions of women . . . Whether we deal with small matters or with large, with the frivolities of ornament and cosmetics or the sanctities of man's place in the universe, we find this great variety of ways, often flatly contradictory one to the other, in which the roles of the two sexes have been patterned.

But we always find the patterning. We know of no culture that has said, articulately, that there is no difference between men and women except in the way they contribute to the creation of the next generation; that otherwise in all respects they are simply human beings with varying gifts, no one of which can be exclusively assigned to either sex.

Are we dealing with a must that we dare not flout because it is rooted so deep in our biological mammalian nature that to flout it means individual and social disease? Or with a must that, although not so deeply rooted, still is so very socially convenient and so well tried that it would be uneconomical to flout it—a must which says, for example, that it is easier to get children born and bred if we stylize the behavior of the sexes very differently, teaching them to walk and dress and act in contrasting ways and to specialize in different kinds of work?[15]

We must also ask: What are the potentialities of sex differences? . . . If little boys have to meet and assimilate the early shock of knowing that they can never create a baby with the sureness and incontrovertibility that is a woman's birthright, how does this make them more creatively ambitious, as well as more dependent upon achievement? If little girls have a rhythm of growth which means that their own sex appears to them as initially less sure than their brothers, and so gives them a little false flick towards compensatory achievement that almost always dies down before the certainty of maternity, this probably does mean a limitation on their sense of ambition? But what positive potentialities are there also?[16]

In these passages from *Male and Female*, a book which became the cornerstone of the feminine mystique, Margaret Mead betrays her Freudian orientation, even though she cautiously prefaces each statement of apparent scientific fact with the small word "if." But it is a very significant "if." For when sexual differences become the basis of your approach to culture and personality, and when you assume that sexuality is the driving force of human personality (an assumption that you took from Freud), and when, moreover, as an anthropologist, you know that there are no true-for-every-culture sexual differences except those involved in the act of procreation, you will inevitably give that one biological difference, the difference in reproductive role, increasing importance in the determination of woman's personality.

Margaret Mead did not conceal the fact that, after 1931, Freudian rubrics, based on the zones of the body, were part of the equipment she took with her on anthropological field

---

[15]   Margaret Mead, *Male and Female*, New York, 1955, pp. 16-18.
[16]   *Ibid.*, p. 26.

trips.[17] Thus she began to equate "those assertive, creative, productive aspects of life on which the superstructure of a civilization depends" with the penis, and to define feminine creativity in terms of the "passive receptivity" of the uterus.

In discussing men and women, I shall be concerned with the primary differences between them, the difference in their reproductive roles. Out of the bodies fashioned for complementary roles in perpetuating the race, what differences in functioning, in capacities, in sensitivities, in vulnerabilities arise? How is what men can do related to the fact that their reproductive role is over in a single act, what women can do related to the fact that their reproductive role takes nine months of gestation, and until recently many months of breast feeding? What is the contribution of each sex, seen as itself, not as a mere imperfect version of the other?

Living in the modern world, clothed and muffled, forced to convey our sense of our bodies in terms of remote symbols like walking sticks and umbrellas and handbags, it is easy to lose sight of the immediacy of the human body plan. But when one lives among primitive peoples, where women wear only a pair of little grass aprons, and may discard even these to insult each other or to bathe in a group, and men wear only a very lightly fastened G-string of beaten bark . . . and small babies wear nothing at all, the basic communications . . . that are conducted between bodies become very real. In our own

---

[17]   *Ibid.*, footnotes, pp. 289f:

I did not begin to work seriously with the zones of the body until I went to the Arapesh in 1931. While I was generally familiar with Freud's basic work on the subject, I had not seen how it might be applied in the field until I read Geza Roheim's first field report, "Psychoanalysis of Primitive Culture Types" . . . I then sent home for abstracts of K. Abraham's work. After I became acquainted with Erik Homburges Erikson's systematic handling of these ideas, they became an integral part of my theoretical equipment.

society, we have now invented a therapeutic method that can laboriously deduce from the recollections of the neurotic, or the untrammelled phantasies of the psychotic, how the human body, its entrances and exits, originally shaped the growing individual's view of the world.[18]

As a matter of fact, the lens of "anatomy is destiny" seemed to be peculiarly right for viewing the cultures and personalities of Samoa, Manus, Arapesh, Mundugumor, Tchambuli, Iatmul and Bali; right as perhaps it never was right, in that formulation, for Vienna at the end of the nineteenth century or America in the twentieth.

In the primitive civilizations of the South Sea islands, anatomy was still destiny when Margaret Mead first visited them. Freud's theory that the primitive instincts of the body determined adult personality could find convincing demonstration. The complex goals of more advanced civilizations, in which instinct and environment are increasingly controlled and transformed by the human mind, did not then form the irreversible matrix of every human life. It must have been much easier to see biological differences between men and women as the basic force in life in those unclothed primitive peoples. But only if you go to such an island with the Freudian lens in your eye, accepting before you start what certain irreverent anthropologists call the toilet-paper theory of history, will you draw from observations in primitive civilizations of the role of the unclothed body, male or female, a lesson for modern women which assumes that the unclothed body can determine in the same way the course of human life and personality in a complex modern civilization.

Anthropologists today are less inclined to see in primitive civilization a laboratory for the observation of our own civilization, a scale model with all the irrelevancies blotted out; civilization is just not that irrelevant.

---

[18]   *Ibid.,* pp. 50 f.

Because the human body is the same in primitive South Sea tribes and modern cities, an anthropologist, who starts with a psychological theory that reduces human personality and civilization to bodily analogies, can end up advising modern women to live through their bodies in the same way as the women of the South Seas. The trouble is that Margaret Mead could not recreate a South Sea world for us to live in: a world where having a baby is the pinnacle of human achievement. (If reproduction were the chief and only fact of human life, would all men today suffer from "uterus envy?")

In Bali, little girls between two and three walk much of the time with purposely thrust-out little bellies, and the older women tap them playfully as they pass. "Pregnant," they tease. So the little girl learns that although the signs of her membership in her own sex are slight, her breasts mere tiny buttons no bigger than her brother's, her genitals a simple inconspicuous fold, some day she will be pregnant, some day she will have a baby, and having a baby is, on the whole, one of the most exciting and conspicuous achievements that can be presented to the eyes of small children in these simple worlds, in some of which the largest buildings are only fifteen feet high, the largest boat some twenty feet long. Furthermore, the little girl learns that she will have a baby not because she is strong or energetic or initiating, not because she works and struggles and tries, and in the end succeeds, but simply because she is a girl and not a boy, and girls turn into women, and in the end—if they protect their femininity—have babies.[19]

To an American woman in the twentieth century competing in a field which demands initiative and energy and work and in which men resent her success, to a woman with less will and ability to compete than Margaret Mead, how tempting is her vision of that South Sea world where a woman succeeds and is envied by man just by being a woman.

---

[19] *Ibid.,* pp. 72 ff.

In our Occidental view of life, woman, fashioned from man's rib, can at the most strive unsuccessfully to imitate man's superior powers and higher vocations. The basic theme of the initiatory cult, however, is that women, by virtue of their ability to make children, hold the secret of life. Man's role is uncertain, undefined, and perhaps unnecessary. By a great effort man has hit upon a method of compensating himself for his basic inferiority. Equipped with various mysterious noise-making instruments, whose potency rests upon their actual forms being unknown to those who hear the sounds—that is, the women and children must never know that they are really bamboo flutes, or hollow logs . . . they can get the male children away from the women, brand them as incomplete and themselves turn boys into men. Women, it is true, make human beings, but only men can make men.[20]

True, this primitive society was a "shaky structure, protected by endless taboos and precautions"—by women's shame, fluttery fear, indulgence of male vanity—and it survived only as long as everyone kept the rules. "The missionary who shows the flutes to the women has broken the culture successfully."[21] But Margaret Mead, who might have shown American men and women "the flutes" of their own arbitrary and shaky taboos, precautions, shames, fears, and indulgence of male vanity, did not use her knowledge in this way. Out of life the way it was—in Samoa, Bali, where all men envied women—she held up an ideal for American women that gave new reality to the shaky structure of sexual prejudice, the feminine mystique.

The language is anthropological, the theory stated as fact is Freudian, but the yearning is for a return to the Garden of Eden: a garden where women need only forget the "divine discontent" born of education to return to a world in which male achievement becomes merely a poor substitute for child-bearing.

---

[20] *Ibid.,* pp. 84 ff.
[21] *Ibid.,* p. 85.

The recurrent problem of civilization is to define the male role satisfactorily enough—whether it be to build gardens or raise cattle, kill game or kill enemies, build bridges or handle bank shares—so that the male may, in the course of his life, reach a solid sense of irreversible achievement of which his childhood knowledge of the satisfactions of child-bearing has given him a glimpse. In the case of women, it is only necessary that they be permitted by the given social arrangements to fulfill their biological role, to attain this sense of irreversible achievement. If women are to be restless and questing, even in the face of childbearing, they must be made so through education.[22]

What the feminine mystique took from Margaret Mead was not her vision of woman's great untested human potential, but this glorification of the female sexual function that has indeed been tested, in every culture, but seldom, in civilized cultures, valued as highly as the unlimited potential of human creativity, so far mainly displayed by man. The vision the mystique took from Margaret Mead was of a world where women, by merely being women and bearing children, will earn the same respect accorded men for their creative achievements—as if possession of uterus and breasts bestows on women a glory that men can never know, even though they labor all their lives to create. In such a world, all the other things that a woman can do or be are merely pale substitutes for the conception of a child. Femininity becomes more than its definition by society; it becomes a value which society must protect from the destructive onrush of civilization like the vanishing buffalo.

Margaret Mead's eloquent pages made a great many American women envy the serene femininity of a bare-breasted Samoan, and try to make themselves into languorous savages, breasts unfettered by civilization's brassieres, and brains undisturbed by pallid man-made knowledge of the goals of human progress.

---

[22] *Ibid.*, pp. 125 ff.

Woman's biological career-line has a natural climax structure that can be overlaid, muted, muffled and publicly denied, but which remains as an essential element in both sexes' view of themselves . . . The young Balinese girl to whom one says, "Your name is I Tewa?" and who draws herself up and answers, "I am Men Bawa" (Mother of Bawa) is speaking absolutely. She is the mother of Bawa; Bawa may die tomorrow, but she remains the mother of Bawa; only if he had died unnamed would her neighbors have called her "Men Belasin," "Mother Bereft." Stage after stage in women's life-histories thus stand, irrevocable, indisputable, accomplished. This gives a natural basis for the little girl's emphasis on being rather than on doing. The little boy learns that he must act like a boy, do things, prove that he is a boy, and prove it over and over again, while the little girl learns that she is a girl, and all she has to do is to refrain from acting like a boy.[23]

And so it goes, on and on, until one is inclined to say—so what? You are born, you grow, you are impregnated, you have a child, it grows; this is true of all cultures, recorded or unrecorded, the one we know from life and the recondite ones which only the far-traveled anthropologist knows. But is this all there is to life for a woman today?

It is not to deny the importance of biology to question a definition of woman's nature that is based so completely on her biological difference from man. Female biology, woman's "biological career-line," may be changeless—the same in Stone Age women twenty thousand years ago, and Samoan women on remote islands, and American women in the twentieth century—but the nature of the human relationship to biology *has* changed. Our increasing knowledge, the increasing potency of human intelligence, has given us an awareness of purposes and goals beyond the simple biological needs of hunger, thirst, and sex. Even these simple needs, in men or women today, are not the same as they were in the Stone Age or in the South

---

[23]   *Ibid.,* pp. 135 ff.

Sea cultures, because they are now part of a more complex pattern of human life.

As an anthropologist, of course, Margaret Mead knew this. And for all her words glorifying the female role, there are other words picturing the wonders of a world in which women would be able to realize their full capabilities. But this picture is almost invariably overlaid with the therapeutic caution, the manipulative superiority, typical of too many American social scientists. When this caution is combined with perhaps an over-evaluation of the power of social science not merely to interpret culture and personality, but to order our lives, her words acquire the aura of a righteous crusade—a crusade against change. She joins the other functional social scientists in their emphasis on adjusting to society as we find it, on living our lives within the framework of the conventional cultural definitions of the male and female roles. This attitude is explicit in the later pages of *Male and Female.*

Giving each sex its due, a full recognition of its special vulnerabilities and needs for protection, means looking beyond the superficial resemblances during the period of later childhood when both boys and girls, each having laid many of the problems of sex adjustment aside, seem so eager to learn, and so able to learn the same things . . . But every adjustment that minimizes a difference, a vulnerability, in one sex, a differential strength in the other, diminishes their possibility of complementing each other, and corresponds— symbolically—to sealing off the constructive receptivity of the female and the vigorous outgoing constructive activity of the male, muting them both in the end to a duller version of human life, in which each is denied the fullness of humanity that each might have had.[24]

No human gift is strong enough to flower fully in a person who is threatened with loss of sex membership . . . No matter with what good will we may embark on a program

---

[24]   *Ibid.,* pp. 274 ff.

of actually rearing both men and women to make their full and special contributions in all the complex processes of civilization—medicine and law, education and religion, the arts and sciences—the task will be very difficult . . .

It is of very doubtful value to enlist the gifts of women if bringing women into fields that have been defined as male frightens the men, unsexes the women, muffles and distorts the contribution the women could make, either because their presence excludes men from the occupation or because it changes the quality of the men who enter it . . . It is folly to ignore the signs which warn us that the present terms in which women are lured by their own curiosities and drives developed under the same educational system as boys . . . are bad for both men and women.[25]

The role of Margaret Mead as the professional spokesman of femininity would have been less important if American women had taken the example of her own life, instead of listening to what she said in her books. Margaret Mead has lived a life of open challenge, and lived it proudly, if sometimes self-consciously, as a woman. She has moved on the frontiers of thought and added to the superstructure of our knowledge. She has demonstrated feminine capabilities that go far beyond childbirth; she made her way in what was still very much a "man's world" without denying that she was a woman; in fact, she proclaimed in her work a unique woman's knowledge with which no male anthropologist could compete. After so many centuries of unquestioned masculine authority, how natural for someone to proclaim a feminine authority. But the great human visions of stopping wars, curing sickness, teaching races to live together, building new and beautiful structures for people to live in, are more than "other ways of having children."

It is not easy to combat age-old prejudices. As a social scientist, and as a woman, she struck certain blows against the

---

[25]   *Ibid.*, pp. 278 ff.

prejudicial image of woman that may long outlast her own life. In her insistence that women are human beings—unique human beings, not men with something missing—she went a step beyond Freud. And yet, because her observations were based on Freud's bodily analogies, she cut down her own vision of women by glorifying the mysterious miracle of femininity, which a woman realizes simply by being female, letting the breasts grow and the menstrual blood flow and the baby suck from the swollen breast. In her warning that women who seek fulfillment beyond their biological role are in danger of becoming desexed witches, she spelled out again an unnecessary choice. She persuaded younger women to give up part of their dearly won humanity rather than lose their femininity. In the end she did the very thing that she warned against, re-creating in her work the vicious circle that she broke in her own life:

We may go up the scale from simple physical differences through complementary distinctions that overstress the role of sex difference and extend it inappropriately to other aspects of life, to stereotypes of such complex activities as those involved in the formal use of the intellect, in the arts, in government, and in religion.

In all these complex achievements of civilization, those activities which are mankind's glory, and upon which depends our hope of survival in this world that we have built, there has been this tendency to make artificial definitions that limit an activity to one sex, and by denying the actual potentialities of human beings limit not only both men and women, but also equally the development of the activity itself . . .

Here is a vicious circle to which it is not possible to assign either a beginning or an end, in which men's overestimation of women's roles, or women's overestimation of men's roles leads one sex or the other to arrogate, to neglect, or even to relinquish part of our so dearly won humanity. Those who would break the circle are themselves a product of it, express some of its defects in their every gesture, may be only strong enough to challenge it, not able actually to break it. Yet once identified, once analyzed, it should be possible to create a climate of opinion in which others, a little less the product of the dark past because they have been reared with a light in their hand that can shine backwards as well as forwards, may in turn take the next step.[26]

Perhaps the feminine protest was a necessary step after the masculine protest made by some of the feminists. Margaret Mead was one of the first women to emerge into prominence in American life after rights for women were won. Her mother was a social scientist, her grandmother a teacher; she had private images of women who were fully human, she had education equal to any man's. And she was able to say with conviction: it's good to be a woman, you don't need to copy man, you can respect yourself as a woman. She made a resounding feminine protest, in her life and in her work. And it was a step forward when she influenced emancipated modern women to choose, with free intelligence, to have babies, bear them with a proud awareness that denied pain, nurse them at the breast and devote mind and body to their care. It was a step forward in the passionate journey—and one made possible by it—for educated women to say "yes" to motherhood as a conscious human purpose and not a burden imposed by the flesh. For, of course, the natural childbirth-breastfeeding movement Margaret Mead helped inspire was not at all a return to primitive earth-mother maternity. It appealed to the independent, educated, spirited American woman—and to her counterparts in western Europe and Russia—because it enabled her to experience childbirth not as a mindless female animal, an object manipulated by the obstetrician, but as a whole person, able to control her own body with her aware mind. Perhaps less important than birth

---

[26]   *Ibid.*, pp. 276-285.

control and the other rights which made woman more equal to man, the work of Margaret Mead helped humanize sex. It took a scientific supersaleswoman to recreate in modern American life even a semblance of the conditions under which primitive tribesmen jealously imitated maternity and bled themselves. (The modern husband goes through the breathing exercises with his wife as she prepares for natural childbirth.) But did she oversell women?

It was, perhaps, not her fault that she was taken so literally that procreation became a cult, a career, to the exclusion of every other kind of creative endeavor, until women kept on having babies because they knew no other way to create. She was often quoted out of context by the lesser functionalists and the women's magazines. Those who found in her work confirmation of their own unadmitted prejudices and fears ignored not only the complexity of her total work, but the example of her complex life. With all the difficulties she must have encountered, pioneering as a woman in the realm of abstract thought that was the domain of man (a one-sentence review of *Sex and Temperament* indicates the resentment she often met: "Margaret, have you found a culture yet where the men had the babies?"), she has never retreated from the hard road to self-realization so few women have traveled since. She told women often enough to stay on that road. If they only heard her other words of warning, and conformed to her glorification of femininity, perhaps it was because they were not as sure of themselves and their human abilities as she was.

Margaret Mead and the lesser functionalists knew the pains, the risks, of breaking through age-old social strictures.[27] This awareness was their justification for qualifying their statements of women's potentiality with the advice that women not compete with men, but seek respect for their uniqueness

---

[27] Margaret Mead, Introduction to *From the South Seas,* New York, 1939, p. xiii. "It was no use permitting children to develop values different from those of their society . . ."

as women. It was hardly revolutionary advice; it did not upset the traditional image of woman any more than Freudian thought upset it. Perhaps it was their intention to subvert the old image; but instead they gave the new mystique its scientific authority.

Ironically, Margaret Mead, in the 1960's, began to voice alarm at the "return of the cavewoman"—the retreat of American women to narrow domesticity, while the world trembled on the brink of technological holocaust. In an excerpt from a book titled *American Women: The Changing Image*, which appeared in the *Saturday Evening Post* (March 3, 1962), she asked:

> Why have we returned, despite our advances in technology, to the Stone Age picture? . . . Woman has gone back, each to her separate cave, waiting anxiously for her mate and children to return, guarding her mate jealously against other women, almost totally unaware of any life outside her door . . . In this retreat into fecundity, it is not the individual woman who is to blame. It is the climate of opinion that has developed in this country . . .

Apparently Margaret Mead does not acknowledge, or perhaps recognize her own role as a major architect of that "climate of opinion." Apparently she has overlooked much of her own work, which helped persuade several generations of able modern American women "in desperate cavewoman style, to devote their whole lives to narrow domesticity—first in schoolgirl dreaming and a search for roles which make them appealingly ignorant, then as mothers and then as grandmothers . . . restricting their activities to the preservation of their own private, and often boring existences."

Even though it would seem that Margaret Mead is now trying to get women out of the home, she still ascribes a sexual specialness to everything a woman does. Trying to seduce them into the modern world of science as "the teacher-mothers of infant scientists," she is still translating the new possibilities open to women and the new problems facing them as members of the human race into sexual terms. But now "those roles which have historically belonged to women" are stretched to include political responsibility for nuclear disarmament—"to cherish not just their own but the children of the enemy." Since, beginning with the same premise and examining the same body of anthropological evidence, she now arrives at a slightly different sexual role for women, one might seriously question the basis upon which she decides the roles a woman should play—and finds it so easy to change the rules of the game from one decade to the next.

Other social scientists have arrived at the astonishing conclusion that "being a woman was no more and no less than being human."[28] But a cultural lag is built into the feminine mystique. By the time a few social scientists were discovering the flaws in "woman's role," American educators had seized upon it as a magic sesame. Instead of educating women for the greater maturity required to participate in modern society—with all the problems, conflicts, and hard work involved, for educators as well as women—they began educating them to "play the role of woman."

---

[28]   Marie Jahoda and Joan Havel, "Psychological Problems of Women in Different Social Roles—A Case History of Problem Formulation in Research," *Educational Record,* Vol. 36, 1955, pp. 325-333.

NELSON MANDELA

1918-

Long Walk to Freedom

1994

Nelson Mandela was born in 1918, as the son of a tribal chief in the Xhosa nation, Chief Henry Mandela. Nelson Mandela attended the University College of Fort Hare and the University of Witwatersrand and graduated with a law degree in 1942. He joined the African National Congress in 1944 and actively opposed the ruling National Party's apartheid policies from 1948. He was tried for treason between 1956 and 1961 but was acquitted in 1961. However, in 1963, he was again arrested along with many other leaders of the ANC and stood trial for plotting to overthrow the government by violence. This time he was found guilty and sentenced to life in prison in 1964. In 1994, he was elected as the first black president of South Africa shortly after the end of apartheid. His winning of the Nobel Peace Prize for his efforts in the anti-apartheid movement was an acknowledgement that Nelson Mandela is one of the great moral and political leaders of our time.

Mandela has written that the African National Congress's motto ("No man or woman who has abandoned apartheid will be excluded from our movement toward a nonracial, united and democratic South Africa based on one-person one-vote on a common voters' roll") sustained him during his many lonely years in prison. These goals still sustain him and direct the course of his life's work. According to Mandela (1994), "It was the dream I cherished when I entered prison at the age of 44, but I was no longer a young man, I was 71, and I could not afford to waste any time" (p. 570).

In his autobiography, published in 1994, Mandela chronicles his life, time spent in prison, and his return to leadership. He spent twenty-seven years in prison, during which time he secretly wrote *Long Walk to Freedom.*

Source:

African National Congress. (2009.) *Nelson Rolihlahla Mandela.* Retrieved from http://www.anc.org.za/people/mandela.html

Selection from:

Mandela, N. (1994). *Long Walk to Freedom: The Autobiography of Nelson Mandela.* (pp. 610-614). Boston: Little, Brown.

112

ALTHOUGH FEW PEOPLE will remember June 3, 1993, it was a landmark in South African history. On that day, after months of negotiations at the World Trade Centre, the multiparty forum voted to set a date for the country's first national, nonracial, one-person-one-vote election: April 27, 1994. For the first time in South African history, the black majority would go to the polls to elect their own leaders. The agreement was that voters would elect four hundred representatives to a constituent assembly, which would both write a new constitution and serve as a parliament. After convening, the first order of business for the assembly would be to elect a president.

The talks had reconvened in April. This time, the twenty-six parties included Inkatha, the Pan Africanist Congress, and the Conservative Party. We had been pressing the government to establish a date for months, and they had been stalling. But now the date was written in stone.

A month later, in July, the multiparty forum agreed on a first draft of an interim constitution. It provided for a bicameral parliament with a four-hundred-member national assembly elected by proportional representation from national and regional party lists and a senate elected indirectly by regional legislatures. Elections to regional legislatures would take place at the same time as national elections, and the regional bodies could draw up their own constitutions consistent with the national constitution.

Chief Buthelezi wanted a constitution drawn up before the election and walked out in protest against the setting of an election date before a constitution was finalized. A second draft interim constitution in August gave greater powers to the regions, but this did not placate either Chief Buthelezi or the Conservative Party. The Conservative Party described the resolutions as hostile to Afrikaner interests. A group called the Afrikaner Volksfront, led by General Constand Viljoen, a former chief of the South African Defense Force, was formed to unite conservative white organizations around the idea of a *volkstaat*, a white homeland.

Just after midnight on November an interim constitution was approved by a plenary session of the multiparty conference. The government and the ANC had cleared the remaining hurdles. The new cabinet would be composed of those winning more than 5 percent of the vote and would make decisions by consensus, rather than the two-thirds majority proposed by the government; national elections would not take place until 1999, so that the government of national unity would serve for five years; and finally, the government gave way on our insistence on a single ballot paper for the election, rather than separate ballots for national and provincial legislatures. Two ballot papers would only confuse a majority of voters, most of whom would be voting for the first time in their lives. In the period leading up to the election, a Transitional Executive Council with members from each party would ensure the right climate for the elections. In effect, the TEC would be the government between December 22 and the election on April 27. An Independent Electoral Commission with extensive powers would be responsible for the administration of the election. We were truly on the threshold of a new era.

I have never cared very much for personal prizes. A man does not become a freedom fighter in the hope of winning awards, but when I was notified that I had won the 1993 Nobel Peace Prize jointly with Mr. de Klerk, I was deeply moved. The Nobel Peace Prize had a special meaning to me because of its involvement with South African history.

I was the third South African since the end of the Second World War to be so honored by the Nobel committee. Chief Albert Luthuli was awarded the prize in 1960. The second was Archbishop Desmond Tutu, who selflessly fought the evils of racism during the most terrible days of apartheid.

The award was a tribute to all South Africans and especially to those who had fought in the struggle; I would accept the award on their behalf. But the Nobel award was one I never thought about. Even during the bleakest years on Robben Island, Amnesty International would not campaign for us on the grounds that we had pursued an armed struggle, and their organization would not represent anyone who had embraced violence. It was for that reason that I assumed the Nobel committee would never consider the man who had started Umkhonto we Sizwe for the peace prize.

I had tremendous respect for the nations of Norway and Sweden. In the 1950s and 1960s, when we went to Western governments seeking contributions to the ANC, we were turned down flat. But in Norway and Sweden, we were greeted with open arms, and given assistance and scholarships and money for legal defense and humanitarian aid for political prisoners.

I used my speech in Norway not only to thank the Nobel committee and sketch out a vision of a future South Africa that was just and equitable, but to pay tribute to my fellow laureate, Mr. F. W. de Klerk.

> He had the courage to admit that a terrible wrong had been done to our country and people through the imposition of the system of apartheid. He had the foresight to understand and accept that all the people of South Africa must, through negotiations and as equal participants in the process, together determine what they want to make of their future.

I was often asked how could I accept the award jointly with Mr. de Klerk after I had criticized him so severely. Although I would not take back my criticisms, I could say that he had made a genuine and indispensable contribution to the peace process. I never sought to undermine Mr. de Klerk, for the practical reason that the weaker he was, the weaker the negotiations process. To make peace with an enemy one must work with that enemy, and that enemy becomes one's partner.

Although the official campaign for the national assembly was not scheduled to begin until February 1994, we started to campaign in earnest after the new constitution was ratified. That did not give us a head start; the National Party began its campaign the day they released me from prison.

Although the polls showed the ANC with a healthy margin, we never took victory for granted. I counseled everyone against over-optimism. We had all read dozens of accounts of parties favored to win who came in second. We faced an experienced, well-organized, and well-financed rival.

Our campaign was under the capable leadership of Popo Molefe, Terror Lekota, and Ketso Gordhan, all veteran UDF activists adept at mass mobilization. The task was a formidable one. We estimated that there would be over twenty million people going to the polls, most of them voting for the first time. Many of our voters were illiterate, and were likely to be intimidated by the mere idea of voting. According to the Independent Electoral Commission, there would be ten thousand polling stations around the country. We sought to train over one hundred thousand people to assist with voter education.

The first stage of our election effort was what was known as People's Forums. ANC candidates would travel all over the country and hold meetings in towns and villages in order to listen to the hopes and fears, the ideas and complaints, of our people. The People's Forums were similar to the town meetings that candidate Bill Clinton held in America on his way to the presidency. The forums were parliaments of the people, not unlike the meetings of chiefs at the Great Place that I witnessed as a boy.

I reveled in the People's Forums. I began in Natal in November, and then went to the PWV area, the northern Transvaal, and the Orange Free State. I attended as many as three or four forums in a day. The people themselves enjoyed them immensely. No one had ever come to solicit their opinion on what should be done in their own country.

After incorporating the suggestions from the forums, we traveled the country delivering our message to the people. Some in the ANC wanted to make the campaign simply a liberation election, and tell the people: Vote for us because we set you free. We decided instead to offer them a vision of the South Africa we hoped to create. We wanted people to vote for the ANC not just because we had fought apartheid for eighty years, but because we were best qualified to bring about the kind of South Africa they hoped to live in. I felt that our campaign should be about the future, not the past.

The ANC drafted a 150-page document known as the Reconstruction and Development Program, which outlined our plan to create jobs through public works; to build a million new houses with electricity and flush toilets; to extend primary health care and ten years of free education to all South Africans; to redistribute land through a land claims court; and to end the value-added tax on basic foodstuffs. We were also committed to extensive affirmative action measures in both the private and public sectors. This document was translated into a simpler manifesto called "A Better Life for All," which in turn became the ANC's campaign slogan.

Just as we told the people what we would do, I felt we must also tell them what we could not do. Many people felt life would change overnight after a free and democratic election, but that would be far from the case. Often, I said to crowds, "Do not expect to be driving a Mercedes the day after the election or swimming in your own backyard pool." I told our supporters. "Life will not change dramatically, except that you will have increased your self-esteem and become a citizen in your own land. You must have patience. You might have to wait five years for results to show." I challenged them; I did not patronize them: "If you want to continue living in poverty without clothes and food," I told them, "then go and drink in the shebeens. But if you want better things, you must work hard. We cannot do it all for you; you must do it yourselves."

I told white audiences that we needed them and did not want them to leave the country. They were South Africans just like ourselves and this was their land, too. I would not mince words about the horrors of apartheid, but I said, over and over, that we should forget the past and concentrate on building a better future for all.

Each rally was also designed to teach people how to vote. The ballot itself was a long, narrow piece of paper with the parties listed in descending order to the left, and then the symbol of the party and a picture of its leader to the right. Voters were to place an X in the box next to the parts of their choice. I would tell audiences, "On election day, look down your ballot and when you see the face of a young and handsome man, mark an X."

SECTION V

THE CONTEXT OF LEADERSHIP

Thus far in this volume, qualities and behaviors of the leader have been given special focus, yet many times the leader's context is just as influential as the leader him or herself. The readings in Section V explore the leader's context. For example, Tolstoy (1869) suggested that the leader, as one of history's slaves, has far less discretion in the leadership process than is usually assumed. As but one of history's slaves, the leader will find that the course of action chosen was frequently determined by historical forces beyond his or her control.

James MacGregor Burns (1978) suggested that the power a leader may have over followers may also depend upon the level of economic development of a society. For societies in which the economy is developing, a more idolatrous form of heroism may be affected by the leader; in turn, followers may believe that the leader can do anything, and they may end up worshiping the leader.

Not just the level of economic development of a nation, but the very "personality" of a country may exert profound influences on what is expected of the leader. For example, Geert Hofstede (1980) conducted extensive survey research to find four critical variables, such as tolerance for uncertainty avoidance, which change from country to country and make a difference in the leadership equation.

Still other forces chip away at the leader's self determination. Kerr and Jermier (1978) argued that there are important reasons why in some circumstances substitutes for leadership (certain attributes of subordinates, tasks, or organizations that provide task guidance and incentives to perform well) will be found to fully replace the influence of the leader—so much so that it might seem that the leader is not needed.

Another aspect of the context of leadership that cues us to look beyond the leader is followership itself. What is the effect of the follower? What does it mean to be an effective follower? Thus, the above contextual variables qualify our understanding of the leader's influence.

SUN TZU

400 B.C.E.-320 B.C.E.

The Art of War

ca. 6th century B.C.E.

Tradition suggests that Sun Tzu, pronounced SOON-zuh and translated as "Master Sun," is the author of *The Art of War*, an ancient Chinese text on military strategy. In elaborating on Taoist strategies, Sun Tzu has had significant influence on Chinese and Asian history and culture, as both an author and a legendary figure.

Sun Tzu's over-2000-year-old work contains lessons for the soldier and has thirteen chapters, each dedicated to a different aspect of warfare. The chapters include discussions of planning an attack, the use of force, the types of terrains and how to navigate in each, and the use of spies. His work has been applied with much success to Western corporate and business strategies and to office politics as well as to politics in general.

Source:

Sun Tzu. (1963). *The art of war.* (S. B. Griffith, Trans.). London: Oxford University Press.

Selection from:

Sun Tzu. (1963). *The art of war.* (S. B. Griffith, Trans.). (pp. 77-89). London: Oxford University Press.

III
OFFENSIVE STRATEGY

SUN TZU said:

1. Generally in war the best policy is to take a state intact; to ruin it is inferior to this.

    Li Ch'üan: Do not put a premium on killing.

2. To capture the enemy's army is better than to destroy it; to take intact a battalion, a company or a five-man squad is better than to destroy them.

3. For to win one hundred victories in one hundred battles is not the acme of skill. To subdue the enemy without fighting is the acme of skill.

4. Thus, what is of supreme importance in war is to attack the enemy's strategy;[1]

    Tu Mu: . . . The Grand Duke said: 'He who excels at resolving difficulties does so before they arise. He who excels in conquering his enemies triumphs before threats materialize.'

    Li Ch'üan: Attack plans at their inception. In the Later Han, K'ou Hsün surrounded Kao Chun[2]. Chun sent

---

[1]   Not, as Giles translates, 'to balk the enemy's plans'.
[2]   This took place during the first century A.D.

his Planning Officer, Huang-fu Wen, to parley. Huang-fu Wen was stubborn and rude and K'ou Hsü beheaded him, and informed Kao Chun: 'Your staff officer was without propriety. I have beheaded him. If you wish to submit, do so immediately. Otherwise defend yourself.' On the same day, Chun threw open his fortifications and surrendered.

All K'ou Hsün's generals said: 'May we ask, you killed his envoy, but yet forced him to surrender his city. How is this?'

K'ou Hsün said: 'Huang-fu Wen was Kao Chun's heart and guts, his intimate counsellor. If I had spared Huang-fu Wen's life, he would have accomplished his schemes, but when I killed him, Kao Chun lost his guts. It is said: "The supreme excellence in war is to attack the enemy's plans."'
All the generals said: 'This is beyond our comprehension.'

5. Next best is to disrupt his alliances:[3]

> *Tu Yu:* Do not allow your enemies to get together.

> *Wang Hsi:* . . . Look into the matter of his alliances and cause them to be severed and dissolved. If an enemy has alliances, the problem is grave and the enemy's position strong; if he has no alliances the problem is minor and the enemy's position weak.

6. The next best is to attack his army.
> *Chia Lin:* . . . The Grand Duke said: 'He who struggles for victory with naked blades is not a good general.'

---

[3]   Not, as Giles translates, 'to prevent the junction of the enemy's forces'.

Wang Hsi: Battles are dangerous affairs.

Chang Yü: If you cannot nip his plans in the bud, or disrupt his alliances when they re about to be consummated, sharpen your weapons to gain the victory.

7. The worst policy is to attack cities. Attack cities only when there is no alternative.[4]

8. To prepare the shielded wagons and make ready the necessary arms and equipment requires at least three months; to pile up earthen ramps against the walls an additional three months will be needed.

9. If the general is unable to control his impatience and orders his troops to swarm up the wall like ants, one-third of them will be killed without taking the city. Such is the calamity of these attacks.

> *Tu Mu:* . . . In the later Wei, the Emperor T'ai Wu led one hundred thousand troops to attack the Sung general Tsang Chih at Yu T'ai. The Emperor first asked Tsang Chih for some wine.[5] Tsang Chih sealed up a pot full of urine and sent it to him. T'ai Wu was transported with rage and immediately attacked the city, ordering his troops to scale the walls and engage in close combat. Corpses piled up to the top of the walls and after thirty days of this the dead exceeded half his force.

---

[4] In this series of verses Sun Tzu is not discussing the art of generalship as Giles apparently thought. These are objectives or policies-*cheng*-in order of relative merit.

[5] Exchange of gifts and compliments was a normal preliminary to battle.

10. Thus, those skilled in war subdue the enemy's army without battle. They capture his cities without assaulting them and overthrow his state without protracted operations.

> *Li Ch'üan*: They conquer by strategy. In the Later Han the Marquis of Tsan, Tsang Kung, surrounded the 'Yao' rebels at Yüan Wu, but during a succession of months was unable to take the city.[6] His officers and men were ill and covered with ulcers. The King of Tung Hai spoke to Tsang Kung, saying: 'Now you have massed troops and encircled the enemy, who is determined to fight to the death. This is no strategy! You should lift the siege. Let them know that an escape route is open and they will flee and disperse. Then any village constable will be able to capture them!' Tsang Rung followed this advice and took Yüan Wu.

11. Your aim must be to take All-under-Heaven intact. Thus your troops are not worn out and your gains will be complete. This is the art of offensive strategy.

12. Consequently, the art of using troops is this: When ten to the enemy's one, surround him;

13. When five times his strength, attack him;

> *Chang Yu*: If my force is five times that of the enemy I alarm him to the front, surprise him to the rear, create an uproar in the east and strike in the west.

14. If double his strength, divide him.[7]

---

[6] *Yao* connotes the supernatural. The Boxers, who believed themselves impervious to foreign lead, could be so described.

[7] Some commentators think this verse 'means to divide one's own force', but that seems a less satisfactory interpretation, as the character *chih* used in the two previous verses refers to the enemy.

Tu Yu: . . . If a two-to-one superiority is insufficient to manipulate the situation, we use a distracting force to divide his army. Therefore the Grand Duke said: 'If one is unable to influence the enemy to divide his forces, he cannot discuss unusual tactics.'

15. If equally matched you may engage him.

Ho Yen-hsi: . . . In these circumstances only the able general can win.

16. If weaker numerically, be capable of withdrawing;

Tu Mu: If your troops do not equal his, temporarily avoid his initial onrush. Probably later you can take advantage of a soft spot. Then rouse yourself and seek victory with determined spirit.

Chang Yü: If the enemy is strong and I am weak, I temporarily withdraw and do not engage.[8] This is the case when the abilities and courage of the generals and the efficiency of troops are equal.

If I am in good order and the enemy in disarray, if I am energetic and he careless, then, even if he be numerically stronger, I can give battle.

17. And if in all respects unequal, be capable of eluding him, for a small force is but booty for one more powerful.[9]

---

[8] Tu Mu and Chang Yü both counsel 'temporary' withdrawal, thus emphasizing the point that offensive action is to be resumed when circumstances are propitious.

[9] Lit.'the strength of a small force is . . .'. This apparently refers to its weapons and equipment.

Chang Yü: . . . Mencius said: 'The small certainly cannot equal the large, nor can the weak match the strong, nor the few the many.'[10]

18. Now the general is the protector of the state. If this protection is all-embracing, the state will surely be strong; if defective, the state will certainly be weak.

> *Chang Yü* . . . The Grand Duke said: 'A sovereign who obtains the right person prospers. One who fails to do so will be ruined.'

19. Now there are three ways in which a ruler can bring misfortune upon his army:[11]

20. When ignorant that the army should not advance, to order an advance or ignorant that it should not retire, to order a retirement. This is described as 'hobbling the army'.

> *Chia Lin*: The advance and retirement of the army can be controlled by the general in accordance with prevailing circumstances. No evil is greater than commands of the sovereign from the court.

21. When ignorant of military affairs, to participate in their administration. This causes the officers to be perplexed.

> *Ts'ao Ts'ao*: . . . An army cannot be run according to rules of etiquette.

> *Tu Mu*: As far as propriety, laws, and decrees are concerned, the army has its own code, which it ordinarily

---

10   CC II (Mencius), i, ch. 7.
11   Here I have transposed the characters meaning 'ruler' and 'army', otherwise the verse would read that there are three ways in which an army can bring misfortune upon the sovereign.

follows. If these are made identical with those used in governing a state the officers will be bewildered.

Chang Yü: Benevolence and righteousness may be used to govern a state but cannot be used to administer an army. Expediency and flexibility are used in administering an army, but cannot be used in governing a state.

22. When ignorant of command problems to share in the exercise of responsibilities. This engenders doubts in the minds of the officers.[12]

Wang Hsi: . . . If one ignorant of military matters is sent to participate in the administration of the army, then in every movement there will be disagreement and mutual frustration and the entire army will be hamstrung. That is why Pei Tu memorialized the throne to withdraw the Army Supervisor; only then was he able to pacify Ts'ao Chou.[13]

Chang Yü: In recent times court officials have been used as Supervisors of the Army and this is precisely what is wrong.

23. If the army is confused and suspicious, neighbouring rulers will cause trouble. This is what is meant by the saying: 'A confused army leads to another's victory.'[14]

---

12   Lit. 'Not knowing [or 'not understanding' or 'ignorant of'] [where] authority [lies] in the army'; or 'ignorant of [matters relating to exercise of] military authority . . .' The operative character is 'authority' or 'power'.

13   The 'Army Supervisors' of the T'ang were in fact political commissars. Pei Tu became Prime Minister in A.D. 815 and in 817 requested the throne to recall the supervisor assigned him, who must have been interfering in army operations.

14   'Feudal Lords' is rendered 'neighbouring rulers'. The commentators agree that a confused army robs itself of victory.

Meng: . . . The Grand Duke said: 'One who is confused in purpose cannot respond to his enemy.'

Li Ch'üan: . . . The wrong person cannot be appointed to command . . . Lin Hsiang—ju, the Prime Minister of Chao, said: 'Chao Kua is merely able to read his father's books, and is as yet ignorant of correlating changing circumstances. Now Your Majesty, on account of his name, makes him the commander-in-chief. This is like glueing the pegs of a lute and then trying to tune it.'

24. Now there are five circumstances in which victory may be predicted:

25. He who knows when he can fight and when he cannot will be victorious.

26. He who understands how to use both large and small forces will be victorious.

> *Tu Yu*: There are circumstances in war when many cannot attack few, and others when the weak can master the strong. One able to manipulate such circumstances will be victorious.

27. He whose ranks are united in purpose will be victorious.

> *Tu Yu*: Therefore Mencius said: 'The appropriate season is not as important as the advantages of the ground; these are not as important as harmonious human relations.'[15]

---

[15]   CC II (Mencius), ii, ch. I p. 85.

28. He who is prudent and lies in wait for an enemy who is not, will be victorious.

> *Ch'en Hao:* Create an invincible army and await the enemy's moment of vulnerability.

> *Ho Yen-hsi:* . . . A gentleman said: 'To rely on rustics and not prepare is the greatest of crimes; to be prepared before-hand for any contingency is the greatest of virtues.'

29. He whose generals are able and not interfered with by the sovereign will be victorious.

> *Tu Yu:* . . . Therefore Master Wang said: 'To make appointments is the province of the sovereign; to decide on battle, that of the general.'

> *Wang Hsi:* . . . A sovereign of high character and intelligence must he able to know the right man, should place the responsibility on him, and expect results.

> *Ho Yen-hsi:* . . . Now in war there may be one hundred changes in each step. When one sees he can, he advances; when he sees that things are difficult, he retires. To say that a general must await commands of the sovereign in such circumstances is like informing a superior that you wish to put out a fire. Before the order to do so arrives the ashes are cold. And it is said one must consult the Army Supervisor in these matters! This is as if in building a house beside the road one took advice from those who pass by. Of course the work would never be completed![16]

---

[16] A paraphrase of an ode which Legge renders:
They are like one taking counsel with wayfarers about building a house
Which consequently will never come to completion.
(CC IV, ii, p. 332, Ode I.)

To put a rein on an able general while at the same time asking him to suppress a cunning enemy is like tying up the Black Hound of Han and then ordering him to catch elusive hares. What is the difference?

30. It is in these five matters that the way to victory is known.

31. Therefore I say: 'Know the enemy and know yourself; in a hundred battles you will never be in peril.

32. When you are ignorant of the enemy but know yourself, your chances of winning or losing are equal.

33. If ignorant both of your enemy and of yourself, you are certain in every battle to be in peril.'

> *Li Ch'üan*: Such people are called 'mad bandits'. What can they expect if not defeat?

IV
DISPOSITIONS[17]

SUN TZU said:

1. Anciently the skilful warriors first made themselves invincible and awaited the enemy's moment of vulnerability.

2. Invincibility depends on one's self; the enemy's vulnerability on him.

---

[17] The character *hsing* means 'shape', 'form', or 'appearance' or in a more restricted sense, 'disposition' or 'formation'. The Martial Classics edition apparently followed Ts'ao Ts'ao and titled the chapter *Chun Hsing*, 'Shape [or 'Dispositions'] of the Army'. As will appear, the character connotes more than mere physical dispositions.

3. It follows that those skilled in war can make themselves invincible but cannot cause an enemy to be certainly vulnerable.

> *Mei Yao-ch'en:* That which depends on me, I can do; that which depends on the enemy cannot be certain.

4. Therefore it is said that one may know how to win, but cannot necessarily do so.

5. Invincibility lies in the defence; the possibility of victory in the attack.[18]

6. One defends when his strength is inadequate; he attacks when it is abundant.

7. The experts in defence conceal themselves as under the ninefold earth; those skilled in attack move as from above the ninefold heavens. Thus they are capable both of protecting themselves and of gaining a complete victory.[19]

> *Tu Yu:* Those expert at preparing defences consider it fundamental to rely on the strength of such obstacles as mountains, rivers and foothills. They make it impossible for the enemy to know where to attack. They secretly conceal themselves as under the nine-layered ground.

Those expert in attack consider it fundamental to rely on the seasons and the advantages of the ground; they use inundations and fire according to the situation. They make

---

18 'Invincibility is [means] defence; the ability to conquer is [means] attack.'

19 The concept that Heaven and Earth each consist of 'hunts' or 'stages' is an ancient one.

it impossible for an enemy to know where to prepare. They release the attack like a lightning bolt from above the nine-layered heavens.

8. To foresee a victory which the ordinary man can foresee is not the acme of skill;

> *Li Ch'üan*: . . . When Han Hsin destroyed Chao State he marched out of the Well Gorge before breakfast. He said: 'We will destroy the Chao army and then meet for a meal.' The generals were despondent and pretended to agree. Han Hsin drew up his army with the river to its rear. The Chao troops climbed upon their breastworks and, observing this, roared with laughter and taunted him: 'The General of Han does not know how to use troops!' Han Hsin then proceeded to defeat the Chao army and after breakfasting beheaded Lord Ch'eng An.

This is an example of what the multitude does not comprehend.[20]

9. To triumph in battle and be universally acclaimed 'Expert' is not the acme of skill, for to lift an autumn down requires no great strength; to distinguish between the sun and moon is no test of vision; to hear the thunderclap is no indication of acute hearing.[21]

> *Chang Yü*: By 'autumn down' Sun Tzu means rabbits' down, which on the coming of autumn is extremely light.

---

[20] Han Hsin placed his army in 'death ground'. He burned his boats and smashed his cooking pots. The river was at the rear, the Chao army to the front. Han Hsin had to conquer or drown.

[21] To win a hard-fought battle or to win one by luck is no mark of skill.

10. Anciently those called skilled in war conquered an enemy easily conquered.[22]

11. And therefore the victories won by a master of war gain him neither reputation for wisdom nor merit for valour.

> *Tu Mu:* A victory gained before the situation has crystallized is one the common man does not comprehend. Thus its author gains no reputation for sagacity. Before he has bloodied his blade the enemy state has already submitted.

> *Ho Yen-hsi:* . . . When you subdue your enemy without fighting who will pronounce you valorous?

12. For he wins his victories without erring. 'Without erring' means that whatever he does insures his victory; he conquers an enemy already defeated.

> *Chen Hao:* In planning, never a useless move; in strategy, no step taken in vain.

13. Therefore the skilful commander takes up a position in which he cannot be defeated and misses no opportunity to master his enemy.

14. Thus a victorious army wins its victories before seeking battle; an army destined to defeat fights in the hope of winning.

> *Tu Mu:* . . . Duke Li Ching of Wei said: 'Now, the supreme requirements of generalship are a clear perception, the harmony of his host, a profound strategy coupled

---

[22] The enemy was conquered easily because the experts previously had created appropriate conditions.

with far-reaching plans, an understanding of the seasons and an ability to examine the human factors. For a general unable to estimate his capabilities or comprehend the arts of expediency and flexibility when faced with the opportunity to engage the enemy will advance in a stumbling and hesitant manner, looking anxiously first to his right and then to his left, and be unable to produce a plan. Credulous, he will place confidence in unreliable reports, believing at one moment this and at another that. As timorous as a fox in advancing or retiring, his groups will be scattered about. What is the difference between this and driving innocent people into boiling water or fire? Is this not exactly like driving cows and sheep to feed wolves or tigers?'

15. Those skilled in war cultivate the Tao and preserve the laws and are therefore able to formulate victorious policies.

> *Tu Mu:* The *Tao* is the way of humanity and justice; 'laws' are regulations and institutions. Those who excel in war first cultivate their own humanity and justice and maintain their laws and institutions. By these means they make their governments invincible.

16. Now the elements of the art of war are first, measurement of space; second, estimation of quantities; third, calculations; fourth, comparisons; and fifth, chances of victory.

17. Measurements of space are derived from the ground.

18. Quantities derive from measurement, figures from quantities, comparisons from figures, and victory from comparisons.

Ho Yen-hsi:[23] 'Ground' includes both distances and type of terrain; 'measurement' is calculation. Before the army is dispatched, calculations are made respecting the degree of difficulty of the enemy's land; the directness and deviousness of its roads; the number of his troops; the quantity of his war equipment and the state of his morale. Calculations are made to see if the enemy can be attacked and only after this is the population mobilized and troops raised.

19. Thus a victorious army is as a hundredweight balanced against a grain; a defeated army as a grain balanced against a hundredweight.

20. It is because of disposition that a victorious general is able to make his people fight with the effect of pent-up waters which, suddenly released, plunge into a bottomless abyss.

Chang Yü: The nature of water is that it avoids heights and hastens to the lowlands. When a dam is broken, the water cascades with irresistible force. Now the shape of an army resembles water. Take advantage of the enemy's unpreparedness; attack him when he does not expect it; avoid his strength and strike his emptiness, and like water, none can oppose you.

---

23   This comment appears in the text after V. 18. The factors emunerated are qualities of 'shape'.

LEO TOLSTOY

1828-1910

War and Peace

1865-1869

Leo Tolstoy, a novelist and philosopher, was born into the nineteenth century Russian aristocracy. He wrote the epic novel, *War and Peace,* between 1865 and 1869. Almost one hundred years after his death, in January, 2007, Tolstoy's *Anna Karenina* (1878) and *War and Peace* were placed on *Time* magazine's list of the ten greatest novels of all time, first and third place respectively (Grossman, 2007).

"Man in connection with the general life of humanity appears subject to laws which determine that life. But the same man apart from that connection appears to be free. How should the past life of nations and of humanity be regarded—as the result of the free, or as the result of the constrained, activity of man? That is a question for history." (Epilogue 2, Chapter VIII). The piece below, excerpted from Tolstoy's great novel, explores the very real limitations imposed upon the leader by powerful historical forces.

Source:

Grossman, L. (2007, January). The ten greatest books of all time. *Time* entertainment. Retrieved from http://www.time.com/time/arts/article/0,8599,1578073,00.html.

Selection from:

Tolstoy, L. *War and peace.* http://www.online-literature.com/. Retrieved with permission 1/15/08. (Original work published 1869.)

Book Nine

Chapter 1
The Year 1812. Rulers and generals are "history's slaves"

From the close of the year 1811 intensified arming and concentrating of the forces of Western Europe began, and in 1812 these forces—millions of men, reckoning those transporting and feeding the army—moved from the west eastwards to the Russian frontier, toward which since 1811 Russian forces had been similarly drawn. On the twelfth of June, 1812, the forces of Western Europe crossed the Russian frontier and war began, that is, an event took place opposed to human reason and to human nature. Millions of men perpetrated against one another such innumerable crimes, frauds, treacheries, thefts, forgeries, issues of false money, burglaries, incendiarisms, and murders as in whole centuries are not recorded in the annals of all the law courts of the world, but which those who committed them did not at the time regard as being crimes.

What produced this extraordinary occurrence? What were its causes? The historians tell us with naive assurance that its causes were the wrongs inflicted on the Duke of Oldenburg, the nonobservance of the Continental System, the ambition of Napoleon, the firmness of Alexander, the mistakes of the diplomatists, and so on.

Consequently, it would only have been necessary for Metternich, Rumyantsev, or Talleyrand, between a levee and an evening party, to have taken proper pains and written a more adroit note, or for Napoleon to have written to Alexander: "My respected Brother, I consent to restore the duchy to the Duke of Oldenburg"—and there would have been no war.

We can understand that the matter seemed like that to contemporaries. It naturally seemed to Napoleon that the war was caused by England's intrigues (as in fact he said on the island of St. Helena). It naturally seemed to members of the English Parliament that the cause of the war was Napoleon's ambition; to the Duke of Oldenburg, that the cause of the war was the violence done to him; to businessmen that the cause of the war was the Continental System which was ruining Europe; to the generals and old soldiers that the chief reason for the war was the necessity of giving them employment; to the legitimists of that day that it was the need of re-establishing *les bons principes*, and to the diplomatists of that time that it all resulted from the fact that the alliance between Russia and Austria in 1809 had not been sufficiently well concealed from Napoleon, and from the awkward wording of Memorandum No. 178. It is natural that these and a countless and infinite quantity of other reasons, the number depending on the endless diversity of points of view, presented themselves to the men of that day; but to us, to posterity who view the thing that happened in all its magnitude and perceive its plain and terrible meaning, these causes seem insufficient. To us it is incomprehensible that millions of Christian men killed and tortured each other either because Napoleon was ambitious or Alexander was firm, or because England's policy was astute or the Duke of Oldenburg wronged. We cannot grasp what connection such circumstances have with the actual fact of slaughter and violence: why because the Duke was wronged, thousands of men from the other side of

Europe killed and ruined the people of Smolensk and Moscow and were killed by them.

To us, their descendants, who are not historians and are not carried away by the process of research and can therefore regard the event with unclouded common sense, an incalculable number of causes present themselves. The deeper we delve in search of these causes the more of them we find; and each separate cause or whole series of causes appears to us equally valid in itself and equally false by its insignificance compared to the magnitude of the events, and by its impotence—apart from the cooperation of all the other coincident causes—to occasion the event. To us, the wish or objection of this or that French corporal to serve a second term appears as much a cause as Napoleon's refusal to withdraw his troops beyond the Vistula and to restore the duchy of Oldenburg; for had he not wished to serve, and had a second, a third, and a thousandth corporal and private also refused, there would have been so many less men in Napoleon's army and the war could not have occurred.

Had Napoleon not taken offense at the demand that he should withdraw beyond the Vistula, and not ordered his troops to advance, there would have been no war; but had all his sergeants objected to serving a second term then also there could have been no war. Nor could there have been a war had there been no English intrigues and no Duke of Oldenburg, and had Alexander not felt insulted, and had there not been an autocratic government in Russia, or a Revolution in France and a subsequent dictatorship and Empire, or all the things that produced the French Revolution, and so on. Without each of these causes nothing could have happened. So all these causes—myriads of causes—coincided to bring it about. And so there was no one cause for that occurrence, but it had to occur because it had to. Millions of men, renouncing their human feelings and reason, had to go from west to east to slay their fellows, just as some centuries previously hordes of men had come from the east to the west, slaying their fellows.

The actions of Napoleon and Alexander, on whose words the event seemed to hang, were as little voluntary as the actions of any soldier who was drawn into the campaign by lot or by conscription. This could not be otherwise, for in order that the will of Napoleon and Alexander (on whom the event seemed to depend) should be carried out, the concurrence of innumerable circumstances was needed without any one of which the event could not have taken place. It was necessary that millions of men in whose hands lay the real power—the soldiers who fired, or transported provisions and guns—should consent to carry out the will of these weak individuals, and should have been induced to do so by an infinite number of diverse and complex causes.

We are forced to fall back on fatalism as an explanation of irrational events (that is to say, events the reasonableness of which we do not understand). The more we try to explain such events in history reasonably, the more unreasonable and incomprehensible do they become to us.

Each man lives for himself, using his freedom to attain his personal aims, and feels with his whole being that he can now do or abstain from doing this or that action; but as soon as he has done it, that action performed at a certain moment in time becomes irrevocable and belongs to history, in which it has not a free but a predestined significance.

There are two sides to the life of every man, his individual life, which is the more free the more abstract its interests, and his elemental hive life in which he inevitably obeys laws laid down for him.

Man lives consciously for himself, but is an unconscious instrument in the attainment of the historic, universal, aims of humanity. A deed done is irrevocable, and its result coinciding in time with the actions of millions of other men assumes an historic significance. The higher a man stands on the social ladder, the more people he is connected with and the more power he has over others, the more evident is the predestination and inevitability of his every action.

"The king's heart is in the hands of the Lord."

A king is history's slave.

History, that is, the unconscious, general, hive life of mankind, uses every moment of the life of kings as a tool for its own purposes.

Though Napoleon at that time, in 1812, was more convinced than ever that it depended on him, "*verser (ou ne pas verser) le sang de ses peuples*"[1]— as Alexander expressed it in the last letter he wrote him—he had never been so much in the grip of inevitable laws, which compelled him, while thinking that he was acting on his own volition, to perform for the hive life—that is to say, for history—whatever had to be performed.

The people of the west moved eastwards to slay their fellow men, and by the law of coincidence thousands of minute causes fitted in and co-ordinated to produce that movement and war: reproaches for the nonobservance of the Continental System, the Duke of Oldenburg's wrongs, the movement of troops into Prussia—undertaken (as it seemed to Napoleon) only for the purpose of securing an armed peace, the French Emperor's love and habit of war coinciding with his people's inclinations, allurement by the grandeur of the preparations, and the expenditure on those preparations and the need of obtaining advantages to compensate for that expenditure, the intoxicating honors he received in Dresden, the diplomatic negotiations which, in the opinion of contemporaries, were carried on with a sincere desire to attain peace, but which only wounded the self-love of both sides, and millions of other causes that adapted themselves to the event that was happening or coincided with it.

When an apple has ripened and falls, why does it fall? Because of its attraction to the earth, because its stalk withers, because it is dried by the sun, because it grows heavier, because

---

[1]   "To shed (or not to shed) the blood of his peoples"

the wind shakes it, or because the boy standing below wants to eat it?

Nothing is the cause. All this is only the coincidence of conditions in which all vital organic and elemental events occur. And the botanist who finds that the apple falls because the cellular tissue decays and so forth is equally right with the child who stands under the tree and says the apple fell because he wanted to eat it and prayed for it. Equally right or wrong is he who says that Napoleon went to Moscow because he wanted to, and perished because Alexander desired his destruction, and he who says that an undermined hill weighing a million tons fell because the last navvy struck it for the last time with his mattock. In historic events the so-called great men are labels giving names to events, and like labels they have but the smallest connection with the event itself.

Every act of theirs, which appears to them an act of their own will, is in an historical sense involuntary and is related to the whole course of history and predestined from eternity.

JAMES MACGREGOR BURNS

1918-

Heroic Leadership

1978

This work is excerpted from Burns' classic book, *Leadership*. Also, please refer to Section I of this volume to learn more about this author. In this piece, Burns steps back to examine the effect of the level of an economy's development on how the leader is perceived by followers. The more a followership needs the leader to be great, the more likely s/he is to be perceived as great and even super-human.

Selection from:

Burns, J. M. (1979.) Heroes and ideologues. In *Leadership*. (pp. 243-248). New York: Harper & Row.

Heroic Leadership

Max Weber concluded that societies passed through a sequence of three "pure" types of authority: the charismatic, the rational-legal, and the traditional. The miraculous, transcending leadership of a religious savior such as Christ or Muhammad was followed by a period in which charisma was routinized and bureaucratized and authority was exercised through legal and "rational" institutions and practices. In time this system evolved into a traditionalist society in which authority was legitimated by usage, precedent, and custom. As this society became more traditionbound and static, the seeds were sown for the birth of a new charismatic leadership and authority. And so the cycle proceeded. Russia seemed to fit Weber's model. The archetypes of traditionalist rule there were the czars, James Davies notes, "who presumed to be exercising power according to long-established custom but for practical purposes recognized no superior earthly authority." Confronted by a delegation of churchmen exhorting him to appoint someone head of the state church, Peter the Great pointed to himself and said, "Here is your patriarch."

The concept of charisma has fertilized the study of leadership. Its very ambiguity has enabled it to be captured by scholars in different disciplines and applied to a variety of situations. The term itself means the endowment of divine grace, but Weber did not make clear whether this gift of grace was a quality possessed by leaders independent of society or a quality dependent on its recognition by followers. The term has taken on a number of different but overlapping meanings: leaders' magical qualities; an emotional bond between leader and led; dependence on a father figure by the masses; popular assumptions that a leader is powerful, omniscient, and virtuous; imputation of enormous supernatural power to leaders (or secular power, or both); and simply popular support for a leader that verges on love. The word has been so overburdened as to collapse under close analysis. It has also become cheapened. Lyndon Johnson would complain that his trouble was that he lacked "charisma" (a word he pronounced with a soft "ch"—to the derision of the intelligentsia).

It is impossible to restore the word to analytic duty; hence I will use the term *heroic leadership* to mean the following: belief in leaders because of their personage alone, aside from their tested capacities, experience, or stand on issues; faith in the leaders' capacity to overcome obstacles and crises: readiness to grant to leaders the powers to handle crises: mass support for such leaders expressed directly—through votes, applause, letters, shaking hands—rather than through intermediaries or institutions. Heroic leadership is not simply a quality or entity possessed by someone: it is a *type of relationship* between leader and led. A crucial aspect of this relationship is the absence of conflict. "Instead of acquiring insight into their deep-lying motives, people seek some release from their conflicts by projecting their fears, aggressions, and aspirations onto some social objects which allow a symbolic solution," Daniel Katz notes. Heroic leadership provides the *symbolic* solution of internal and external conflict.

Heroic leaders—in contrast with leaders who are merely enjoying popular favor—usually arise in societies undergoing profound crisis. Existing mechanisms of conflict resolution have broken down; traditions, established authority, old legitimations, customary ways of doing things—all are under heavy strain. Mass alienation and social atomization are rising. Intense psychological and material needs go unfulfilled. Long-held values are ready to be replaced or transformed. A variety of secondary leaders come to the fore to raise expectations and sharpen demands. In short, a crisis in trust and legitimacy overwhelms the system's rulers, ideology, and institutions. Then there appears a leader or leadership group, equipped with rare gifts of compassion and competence—dynamic, resourceful, responsive—that rebels against authority and tradition.

Of numerous instances of the rise of such leadership, the case of the Mahdi of the Sudan is one of the most striking. The eighteenth and early nineteenth centuries saw the emergence of powerful religious movements with heavy puritanical overtones in the borderlands of the imperial Ottoman domain, in Arabia, Libya, and especially the Sudan. Society was becoming atomized as traditional Islamic belief systems became fragmented. "Foreign" invaders and conquerors further threatened old loyalties by seeking to impose "alien" legal and penal ways on native populations. A host of religious proselytizers exploited and abetted the unrest. It had long been a popular myth that "the guided one" would come to save the Islamic community.

Muhammad Ahmad was born the son of a poor Dongolese boatbuilder. Orphaned in his early years, he was sent to live with an uncle. "As a child he displayed unusual motivation and a prodigious mind that enabled him to recite the entire Qur'an at the age of nine." Denied an education at the prestigious university of Al-Azhar, he remained in the Sudan and lived as an ascetic in an established order. Becoming in time a full-time proselytizer with a reputation for great piety, humility, and asceticism, he turned against the established rulers, accusing them of impious practices such as music and dancing. Expelled from his order, he joined a rival one and soon became its head. He declared himself the Mahdi on the claim that during a vision the Prophet Muhammad had appointed him successor of Allah's apostle.

The message of the new Mahdi was direct and explicit: a return to puritanical Islam, a rejection of sinful pursuits in favor of perpetual asceticism. The government saw this as a political as well as a religious threat and dispatched an army to put down the usurper and his followers. The defeat of this army and a series of victories in succeeding months brought more recruits to the Mahdi's cause. But his main strength seemed to lie in the force of his message, his ability to adapt it to the needs of different classes and groups, his promise of salvation to believers who fell in battle, and his ability to win sophisticated theological debates with the opposition. He won world renown—and opprobrium in Britain—when his forces took Khartoum and slew the British hero General Charles Gordon. The Mahdi himself died not long after the fall of Khartoum. The succession proceeded peacefully for a time, but it was challenged later, and the dramatic episode came to an end when the British under Kitchener reconquered the Sudan.

The extent of actual change brought about by the Mahdi remains a subject of debate. The extent of "value transformation" in itself could not be measured, though it is noteworthy that more than ten thousand of the Mahdi's followers threw themselves against the British machine guns in the last big stand. "At the zenith of his power, the leader died without an opportunity to see through the process of rebuilding (routinization) that had barely started," Richard Dekmejian and Margaret Wyszomirski conclude. "As a result, the task of the comprehensive, spiritual-social reconstruction of Sudanese society that the Mahdi intended never became a reality. In other words, the crucial social integration and spiritual homogenization of the tribal Sudanese was aborted." One can question whether lasting social transformation would have taken place even if the Mahdi had lived, given the theological emphasis of his message and the puritanical, anti-modern cast of his doctrine. The Mahdi was not, in the end, an agent for social change.

Heroic leadership plays a vital role in transitional or developing societies, where even the more idolatrous form of heroic leadership may meet the special needs of both leaders and followers. The idols are usually motivated by powerful needs for affection, esteem, and self-actualization. They want and need an audience, and an audience needs them. Followers flock to see such heroes, crowd in to touch their hands or the hems of their garments. The spectators are moved by their own needs—by their need to overcome their frustrations through projecting their fears, hopes, and aggressions onto heroes who can provide at least symbolic solutions: by their need for identification with the mighty and the awesome; by their need for esteem from performers who bestow recognition and flattery on them—and thus by their need for self-esteem. The heroes personalize movements and symbolize ideas. In some elections in "new nations" illiterate persons who cannot recognize the name of a candidate or a party, and perhaps not even a party device such as a cow, can still decide by choosing from small balls bearing the likenesses of the candidates.

The idolatrous form of heroic leadership can serve, in Robert C. Tucker's words, as "essentially a fulcrum of the transition from colonial-ruled traditional society to politically independent modern society." Lucian W. Pye noted, in his study of Burmese transitional politics, that questions of personal loyalty and identification are central and the bond between idolized leader and follower is generally an affective and emotional one. Symbols of national unity and personal support overshadow policy issues. It is far easier, according to Pye, to communicate emotional and personal support than substantive government programs. But this kind of relationship, Pye points out, is "likely to wear thin"; expectations are built up that are hard for idolized leaders to follow.

"The people believe that just because I am important there is nothing that I can't do," one Burmese politician complained. "If I don't do something for them they say that I am either mean to them or that I am a weak leader and they should find another. Our people have no idea at all how hard it is to do anything."

The question remains whether the hero can do anything more for idol-worshipers than incite and appease emotional or psychological needs. This may be important—for some spectators all-important—for the psychic investment of the "follower" in the "leader" may be very high while the reverse relationship may be slight. The effect on the hero-worshiper's life or happiness may be insubstantial and fleeting, while the performer easily moves on to new audiences. The cardinal question is whether the idolized hero can help develop in "new nations" the political movements or parties that convert personal followings into durable ones, personal affect and symbol into policy and program. The record is mixed. Some of the Roman emperors who claimed—or had imputed to them—godlike powers had little interest in identifying with or responding to the lasting "real needs" of their people. Muhammad was an idolized religious leader but, like Moses, he left a legacy of social and political values—including that of equality (except between the sexes)—that helped shape Islamic thought and behavior. Napoleon encouraged a cult of personality but, like Moses, he bequeathed France a legal code. Atatürk, often envisioned as a "charismatic" leader because of his courage and his narrow escapes, was even more a cautious, calculating leader—"an organization man thrown into a charismatic situation," Dankwart A. Rustow labeled him. Nkrumah—handsome, graceful, warm, responsive, of voice "both deep and melodious"—viewed himself as a cross between Gandhi and Lenin in the tradition of great "thinker-politicians." An article in the Ghana press proclaimed that Nkrumah had "revealed himself like a Moses—yea, a greater Moses . . . With the support of all African leaders he will help to lead his people across the Red Sea of imperialist massacre and suffering." But in the end, David Apter says, "Nkrumah lacked the imagination and skill to develop a country. He was a revolutionary without a plan—a visionary, but not a builder."

The "developed" nations are by no means free of hero-idolatry. A poem in *Pravda* in 1936 sang to Stalin:

> O, thou great leader of the peoples/ Thou who gayest man his life/
> Thou who fructified the lands . . . O, father . . .
> Thou art the sun . . .

And a poem in *Women of China* (Peking) in 1961 praised Mao Tse-tung:

> You are rain for the planting season, Breeze for the hottest noon/
> You are the red sun that never sets . . .   .

In the United States the "jumpers" of 1960 hopped up and down, screaming in frenzy, as John F. Kennedy and his entourage approached during the presidential campaign of that year. One can doubt that these teenagers and subteenagers were whooping it up for Kennedy because of his stand on old-age pensions or on Latin America policy. Over the succeeding decade pictures of John and Jacqueline Kennedy decorated the front covers of literally tens of millions of copies of popular magazines. He was handsome, with a boyish grin, but in 1960 Kennedy had little connection with the basic needs, expectations, and values of the young people. Kennedy's appearance and performance titillated them; that was enough.

Some years before this phenomenon, a California longshoreman-philosopher, Eric Hoffer, was analyzing "true believers" as he had seen and read about them. He dissected the groups that seemed most susceptible to leadership that "articulates and justifies the resentment dammed up in the souls of the frustrated"; the misfits, the inordinately selfish, the bored, the sinners, and the different varieties of the poor. He was more interested in the led—the kind of people he watched and listened to daily—than the leaders. He noted that the "total surrender of a distinct self "is a prerequisite for the attainment of both unity and self-sacrifice; that to the frustrated, "freedom from responsibility is more attractive than freedom from restraint"; that they surrendered to leaders because leaders could take them away from their unwanted selves. People lost themselves in mass movements to escape individual responsibility—to be free of freedom.

The "escape from freedom" is also an escape from conflict; the spectator can love the performer without hating anyone else. (It is easier not to choose up sides.) The halo surrounding Number One bathes the political landscape in a glow of harmony and consent. Purpose, which needs to be sharpened in conflict, is also lacking. While emotional needs in hero and spectator may be deeply involved, no central purpose, no collective intent other than short-run psychic dependency and gratification unites performer and spectator. And if there is no transcending purpose, there is no real change that can be related to or measured by original purpose.

Idolized heroes are not, then, authentic leaders because no true relationship exists between them and the spectators—no relationship characterized by deeply held motives, shared goals, rational conflict, and lasting influence in the form of change.

JOHN JERMIER

1946-

STEVEN KERR

1941-

Substitutes for leadership:
Their meaning and measurement

1978

Steven Kerr currently works at Goldman Sachs as the chief learning officer and a managing director. Previously, he was vice president of corporate leadership development and chief learning officer at GE. Kerr also has teaching and research experience in the business schools of the Ohio State University, the University of Michigan, and the University of Southern California. He is a former president of the Academy of Management.

John M. Jermier teaches organizational behavior at the University of South Florida (USF) in Tampa and holds an affiliate professor appointment on USF's faculty of Environmental Science and Policy. Jermier is a former chair of the Organizations and the Natural Environment Division of the Academy of Management. As well as co-editing

Organization & Environment, Jermier serves on the editorial review boards of *Human Relations, Organization, Organization Science, Leadership Quarterly, Leadership,* and the *Journal of Workplace Rights.*

In the following reading, "substitutes for leadership" is proposed as a set of contingency variables that work to neutralize the need for leadership. Under what conditions might leadership be deemed unnecessary?

Sources:

Performance and Reward Centre. (2009). *PARC Programme 2008.* Retrieved from http://www.parcentre.com/uploads/media/PARC_Programme_2008__final_.pdf

Sage Publications. (2009). *John Jermier.* Retrieved from www.sagepub.com/editor Details.nav?contribId=514039.

Selection from:

Jermier, J. & Kerr, S. (1978). Substitutes for leadership: Their meaning and measurement. *Organizational Behavior and Human Performance. 22*(3), 377-380.

SUBSTITUTES FOR LEADERSHIP

A wide variety of individual, task, and organizational characteristics have been found to influence relationships between leader behavior and subordinate satisfaction, morale, and performance. Some of these variables (for example, job pressure and subordinate expectations of leader behavior) act primarily to influence which leadership style will best permit the hierarchical superior to motivate, direct, and control subordinates. The effect of others, however, is to act as "substitutes for leadership," tending to negate the leader's ability to either improve or impair subordinate satisfaction and performance.

Substitutes for leadership are apparently prominent in many different organizational settings, but their existence is not explicated in any of the dominant leadership theories. As a result, data describing formal superior-subordinate relationships are often obtained in situations where important substitutes exist. These data logically ought to be, and usually are, insignificant, and are useful primarily as a reminder that when leadership styles are studied in circumstances where the choice of style is irrelevant, the effect is to replace the potential power of the leadership construct with the unintentional comedy of the "Law of the instrument."[1]

What is needed, then, is a taxonomy of situations where we should not be studying "leadership" (in the formal hierarchical sense) at all. Development of such a taxonomy is still at an early stage, but Woodward (1973) and Miner (1975) have laid important groundwork through their classifications of control, and some effects of nonleader sources of clarity have been considered by Hunt (Note 2) and Hunt and Osborn (1975). Reviews of the leadership literature by House and Mitchell (1974) and Kerr *et al.* (1974) have also proved pertinent in this regard, and suggest that individual, task, and organizational characteristics of the kind outlined in Table 1 will help to determine whether or not hierarchical leadership is likely to matter.

Conceptual domain of substitutes for leadership. Since Table 1 is derived from previously-conducted studies, substitutes are only suggested for the two leader behavior styles which dominate the research literature. The substitutes construct probably has much wider applicability, however, perhaps to hierarchical leadership in general.

It is probably useful to clarify some of the characteristics listed in Table 1. "Professional orientation" is considered a potential substitute for leadership because employees with

---

[1] Abraham Kaplan (1964, p. 28) has observed: "Give a small boy a hammer, and he will find that everything he encounters needs pounding."

such an orientation typically cultivate horizontal rather than vertical relationships, give greater credence to peer review processes, however informal, than to hierarchical evaluations, and tend to develop important referents external to the employing organization (Filley, House, & Kerr, 1976). Clearly, such attitudes and behaviors can sharply reduce the influence of the hierarchical superior.

"Methodologically invariant" tasks may result from serial interdependence, from machine-paced operations, or from work methods which are highly standardized. In one study (House, Filley, & Kerr, 1971. p. 26), invariance was found to derive from a network of government contracts which "specified not only the performance requirements of the end product, but also many of the management practices and control techniques that the company must follow in carrying out the contract."

Invariant methodology relates to what Miner (1975) describes as the "push" of work. Tasks which are "intrinsically satisfying" (another potential substitute listed in Table 1) contribute in turn to the "pull" of work. Miner believes that for "task control" to be effective, a force comprised of both the push and pull of work must be developed. At least in theory, however, either type alone may act as a substitute for hierarchical leadership.

TABLE 1
SUBSTITUTES FOR LEADERSHIP

Characteristic	Will tend to neutralize	
	Relationship-Oriented, Supportive, People-Centered Leadership: Consideration, Support, and Interaction Facilitation	Task-Oriented, Instrumental, Job-Centered Leadership: Initiating Structure, Goal Emphasis, and Work Facilitation
of the subordinate		
ability, experience, training, knowledge		X
need for independence	X	X
"professional" orientation	X	X
indifference toward organizational rewards	X	X
of the task		
unambiguous and routine		X
methodologically invariant		X
provides its own feedback con- cerning accomplishment		X
intrinsically satisfying	X	
of the organization		
formalization (explicit plans, goals, and areas of responsibility)		X

inflexibility (rigid, unbending rules and procedures)		X
highly-specified and active advisory and staff functions		X
closely-knit, cohesive work groups	X	X
organizational rewards not within the leader's control	X	X
spatial distance between superior and subordinates	X	X

Performance feedback provided by the work itself is another characteristic of the task which potentially functions in place of the formal leader. It has been reported that employees with high growth need strength in particular derive beneficial psychological states (internal motivation, general satisfaction, work effectiveness) from clear and direct knowledge of the results of performance (Hackman & Oldham, 1976; Oldham, 1976). Task-provided feedback is often: (1) the most immediate source of feedback given the infrequency of performance appraisal sessions (Hall & Lawler, 1969); (2) the most accurate source of feedback given the problems of measuring the performance of others (Campbell, Dunnette, Lawler, & Weick, 1970); and (3) the most self-evaluation evoking and intrinsically motivating source of feedback given the controlling and informational aspects of feedback from others (DeCharms, 1968; Deci, 1972, 1975; Greller & Herold, 1975). For these reasons, the formal leader's function as a provider of role structure through performance feedback may be insignificant by comparison.

Cohesive, interdependent work groups and active advisory and staff personnel also have the ability to render the formal leader's performance feedback function inconsequential. Inherent in mature group structures are stable performance norms and positional differentiation (Bales & Strodtbeck, 1951; Borgatta & Bales, 1953; Stogdill, 1959; Lott & Lott, 1965; Zander, 1968). Task-relevant guidance and feedback from others may he provided directly by the formal leader, indirectly by the formal leader through the primary work group members, directly by the primary work group members, by staff personnel, or by the client. If the latter four instances prevail, the formal leader's role may be quite trivial. Cohesive work groups are, of course, important sources of affiliative need satisfaction.

Programming through impersonal modes has been reported to be the most frequent type of coordination strategy employed under conditions of low-to-medium task uncertainty and low task interdependence (Van de Ven, Delbecq, & Koenig, 1976). Thus, the existence of written work goals, guidelines, and groundrules (organizational formalization) and rigid rules and procedures (organizational inflexibility) may serve as substitutes for leader-provided coordination under certain conditions. Personal and group coordination modes involving the formal leader may become important only when less costly impersonal strategies are not suitable.

GEERT HOFSTEDE

1928-

Motivation, Leadership, and Organization: Do American Theories Apply Abroad?

1980

Born at Haarlem, the Netherlands, Geert Hofstede is an influential Dutch writer and Professor Emeritus of Organizational Anthropology and International Management at the University of Maastricht in the Netherlands.

Towards the end of the 1960s and into the 1970s, Hofstede started attitude survey research in IBM offices all over the world. In 1980 he published *Culture's Consequences,* describing fundamental differences among people of various nationalities. Do we assume that deep down all people are the same? His work provides cultural insights so that interactions between people from other countries can be more effective.

Hofstede's premise pertinent to the work included in this volume is that we are all influenced by our environments more than we realize. In his research, Hofstede studied national culture differences across subsidiaries of a multi-national corporation (IBM) in sixty-four countries. Thus, he was able to derive generalizations about national differences from data gathered from individual employees. Then he generated a set of four independent dimensions of national culture difference: power distance, individualism, masculinity, and uncertainty avoidance; these concepts are developed more fully in the following excerpt.

Selection from:

Hofstede, G. (1980). Motivation, leadership, and organization: Do American theories apply abroad? *Organizational Dynamics, 9*(1), 42-63.

————

Many of the differences in employee motivation, management styles, and organizational structures of companies throughout the world can be traced to differences in the collective mental programming of people in different national cultures.

A well-known experiment used in organizational behavior courses involves showing the class an ambiguous picture—one that can be interpreted in two different ways. One such picture represents either an attractive young girl or an ugly old woman, depending on the way you look at it. Some of my colleagues and I use the experiment, which demonstrates how different people in the same situation may perceive quite different things. We start by asking half of the class to close their eyes while we show the other half a slightly altered version of the picture—one in which only the young girl can be seen—for only five seconds. Then we ask those who just saw the young girl's picture to close their eyes while we give the other half of the class a five-second look at a version in which only the old woman can be seen. After this preparation we show the ambiguous picture to everyone at the same time.

The results are amazing—most of those "conditioned" by seeing the young girl first see only the young girl in the ambiguous picture, and those "conditioned" by seeing the old woman tend to see only the old woman. We then ask one of those who perceive the old woman to explain to one of those who perceive the young girl what he or she sees, and vice versa, until everyone finally sees both images in the picture. Each group usually finds it very difficult to get its views across to the other one and sometimes there's considerable irritation at how "stupid" the other group is.

CULTURAL CONDITIONING

I use this experiment to introduce a discussion on cultural conditioning. Basically, it shows that in five seconds I can condition half a class to see something different from what the other half sees. If this is so in the simple classroom situation, how much stronger should differences in perception of the same reality be between people who have been conditioned by different education and life experience—not for five seconds, but for twenty, thirty, or forty years?

I define culture as the collective mental programming of the people in an environment. Culture is not a characteristic of individuals; it encompasses a number of people who were conditioned by the same education and life experience. When we speak of the culture of a group, a tribe, a geographical region, a national minority, or a nation, culture refers to the collective mental programming that these people have in common; the programming that is different from that of other groups, tribes, regions, minorities or majorities, or nations.

Culture, in this sense of collective mental programming, is often difficult to change; if it changes at all, it does so slowly. This is so not only because it exists in the minds of the people but, if it is shared by a number of people, because it has become crystallized in the institutions these people have built together: their family structures, educational structures, religious organizations, associations, forms of government, work organizations, law, literature, settlement patterns, buildings and even, as I hope to show, scientific theories. All of these reflect common beliefs that derive from the common culture.

Although we are all conditioned by cultural influences at many different levels—family, social, group, geographical region, professional environment—this article deals specifically with the influence of our national environment: that is, our country. Most countries' inhabitants share a national character that's more clearly apparent to foreigners than to the nationals themselves; it represents the cultural mental programming that the nationals tend to have in common.

NATIONAL CULTURE IN FOUR DIMENSIONS

The concept of national culture or national character has suffered from vagueness. There has been little consensus on what represents the national culture of, for example, Americans, Mexicans, French, or Japanese. We seem to lack even the terminology to describe it. Over a period of six years, I have been involved in a large research project on national cultures. For a set of 40 independent nations, I have tried to determine empirically the main criteria by which their national cultures differed. I found four such criteria, which I label dimensions; these are Power Distance, Uncertainty Avoidance, Individualism-Collectivism, and Masculinity-Femininity. To understand the dimensions of national culture, we can compare it with the dimensions of personality we use when we describe individuals' behavior. In recruiting, an organization often tries to get an impression of a candidate's dimensions of personality, such as intelligence (high-low); energy level (active-passive); and emotional stability (stable-unstable). These distinctions can be refined through the use of certain tests, but it's essential to have a set of criteria whereby the characteristics of individuals can be meaningfully described. The dimensions of national culture I use represent a corresponding set of criteria for describing national cultures.

Characterizing a national culture does not, of course, mean that every person in the nation has all the characteristics assigned to that culture. Therefore, in describing national cultures we refer to the common elements within each nation—the national norm—but we are not describing individuals. This should be kept in mind when interpreting the four dimensions explained in the following paragraphs.

Power distance

The first dimension of national culture is called *Power Distance*. It indicates the extent to which a society accepts the fact that power in institutions and organizations is distributed unequally. It's reflected in the values of the less powerful employees of society as well as in those of the more powerful ones. A fuller picture of the difference between small Power Distance and large Power Distance societies is shown in Figure 1. Of course, this shows only the extremes; most countries fall somewhere in between.

Uncertainty avoidance

The second dimension, *Uncertainty Avoidance*, indicates the extent to which a society feels threatened by uncertain and ambiguous situations and tries to avoid these situations by providing greater career stability, establishing more formal rules, not tolerating deviant ideas and behaviors, and believing in absolute truths and the attainment of expertise. Nevertheless, societies in which uncertainty avoidance is strong are also characterized by a higher level of anxiety and aggressiveness that creates, among other things, a strong inner urge in people to work hard. (See Figure 2).

Individualism-Collectivism

The third dimension encompasses *Individualism* and its opposite, *Collectivism*. Individualism implies a loosely knit social framework in which people are supposed to take care of themselves and of their immediate families only, while collectivism is characterized by a tight social framework in which people distinguish between in-groups and out-groups; they expect their in-group (relatives, clan, organizations) to look after them, and in exchange for that they feel they owe absolute loyalty to it. A fuller picture of this dimension is presented in Figure 3.

Masculinity

The fourth dimension is called *Masculinity* even though, in concept, it encompasses its opposite pole, *Femininity*. Measurements in terms of this dimension express the extent to which the dominant values in society are "masculine"—that is, assertiveness, the acquisition of money and things, and not caring for others, the quality of life, or people. These values were labeled "masculine" because, *within* nearly all societies, men scored higher in terms of the values' positive sense than of their negative sense (in terms of assertiveness, for example, rather than its lack)—even though the society as a whole might veer toward the "feminine" pole. Interestingly, the more an entire society scores to the masculine side, the wider the gap between its "men's" and "women's" values (see Figure 4).

THE RESEARCH DATA

The four dimensions of national culture were found through a combination of theoretical reasoning and massive statistical analysis, in what is most likely the largest survey material ever obtained with a single questionnaire. This survey material was collected between 1967 and 1973 among employees of subsidiaries of one large U.S.-based multinational corporation (MNC) in 40 countries around the globe. The total data bank contains more than 116,000 questionnaires collected from virtually everyone in the corporation, from unskilled workers to research Ph.D.s and top managers. Moreover, data were collected twice—first during a period from 1967 to 1969 and a repeat survey during 1971 to 1973. Out of a total of about 150 different survey questions (of the precoded answer type), about 60 deal with the respondents' beliefs and values; these were analyzed for the present study. The questionnaire was administered in the language of each country; a total of 20 language versions had to be made. On the basis of these data, each of the 40 countries could be given an index score for each of the four dimensions.

I was wondering at first whether differences found among employees of one single corporation could be used to detect truly national culture differences. I also wondered what effect the translation of the questionnaire could have had. With this in mind, I administered a number of the same questions in 1971-1973 to an international group of about 400 managers from different public and private organizations following management development courses in Lausanne, Switzerland. This time, all received the questionnaire in English. In spite of the different mix of respondents and the different language used, I found largely the same differences between countries in the manager group that I found among the multinational personnel. Then I started looking for other studies, comparing aspects of national character across a number of countries on the basis of surveys using other questions and other respondents (such as students) or on representative public opinion polls. I found 13 such studies; these compared between 5 and 19 countries at a time. The results of these studies showed a statistically significant similarity (correlation) with one or more of the four dimensions. Finally, I also looked for national indicators (such as per capita national income, inequality of income distribution, and government spending on development aid) that could logically be supposed to be related to one or more of the dimensions. I found 31 such indicators—of which the values were available for between 5 and 40 countries—that were correlated in a statistically significant way with at least one of the dimensions. All these additional studies (for which the data were collected by other people, not by me) helped make the picture of the four dimensions more complete. Interestingly, very few of these studies had even been related to each other before, but the four dimensions provide a framework that shows how they can be fit together like pieces of a huge puzzle. The fact that data obtained within a single MNC have the power to uncover the secrets of entire national cultures can be understood when it's known that the respondents form well-matched samples from their nations: They are employed by the same firm (or its subsidiary); their jobs are similar (I consistently compared the same occupations across the different countries); and their age categories and sex composition were similar—only their nationalities differed. Therefore, if we look at the differences in survey answers between multinational employees in countries A, B, C, and so on, the general factor that can account for the differences in the answers is national culture.

Figure 1
THE POWER DISTANCE DIMENSION

Small Power Distance	Large Power Distance
Inequality in society should be minimized	There should be an order of inequality in this world in which everybody has a rightful place; high and low are protected by this order.
All people should be interdependent.	A few people should be independent; most should be dependent.
Hierarchy means an inequality of roles, established for convenience.	Hierarchy means existential inequality.
Superiors consider subordinates to be "people like me."	Superiors consider subordinates to be a different kind of people.
Subordinates consider superiors to be "people like me."	Subordinates consider superiors as a different kind of people.
Superiors are accessible.	Superiors are inaccessible.
The use of power should be legitimate and is subject to the judgment as to whether it is good or evil.	Power is a basic fact of society that antedates good or evil. Its legitimacy is irrelevant.
All should have equal rights.	Power-holders are entitled to privileges.
Those in power should try to look less powerful than they are.	Those in power should try to look as powerful as possible.
The system is to blame.	The underdog is to blame.
The way to change a social system is to redistribute power.	The way to change a social system is to dethrone those in power.
People at various power levels feel less threatened and more prepared to trust people.	Other people are a potential threat to one's power and can rarely be trusted.
Latent harmony exists between the powerful and the powerless.	Latent conflict exists between the powerful and the powerless.
Cooperation among the powerless can be based on solidarity.	Cooperation among the powerless is difficult to attain because of their low-faith-in-people norm.

Figure 2

THE UNCERTAINY AVOIDANCE DIMENSION

Weak Uncertainty Avoidance	Strong Uncertainty Avoidance
The uncertainty inherent in life is more easily accepted and each day is taken as it comes.	The uncertainty inherent in life is felt as a continuous threat that must be fought.
Ease and lower stress are experienced.	Higher anxiety and stress are experienced.
Time is free.	Time is money.
Hard work, as such, is not a virtue.	There is an inner urge to work hard.
Aggressive behavior is frowned upon.	Aggressive behavior of self and others is accepted.
Less showing of emotions is preferred.	More showing of emotions is preferred.
Conflict and competition can be contained on the level of fair play and used constructively.	Conflict and competition can unleash aggression and should therefore be avoided.
More acceptance of dissent is entailed.	A strong need for consensus is involved.
Deviation is not considered threatening; greater tolerance is shown.	Deviant persons and ideas are dangerous; intolerance holds sway.
The ambiance is one of less nationalism.	Nationalism is pervasive.
More positive feelings toward younger people are seen.	Younger people are suspect.
There is more willingness to take risks in life.	There is great concern with security in life.
The accent is on relativism, empiricism.	The search is for ultimate, absolute truths and values.
There should be as few rules as possible.	There is a need for written rules and regulations.
If rules cannot he kept, we should change them.	If rules cannot be kept, we are sinners and should repent.
Belief is placed in generalists and common sense.	Belief is placed in experts and their knowledge.
The authorities are there to serve the citizens.	Ordinary citizens are incompetent compared with the authorities.

Figure 3
THE INDIVIDUALISM DIMENS

Collectivist	Individualist
In society, people are born into extended families or clans who protect them in exchange for loyalty.	In society, e' supposed to himself/herself and ... immediate family.
"We" consciousness holds sway.	"I" consciousness holds sway.
Identity is based in the social system.	Identity is based in the individual.
There is emotional dependence of individual on organizations and institutions.	There is emotional independence of individual from organizations or institutions.
The involvement with organizations is moral.	The involvement with organizations is calculative.
The emphasis is on belonging to organizations; membership is the ideal.	The emphasis is on individual initiative and achievement; leadership is the ideal.
Private life is invaded by organizations and clans to which one belongs; opinions are predetermined.	Everybody has a right to a private life and opinion.
Expertise, order, duty, and security are provided by organization or clan.	Autonomy, variety, pleasure, and individual financial security are sought in the system.
Friendships are predetermined by stable social relationships, but there is need for prestige within these relationships.	The need is for specific friendships.
Belief is placed in group decisions.	Belief is placed in individual decisions.
Value standards differ for in-groups and out-groups (particularism).	Value standards should apply to all (universalism).

Figure 4
THE MASCULINITY DIMENSION

Feminine	Masculine
Men needn't be assertive, but can also assume nurturing roles.	Men should be assertive. Women should be nurturing.
Sex roles in society are more fluid.	Sex roles in society are clearly differentiated.
There should be equality between the sexes.	Men should dominate in society.
Quality of life is important.	Performance is what counts.
You work in order to live.	You live in order to work.
People and environment are important.	Money and things are important.
Interdependence is the ideal.	Independence is the ideal.
Service provides the motivation.	Ambition provides the drive.
One sympathizes with the unfortunate.	One admires the successful achiever.
Small and slow are beautiful.	Big and fast are beautiful.
Unisex and androgyny are ideal.	Ostentatious manliness ("machismo") is appreciated.

A SET OF CULTURAL MAPS OF THE WORLD

Research data were obtained by comparing the beliefs and values of employees within the subsidiaries of one large multinational corporation in 40 countries around the world. These countries represent the wealthy countries of the West and the larger, more prosperous of the Third World countries. The Socialist block countries are missing, but data are available for Yugoslavia (where the corporation is represented by a local, self-managed company under Yugoslavian law). It was possible, on the basis of mean answers of employees on a number of key questions, to assign an index value to each country on each dimension. As described in the box above, these index values appear to be related in a statistically significant way to a vast amount of other data about these countries, including both research results from other samples and national indicator figures.

Because of the difficulty of representing four dimensions in a single diagram, the position of the countries of the dimensions is shown in Figures 5, 6, and 7 for two dimensions at a time. The vertical and horizontal axes and the circles around clusters of countries have been drawn subjectively, in order to show the degree of proximity of geographically or historically related countries. The three diagrams thus represent a composite set of cultural maps of the world.

Of the three "maps," those in Figure 5 (Power Distance X Uncertainty Avoidance) and Figure 7 (Masculinity X Uncertainty Avoidance) show a scattering of countries in all corners—that is, all combinations of index values occur. Figure 6 (Power Distance X Individualism), however, shows one empty corner: The combination of Small Power Distance and Collectivism does not occur. In fact, there is a tendency for large Power Distance to be associated with Collectivism and for Small Power Distance with Individualism. However, there is a third factor that should be taken into account here: national wealth. Both Small Power Distance and Individualism go together with greater national wealth (per capita gross national product). The relationship between Individualism and Wealth is quite strong, as Figure 6 shows. In the upper part (Collectivist) we find only the poorer countries, with Japan as a borderline. In the lower part (Individualism), we find only the wealthier countries. If we look at the poorer and the wealthier countries separately, there is no longer any relationship between Power Distance and Individualism.

THE CULTURAL RELATIVITY OF MANAGEMENT THEORIES

Of particular interest in the context of this discussion is the relative position of the United States on the four dimensions. Here is how the United States rates:

- On *Power Distance* at rank 15 out of the 40 countries (measured from below), it is below average but it is not as low as a number of other wealthy countries.
- On *Uncertainty Avoidance* at rank 9 out of 40, it is well below average.
- On *Individualism* at rank 40 out of 40, the United States is the single most individualist country of the entire set (followed closely by Australia and Great Britain).
- On *Masculinity* at rank 28 out of 40, it is well above average.

For about 60 years, the United States has been the world's largest producer and exporter of management theories covering such key areas as motivation, leadership, and organization. Before that, the centers of theorizing about what we now call "management" lay in the Old World. We can trace the history of management thought as far back as we want—at least to parts of the Old Testament of the Bible, and to ancient Greece (Plato's *The Laws* and *The Republic,* 350 B.C.), Sixteenth-century European "Management" theorists include Niccolò Machiavelli (Italy) and Thomas More (Great Britain); early twentieth-century theorists include Max Weber (Germany) and Henri Fayol (France).

Today we are all culturally conditioned. We see the world in the way we have learned to see it. Only to a limited extent can we, in our thinking, step out of the boundaries imposed by our cultural conditioning. This applies to the author of a theory as much as it does to the ordinary citizen: Theories reflect the cultural environment in which they are written. If this is true, Italian, British, German, and France of their day, and American theories reflect the culture of the United States of its day. Since most present-day theorists are middle-class intellectuals, their theories reflect a national intellectual middle-class background.

Now we ask the question: To what extent do theories developed in one country and reflecting the cultural boundaries of that country apply to other countries? Do American management theories apply to Japan? In India? No management theorist, to my knowledge, has ever explicitly addressed himself or herself to this issue. Most probably assume that their theories are universally valid. The availability of a conceptual framework built on four dimensions of national culture, in conjunction with the cultural maps of the world, makes it possible to see more clearly where and to what extent theories developed in one country are likely to apply elsewhere. In the remaining sections of the article I shall look from this viewpoint at most popular American theories of management in the areas of motivation, leadership, and organization.

MOTIVATION

Why do people behave as they do? There is a great variety of theories of human motivation. According to Sigmund Freud, we are impelled to act by unconscious forces within us, which he called our id. Our conscious conception of ourselves—our ego—tries to control these forces, and an equally unconscious internal pilot—our superego—criticizes the thoughts and acts of our ego and causes feelings of guilt and anxiety when the ego seems to be giving in to the id. The superego is the product of early socialization, mainly learned from our parents when we were young children.

Freud's work has been extremely influential in psychology, but he is rarely quoted in the context of management theories. The latter almost exclusively refer to motivation theories developed later in the United States, particularly those of David McClelland, Abraham Maslow, Frederick Herzberg, and Victor Vroom. According to McClelland, we perform because we have a need to achieve (the achievement motive). More recently, McClelland has also paid a lot of attention to the power motive. Maslow has postulated a hierarchy of human needs, from more "basic" to "higher": most basic are physiological needs, followed by security, social needs, esteem needs and, finally, a need for "self-actualization." The latter incorporates McClelland's theory of achievement, but is defined in broader terms. Maslow's theory of the hierarchy of needs postulates that a higher need will become active only if the lower needs are sufficiently satisfied. Our acting is basically a rational activity by which we expect to fulfill successive levels of needs. Herzberg's two-factor theory of motivation distinguishes between hygienic factors (largely corresponding to Maslow's lower needs—physiological, security, social) and motivators (Maslow's higher needs—esteem, self-actualization); the hygienic factors have only the potential to motivate negatively (demotivate—they are necessary but not sufficient conditions), while only the motivators have the potential to motivate positively. Vroom has formalized the role of "expectancy" in motivation; he opposes "expectancy" theories and "drive" theories. The former see people as being *pulled* by the expectancy of some kind of result from their acts, mostly consciously. The latter (in accordance with Freud's theories) see people as *pushed* by inside forces—often unconscious ones.

Let us now look at these theories through culture-conscious glasses. Why has Freudian thinking never become popular in U.S. management theory, as has the thinking of McClelland, Maslow, Herzberg, and Vroom? To what extent do these theories reflect different cultural patterns? Freud was part of an Austrian middle-class culture at the turn of the century. If we compare present-day Austria and the United States on our cultural maps, we find the following:

- Austria scores considerably lower on Power Distance.
- Austria scores considerably higher on Uncertainty Avoidance.
- Austria scores considerably lower on Individualism.
- Austria scores considerably higher on Masculinity.

We do not know to what extent Austrian culture has changed since Freud's time, but evidence suggests that cultural patterns change very slowly. It is, therefore, not likely to have been much different from today's culture. The most striking thing about present-day Austrian culture is that it combines a fairly high Uncertainty Avoidance with a very low Power Distance (see Figure 5). Somehow the combination of high Uncertainty Avoidance with high Power Distance is more comfortable (we find this in Japan and in all Latin and Mediterranean countries—see Figure 5). Having a powerful superior whom we can both praise and blame is one way of satisfying a strong need for avoiding uncertainty. The Austrian culture, however (together with the German, Swiss, Israeli, and Finnish cultures) cannot rely on an external boss to absorb its uncertainty. Thus Freud's superego acts naturally as an inner uncertainty—absorbing device, an internalized boss. For strong Uncertainty Avoidance countries like Austria, working hard is caused by an inner urge—it is a way of relieving stress. (See Figure 2.) The Austrian superego is reinforced by the country's relatively low level of Individualism (see Figure 6). The inner feeling of obligation to society plays a much stronger role in Austria than in the United States. The ultrahigh Individualism of the United States leads to a need to explain every act in terms of self-interest, and expectancy theories of motivation do provide this explanation—we always do something *because* we expect to obtain the satisfaction of some need.

The comparison between Austrian and U.S. culture has so far justified the popularity of expectancy theories of motivation in the United States. The combination in the United States of weak Uncertainty Avoidance and relatively high Masculinity can tell us more about why the achievement motive has become so popular in that country. David McClelland, in his book *The Achieving Society*, sets up scores reflecting how strong achievement need is in many countries by analyzing the content of children's stories used in those countries to teach the young to read. It now appears that there is a strong relationship between McClelland's need for achievement country scores and the combination of weak Uncertainty Avoidance and strong Masculinity charted in Figure 7. (McClelland's data were collected for two historic years—1925 and 1950—but only his 1925 data relate to the cultural map in Figure 7. It is likely that the 1925 stories were more traditional, reflecting deep underlying cultural currents; the choice of stories in 1950 in most countries may have been affected by modernization currents in education, often imported from abroad.)

Countries in the upper righthand corner of Figure 7 received mostly high scores on achievement need in McClelland's book; countries in the lower lefthand corner of Figure 7 received low scores. This leads us to the conclusion that the concept of the achievement motive presupposes two cultural choices—a willingness to accept risk (equivalent to weak Uncertainty Avoidance; see Figure 2) and a concern with performance (equivalent to strong Masculinity; see Figure 4). This combination is found exclusively in countries in the Anglo-American group and in some of their former colonies (Figure 7). One striking thing about the concept of achievement is that the word itself is hardly translatable into any language other than English; for this reason, the word could not be used in the questionnaire of the multi-national corporation used in my research. The English-speaking countries all appear in the upper righthand corner of Figure 7.

If this is so, there is reason to reconsider Maslow's hierarchy of human needs in the light of the map shown in Figure 7. Quadrant 1 (upper righthand corner) in Figure 7 stands for *achievement motivation,* as we have seen (performance plus risk). Quadrant 2 distinguishes itself from quadrant 1 by strong Uncertainty Avoidance, which means *security motivation* (performance plus security). The countries on the feminine side of Figure 7 distinguish themselves by a focusing on quality of life rather than on performance and on relationships between people rather than on money and things (see Figure 4). This means *social motivation*: quality of life plus security in quadrant 3, and quality of life plus risk in quadrant 4. Now, Maslow's hierarchy puts self-actualization (achievement) plus esteem above social needs above security needs. This, however, is not the description of a universal human motivation process—it is the description of a value system, the value system of the U.S. middle class to which the author belonged. I suggest that if we want to continue thinking in terms of a hierarchy for countries in the lower righthand corner of Figure 7 (quadrant 2), security needs should rank at the top; for countries in the upper lefthand corner (quadrant 4), social needs should rank at the top, and for countries in the lower lefthand corner (quadrant 3) *both* security and social needs should rank at the top.

One practical outcome of presenting motivation theories is the movement toward humanization of work—an attempt to make work more intrinsically interesting to the workers. There are two main currents in humanization of work—one, developed in the United States and called *job enrichment*, aims at restructuring individual jobs. A chief proponent of job enrichment is Frederick Herzberg. The other current, developed in Europe and applied mainly in Sweden and Norway, aims at restructuring work into group work—forming, for example, such semiautonomous teams as those seen in the experiments at Volvo. Why the difference in approaches? What is seen as a "human" job depends on a society's prevailing model of humankind. In a more masculine society like the United States, humanization takes the form of masculinization, allowing individual performance. In the more feminine societies of Sweden and Norway, humanization takes the form of femininization—it is a means toward more wholesome interpersonal relationships in its deemphasis of interindividual competition.

THE 40 COUNTRIES							
(Showing Abbreviations used in Figures 5, 6, and 7.)							
ARG	Argentina	FRA	France	JAP	Japan	SIN	Singapore
AUL	Australia	GBR	Great Britain	MEX	Mexico	SPA	Spain
AUT	Austria	GER	Germany (West)	NET	Netherlands	SWE	Sweden
BEL	Belgium	GRE	Greece	NOR	Norway	SWI	Switzerland
BRA	Brazil	HOK	Hong Kong	NZL	New Zealand	TAI	Taiwan
CAN	Canada	IND	India	PAK	Pakistan	THA	Thailand
CHL	Chili	IRA	Iran	PER	Peru	TUR	Turkey
COL	Colombia	IRE	Ireland	PHI	Philippines	USA	United States
DEN	Denmark	ISR	Israel	POR	Portugal	VEN	Venezuela
FIN	Finland	ITA	Italy	SAF	South Africa	YUG	Yugoslavia

LEADERSHIP

One of the oldest theorists of leadership in world literature is Machiavelli (1468-1527). He described certain effective techniques for manipulation and remaining in power (including deceit, bribery, and murder) that gave him a bad reputation in later centuries. Machiavelli wrote in the context of the Italy of his day, and what he described is clearly a large Power Distance situation. We still find Italy on the larger Power Distance side of Figure 5 (with all other Latin and Mediterranean countries), and we can assume from historical evidence that Power Distances in Italy during the sixteenth century were considerably larger than they are now. When we compare Machiavelli's work with that of his contemporary, Sir Thomas More (1478-1535), we find cultural differences between ways of thinking in different countries even in the sixteenth century. The British More described in *Utopia* a state based on consensus as a "model" to criticize the political situation of his day. But practice did not always follow theory, of course: More, deemed too critical, was beheaded by order of King Henry VIII, while Machiavelli the realist managed to die peacefully in his bed. The difference in theories is nonetheless remarkable.

In the United States a current of leadership theories has developed. Some of the best known were put forth by the late Douglas McGregor (Theory X versus Theory Y), Rensis Likert (System 4 management), and Robert R. Blake with Jane S. Mouton (the Managerial Grid). What these theories have in common is that they all advocate participation in the manager's decisions by his/her subordinates (participative management); however, the initiative toward participation is supposed to be taken by the manager. In a worldwide perspective (Figure 5), we can understand these theories from the middle position of the United States on the Power Distance side (rank 15 out of 40 countries). Had the culture been one of larger Power Distance, we could have expected more "Machiavellian" theories of leadership. In fact, in the management literature of another country with a larger Power Distance index score, France, there is little concern with participative management American style, but great concern with who has the power. However, in countries with smaller Power Distances than the United States (Sweden, Norway, Germany, Israel), there is considerable sympathy for models of management in which even the initiatives are taken by the subordinates (forms of industrial democracy) and with which there's little sympathy in the United States. In the approaches toward "industrial democracy" taken in these countries, we notice their differences on the second dimension, Uncertainty Avoidance. In weak Uncertainty Avoidance countries like Sweden, industrial democracy was started in the form of local experiments and only later was given a legislative framework. In strong Uncertainty Avoidance countries like Germany, industrial democracy was brought about by legislation first and then had to be brought alive in the organizations ("Mitbestimmung").

The crucial fact about leadership in any culture is that it is a complement to subordinateship. The Power Distance Index scores in Figure 5 are, in fact, based on the values of people as *subordinates*, not on the values of superiors. Whatever a naïve literature on leadership may give us to understand, leaders cannot choose their styles at will; what is feasible depends to a large extent on the cultural conditioning of a leader's subordinates. Along these lines, Figure 8 describes the type of subordinateship that, other things being equal, a leader can expect to meet in societies at three different levels of Power Distance—subordinateship to which a leader must respond. The middle level represents what is most likely found in the United States.

Neither McGregor, nor Liken, nor Blake and Mouton allow for this type of cultural proviso—all three tend to be prescriptive with regard to a leadership style that, at best, will work with U.S. subordinates and with those in cultures—such as Canada or Australia—that have not too different Power Distance levels (Figure 5). In fact, my research shows that subordinates in larger Power Distance countries tend to agree more frequently with Theory Y.

A U.S. theory of leadership that allows for a certain amount of cultural relativity, although indirectly, is Fred Fiedler's contingency theory of leadership. Fiedler states that different leader personalities are needed for "difficult" and "easy" situations, and that a cultural gap between superior and subordinates is one of the factors that makes a situation "difficult." However, this theory does not address the kind of cultural gap in question.

In practice, the adaptation of managers to higher Power Distance environments does not seem to present too many problems. Although this is an unpopular message—one seldom professed in management development courses—managers moving to a larger Power Distance culture soon learn that they have to behave more autocratically in order to be effective, and tend to do so; this is borne out by the colonial history of most Western countries. But it is interesting that the Western ex-colonial power with the highest Power Distance norm—France—seems to be most appreciated by its former colonies and seems to maintain the best postcolonial relationships with most of them. This suggests that subordinates in a large Power Distance culture feel even more comfortable with superiors who are real autocrats than with those whose assumed autocratic stance is out of national character.

The operation of a manager in an environment with a Power Distance norm lower than his or her own is more problematic. U.S. managers tend to find it difficult to collaborate wholeheartedly in the "industrial democracy" processes of such countries as Sweden, Germany, and even the Netherlands. U.S. citizens tend to consider their country as the example of democracy, and find it difficult to accept that other countries might wish to develop forms of democracy for which they feel no need and that make major inroads upon managers' (or leaders') prerogatives. However, the very idea of management prerogatives is not accepted in very low Power Distance countries. This is, perhaps, best illustrated by a remark a Scandinavian social scientist is supposed to have made to Herzberg in a seminar: "You are against participation for the very reason we are in favour of it—one doesn't know where it will stop. We think that is good."

One way in which the U.S. approach to leadership has been packaged and formalized is management by objectives (MBO), first advocated by Peter Drucker in 1955 in *The Practice of Management*. In the United States, MBO has been used to spread a pragmatic results orientation throughout the organization. It has been considerably more successful where results are objectively measurable than where they can only be interpreted subjectively, and, even in the United States, it has been criticized heavily. Still, it has been perhaps the single most popular management technique "made in U.S.A." Therefore, it can be accepted as fitting U.S. culture. MBO presupposes:

- That subordinates are sufficiently independent to negotiate meaningfully with the boss (not-too-large Power Distance).

- That both are willing to take risks (weak Uncertainty Avoidance).
- That performance is seen as important by both (high Masculinity).

Let us now take the case of Germany, a below-average Power Distance country. Here, the dialogue element in MBO should present no problem. However, since Germany scores considerably higher on Uncertainty Avoidance, the tendency toward accepting risk and ambiguity will not exist to the same extent. The idea of replacing the arbitrary authority of the boss with the impersonal authority of mutually agreed-upon objectives, however, fits the small Power Distance/strong Uncertainty Avoidance cultural cluster very well. The objectives become the subordinates' "superego." In a book of case studies about MBO in Germany, Ian R. G. Ferguson states that "MBO has acquired a different flavour in the German-speaking area, not least because in these countries the societal and political pressure towards increasing the value of man in the organization on the right to co-determination has become quite clear. Thence, MBO has been translit-erated into Management by Joint Goal Setting (Führung durch Zielvereinbarung)." Ferguson's view of MBO fits the ideological needs of the German-speaking countries of the moment. The case studies in his book show elaborate formal systems with extensive ideological justification: the stress on *team* objectives is quite strong, which is in line with the lower individualism in these countries.

The other area in which specific information on MBO is available is France. MBO was first introduced in France in the early 1960s, but it became extremely popular for a time after the 1968 student revolt. People expected that this new technique would lead to the long-overdue democratization of organizations. Instead of DPO (Direction par Objectifs), the French name for MBO became DPPO (Direction *Participative* par Objectifs). So in France, too, societal developments affected the MBO system. However, DPPO remained, in general, as much a vain slogan as did Liberté, Egalité, Fraternité (Freedom, Equality, Brotherhood) after the 1789 revolt. G. Franck wrote in 1973 " . . . I think that the career of DPPO is terminated, or rather that it has never started, and it won't ever start as long as we continue in France our tendency to confound ideology and reality . . ." In a postscript to Franck's article, the editors of *Le Management* write: "French blue—and white-collar workers, lower-level and higher-level managers, and 'patrons' all belong to the same cultural system which maintains dependency relations from level to level. Only the deviants really dislike this system. The hierarchical structure protects against anxiety; DPO, however, generates anxiety . . ." The reason for the anxiety in the French cultural context is that MBO presupposes a depersonalized authority in the form of internalized objectives; but French people, from their early childhood onward, are accustomed to large Power Distances, to an authority that is highly personalized. And in spite of all attempts to introduce Anglo-Saxon management methods, French superiors do not easily decentralize and do not stop short-circuiting intermediate hierarchical levels, nor do French subordinates expect them to. The developments of the 1970s have severely discredited DPPO, which probably does injustice to the cases in which individual French organizations or units, starting from less exaggerated expectations, have benefited from it.

In the examples used thus far in this section, the cultural context of leadership may look rather obvious to the reader. But it also works in more subtle, less obvious ways. Here's an example from the area of management decision making: A prestigious U.S. consulting firm was asked to analyze the decision-making processes in a large Scandinavian "XYZ" corporation. Their report criticized the corporation's decision-making style, which they characterized as being, among other things, "intuitive" and "consensus based." They compared "observations of traditional XYZ practices" with "selected examples of practices in other companies." These "selected examples," offered as a model, were evidently taken from their U.S. clients and reflect the U.S. textbook norm—"fact based" rather than intuitive management, and "fast decisions based on clear responsibilities" rather than the use of informal, personal contacts and the concern for consensus.

Is this consulting firm doing its Scandinavian clients a service? It follows from Figure 7 that where the United States and the Scandinavian culture are wide apart is on the Masculinity dimension. The use of intuition and the concern for consensus in Scandinavia are "feminine" characteristics of the culture, well embedded in the total texture of these societies. Stressing "facts" and "clear responsibilities" fits the "masculine" U.S. culture. From a neutral viewpoint, the reasons for criticizing the U.S. decision-making style are as good as those for criticizing the Scandinavian style. In complex decision-making situations, "facts" no longer exist independently from the people who define them, so "fact-based management" becomes a misleading slogan. Intuition may not be a bad method of deciding in such cases at all. And if the implementation of decisions requires the commitment of many people, even a consensus process that takes more time is an asset rather than a liability. But the essential element overlooked by the consultant is that decisions have to be made in a way that corresponds to the values of the environment in which they have to be effective. People in this consulting firm lacked insight into their own cultural biases. This does not mean that the Scandinavian corporation's management need not improve its decision making and could not learn from the consultant's experience. But this can be done only through a mutual recognition of cultural differences, not by ignoring them.

ORGANIZATION

The Power Distance X Uncertainty Avoidance map (Figure 5) is of vital importance for structuring organizations that will work best in different countries. For example, one U.S.-

based multinational corporation has a worldwide policy that salary-increase proposals should be initiated by the employee's direct superior. However, the French management of its French subsidiary interpreted this policy in such a way that the superior's superior's superior—three levels above—was the one to initiate salary proposals. This way of working was regarded as quite natural by both superiors and subordinates in France. Other factors being equal, people in large Power Distance cultures prefer that decisions be centralized because even superiors have strong dependency needs in relation to their superiors; this tends to move decisions up as far as they can go (see Figure 8). People in small Power Distance cultures want decisions to be decentralized.

While Power Distance relates to centralization, Uncertainty Avoidance relates to formalization—the need for formal rules and specialization, the assignment of tasks to experts. My former colleague O. J. Stevens at INSEAD has done an interesting research project (as yet unpublished) with M.B.A. students from Germany, Great Britain, and France. He asked them to write their own diagnosis and solution for a small case study of an organizational problem—a conflict in one company between the sales and product development departments. The majority of the French referred the problem to the next higher authority (the president of the company); the Germans attributed it to the lack of a written policy, and proposed es-tablishing one; the British attributed it to a lack of interpersonal communication, to be cured by some kind of group training.

Stevens concludes that the "implicit model" of the organization for most French was a pyramid (both centralized and formal); for most Germans, a well-oiled machine (formalized but not centralized); and for most British, a village market (neither formalized nor centralized). This covers three quadrants (2, 3, and 4) in Figure 5. What is missing is an "implicit model" for quadrant 1, which contains four Asian countries, including India. A discussion with an Indian colleague leads me to place the family (centralized, but not formalized) in this quadrant as the "implicit model" of the organization. In fact, Indian organizations tend to be formalized as far as relationships between people go (this is related to Power Distance), but not as far as workflow goes (this is Uncertainty Avoidance).

The "well-oiled machine" model for Germany reminds us of the fact that Max Weber, author of the first theory of bureaucracy, was a German. Weber pictures bureaucracy as a highly formalized system (strong Uncertainty Avoidance), in which, however, the rules protect the lower-ranking members against abuse of power by their superiors. The superiors have no power by themselves, only the power that their bureaucratic roles have given them as incumbents of the roles—the power is in the role, not in the person (small Power Distance).

The United States is found fairly close to the center of the map in Figure 5, taking an intermediate position between the "pyramid," "machine," and "market" implicit models—a position that may help explain the success of U.S. business operations in very different cultures. However, according to the common U.S. conception of organization, we might say that *hierarchy is not a goal by itself* (as it is in France) and that *rules are not a goal by themselves*. Both are means toward obtaining results, to be changed if needed. A breaking away from hierarchic and bureaucratic traditions is found in the development toward matrix organizations and similar temporary or flexible organization systems.

Another INSEAD colleague, André Laurent, has shown that French managers strongly disbelieve in the feasibility of matrix organizations, because they see them as violating the "holy" principle of unit of command. However, in the French subsidiary of a multinational corporation that has a long history of successful matrix management, the French managers were quite positive toward it; obviously, then, cultural barriers to organizational innovation can be overcome. German managers are not too favorably disposed toward matrix organizations either, feeling that they tend to frustrate their need for organizational clarity. This means that matrix organizations will be accepted *if* the roles of individuals within the organization can be defined without ambiguity.

The extreme position of the United States on the Individualism scale leads to other potential conflicts between the U.S. way of thinking about organizations and the values dominant in other parts of the world. In the U.S. Individualist conception, the relationship between the individual and the organization is essentially calculative, being based on enlightened self-interest. In fact, there is a strong historical and cultural link between Individualism and Capitalism. The capitalist system—based on self-interest and the market mechanism—was "invented" in Great Britain, which is still among the top three most Individualist countries in the world. In more Collectivist societies, however, the link between individuals and their traditional organizations is not calculative, but moral: It is based not on self-interest, but on the individual's loyalty toward the clan, organization, or society—which is supposedly the best guarantee of that individual's ultimate interest. "Collectivism" is a bad word in the United States, but "individualism" is as much a bad word in the writings of Mao Tse-tung, who writes from a strongly Collectivist cultural tradition (see Figure 6 for the Collectivist scores of the Chinese majority countries Taiwan, Hong Kong, and Singapore). This means that U.S. organizations may get themselves into considerable trouble in more Collectivist environments if they do not recognize their local employees' needs for ties of mutual loyalty between company and employee. "Hire and fire" is very ill perceived in these countries, if firing isn't prohibited by law altogether. Given the value position of people in more Collectivist cultures, it should not be seen as surprising if they prefer other types of economic order to capitalism—if capitalism cannot get rid of its Individualist image.

CONSEQUENCES FOR POLICY

So far we have seriously questioned the universal validity of management theories developed in one country—in most instances here, the United States.

On a practical level, this has the least consequence for organizations operating entirely within the country in which the theories were born. As long as the theories apply within the United States, U.S. organizations can base their policies for motivating employees, leadership, and organization development on these policies. Still, some caution is due. If differences in environmental culture can be shown to exist between countries, and if these constrain the validity of management theories, what about the subcultures and countercultures within the country? To what extent do the familiar theories apply when the organization employs people for whom the theories were not, in the first instance, conceived—such as members of minority groups with a different educational level, or belonging to a different generation? If culture matters, an organization's policies can lose their effectiveness when its cultural environment changes.

No doubt, however, the consequences of the cultural relativity of management theories are more serious for the multinational organization. The cultural maps in Figures 5, 6, and 7 can help predict the kind of culture difference between subsidiaries and mother company that will need to be met. An important implication is that identical personnel policies may have very different effects in different countries—and within countries for different subgroups of employees. This is not only a matter of different employee values; there are also, of course, differences in government policies and legislation (which usually reflect quite clearly the country's different cultural position). And there are differences in labor market situations and labor union power positions.

These differences—tangible as well as intangible—may have consequences for performance, attention to quality, cost, labor turnover, and absenteeism. Typical universal policies that may work out quite differently in different countries are those dealing with financial incentives, promotion paths, and grievance channels.

The dilemma for the organization operating abroad is whether to adapt to the local culture or try to change it. There are examples of companies that have successfully changed local habits, such as in the earlier mention of the introduction of matrix organization in France. Many Third World countries want to transfer new technologies from more economically advanced countries. If they are to work at all, these technologies must presuppose values that may run counter to local traditions, such as a certain discretion of subordinates toward superiors (lower Power Distance) or of individuals toward in-groups (more Individualism). In such a case, the local culture has to be changed; this is a difficult task that should not be taken lightly. Since it calls for a conscious strategy based on insight into the local culture, it's logical to involve acculturated locals in strategy formulations. Often, the original policy will have to be adapted to fit local culture and lead to the desired effect. We saw earlier how, in the case of MBO, this has succeeded in Germany, but generally failed in France.

A final area in which the cultural boundaries of home-country management theories are important is the training of managers for assignments abroad. For managers who have to operate in an unfamiliar culture, training based on home-country theories is of very limited use and may even do more harm than good. Of more importance is a thorough familiarization with the other culture, for which the organization can use the services of specialized crosscultural training institutes—or it can develop its own program by using host-country personnel as teachers.

ACKNOWLEDGMENTS

This article is based on research carried out in the period 1973-78 at the European Institute for Advanced Studies in Management, Brussels. The article itself was sponsored by executive search consultants Berndtson International S.A., Brussels. The author acknowledges the helpful comments of Mark Cantley, André Laurent, Ernest C. Miller, and Jennifer Robinson on an earlier version of it.

Figure 5
The Position of the 40 Countries
On the Power Distance and Uncertainty Avoidance Scales

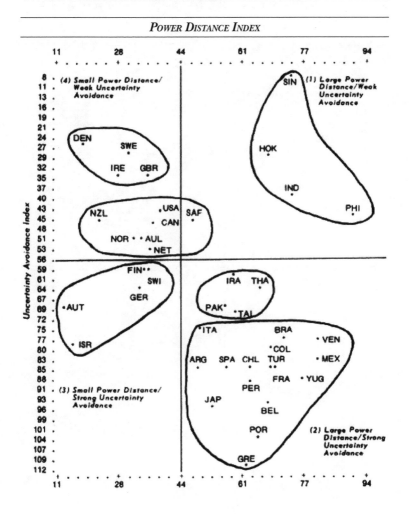

Figure 6
THE POSITION OF THE 40 COUNTRIES
ON THE POWER DISTANCE AND INDIVIDUALISM SCALES

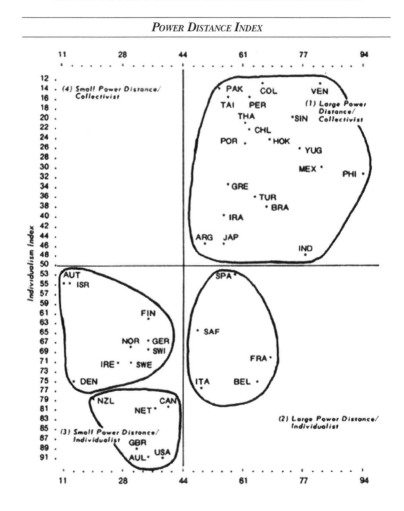

Figure 7
The Position of the 40 Countries
On the Uncertainty Avoidance and Masculinity Scales

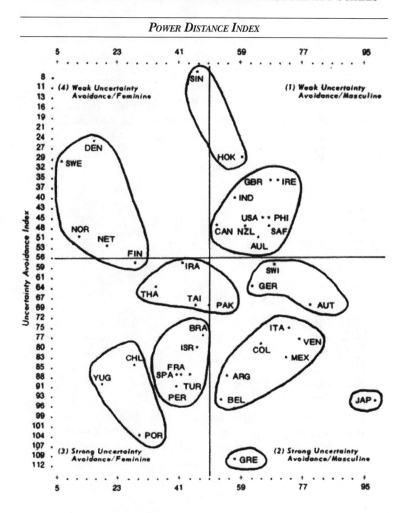

Figure 8

SUBORDINATESHIP FOR THREE LEVELS OF POWER DISTANCE

Small Power Distance	Medium Power Distance (United States)	Large Power Distance
Subordinates have weak dependence needs.	Subordinates have medium dependence needs.	Subordinates have strong dependence needs.
Superiors have weak dependence needs toward their superiors.	Superiors have medium dependence needs toward their superiors.	Superiors have strong dependence needs toward their superiors.
Subordinates expect superiors to consult them and may rebel or strike if superiors are not seen as staying within their legitimate role.	Subordinates expect superiors to consult them but will accept autocratic behavior as well.	Subordinates expect superiors to act autocratically.
Ideal superior to most is a loyal democrat.	Ideal superior to most is a resourceful democrat.	Ideal superior to most is a benevolent autocrat or paternalist.
Laws and rules apply to all and privileges for superiors are not considered acceptable.	Laws and rules apply to all, but a certain level of privileges for superiors is considered normal.	Everybody expects superiors to enjoy privileges; laws and rules differ for superiors and subordinates.
Status symbols are frowned upon and will easily come under attack from subordinates.	Status symbols for superiors contribute moderately to their authority and will be accepted by subordinates.	Status symbols are very important and contribute strongly to the superior's authority with the subordinates.

SELECTED BIBLIOGRAPHY

The first U.S. book about the cultural relativity of U.S. management theories is still to be written, I believe—which lack in itself indicates how difficult it is to recognize one's own cultural biases. One of the few U.S. books describing the process of cultural conditioning for a management readership is Edward T. Hall's *The Silent Language* (Fawcett, 1959, but reprinted since). Good reading also is Hall's article "The Silent Language in Overseas Business" (*Harvard Business Review*, May-June 1960). Hall is an anthropologist and therefore a specialist in the study of culture. Very readable on the same subject are two books by the British anthropologist Mary Douglas, *Natural Symbols: Exploration in Cosmology* (Vintage, 1973) and the reader *Rules and Meanings: The Anthropology of Everyday Knowledge* (Penguin, 1973). Another excellent reader is Theodore D. Weinshall's *Culture and Management* (Penguin, 1977).

On the concept of national character, some well-written professional literature is Margaret Mead's "National Character," in the reader by Sol Tax, *Anthropology Today* (University of Chicago Press, 1962), and Alex Inkeles and D. J. Levinson's, "National Character," in Lindzey and Aronson's *Handbook of Social Psychology*, second edition, volume 4, (Addison-Wesley, 1969). Critique on the implicit claims of universal validity of management theories comes from some foreign authors: An important article is Michel Brossard and Marc Maurice's "Is There a Universal Model of Organization Structure?" (*International Studies of Management and Organization*, Fall 1976). This journal is a journal of translations from non-American literature, based in New York, that often contains important articles on management issues by non-U.S. authors that take issue with the dominant theories. Another article is Gunnar Hjelholt's "Europe Is Different," in Geert Hofstede and M. Sami Kassem's reader, *European Contributions to Organization Theory* (Assen Netherlands: Von Gorcum, 1976).

Some other references of interest: Ian R. G. Ferguson's *Management by Objectives in Deutschland,* (Herder and Herder, 1973) (in German); G. Franck's "Epitaphe pour la DPO," in *Le Management,* November 1973 (in French); and D. Jenkins's *Blue—and White-Collar Democracy,* (Doubleday, 1973).

Note: Details of Geert Hofstede's study of national cultures has been published in his book, *Culture's Consequences: International Differences in Work-Related Values* (Beverly Hills: Sage Publications, 1980).

IRA CHALEFF

1945-

The Courageous Follower

1998

Ira Chaleff is the founder and president of Executive Coaching and Consulting Associates, Washington, DC, which specializes in coaching political leaders. He is a founding partner of the Institute for Business Technology, US, which focuses on worker efficiency and workload management. He co-edited *The Art of Followership: How Great Followers Make Great Leaders and Organizations* (2008), and his work with political leaders led to his well-received text, *The Courageous Follower: Standing Up To and For Our Leaders* (1998). For all these reasons as well as for his teaching experience at Georgetown University and for his founding of the Followership Learning Community at the International Leadership Association, *Leadership Excellence* magazine acknowledged Chaleff as one of the 100 Best Thinkers on Leadership. Chaleff prompts us to consider whether someone can be an effective leader if s/he has not first been an effective follower.

Source:

Executive Coaching & Consulting Associates. (n.d.) *Ira Chaleff, Executive Coach, President.* Retrieved from http://www.exe-coach.com/ira.htm

Selection from:

Chaleff, Ira. (1998). *The courageous follower: Standing up to and for our leaders.* (pp. 1-8.) San Francisco: Berrett-Koehler.

There are four dimensions in which a courageous follower operates within a group, and a fifth dimension outside of the group. The model will explore each of these dimensions as a way to compare our current followership practices with how we might develop the follower role.

THE FIVE DIMENSIONS
OF COURAGEOUS FOLLOWERSHIP

THE COURAGE TO ASSUME RESPONSIBILITY

Courageous followers assume responsibility for themselves and the organization. They do not hold a paternalistic image of the leader or organization; they do not expect the leader or organization to provide for their security and growth, or to give them permission to act. Courageous followers discover or create opportunities to fulfill their potential and maximize their value to the organization. They initiate values-based action to improve the organization's external activities and its internal processes. The "authority" to initiate comes from the courageous follower's understanding and ownership of the common purpose, and from the needs of those the organization serves.

THE COURAGE TO SERVE

Courageous followers are not afraid of the hard work required to serve a leader. They assume new or additional responsibilities to unburden the leader and serve the organization. They stay alert for areas in which their strengths complement the leader's and assert themselves in these areas. Courageous followers stand up for their leader and the tough decisions a leader must make if the organization is to achieve its purpose. They are as passionate as the leader in pursuing the common purpose.

THE COURAGE TO CHALLENGE

Courageous followers give voice to the discomfort they feel when the behaviors or policies of the leader or group conflict with their sense of what is right. They are willing to stand up, to stand out, to risk rejection, to initiate conflict in order to examine the actions of the leader and group when appropriate. They are willing to deal with the emotions their challenge evokes in the leader and group. Courageous followers value organizational harmony and their relationship with the leader, but not at the expense of the common purpose and their integrity.

THE COURAGE TO PARTICIPATE
IN TRANSFORMATION

When behavior that jeopardizes the common purpose remains unchanged, courageous followers recognize the need for transformation. They champion the need for change and stay with the leader and group while they mutually struggle with the difficulty of real change. They examine their own need for transformation and become full participants in the change process as appropriate.

THE COURAGE TO LEAVE

Courageous followers know when it is time to separate from a leader and group. Self-growth or organizational growth may require a courageous follower to eventually leave even the most enlightened and effective of leaders. When leaders are ineffective or their actions are detrimental to the common purpose and they are not open to transformation, the need for separation becomes more compelling. Courageous followers are prepared to withdraw support from, even to disavow or oppose destructive leaders, despite high personal risk.

The world is fitfully evolving to a more egalitarian culture. Leadership and followership are evolving. As in any evolutionary process, the prospects for the emerging stage of development often look dubious. There will be times while reading this book when you might wince at suggested behaviors and think, "Get real!" For some leaders the suggested approach will be unreal. For others, who have allowed contemporary cultural changes to seep into their patterning, the approach presented here may be startling, but will also be fresh and welcome. The leader's reactions are of secondary importance, however, to the actions of the follower. That is why this book focuses on the courage of the follower; we are not talking about comfortable, risk-free behavior.

Most of us will have ample opportunity to experiment with and develop new models of courageous followership in the course of "ordinary" living. We will help our organizations compete more efficiently, make them more "employee-friendly," and help our community groups function more responsively.

But the extraordinary also occurs: the opportunity to help a leader make a bold peace initiative, the discovery of abusive practices that demand reversal, the chance to influence leadership practices that may bring an organization to a crossroads in choosing the values by which it will live. To the degree we have become strong and comfortable with new models of followership, those models will serve us well when we find ourselves in situations where the consequences are profound.

Whether we are dealing with the ordinary or extraordinary, the challenge a follower faces is significant . . .

Section VI

Leadership And Ethics

The many definitions of leadership that have been explored in Section I of this volume do not include much discussion of ethics (concerning human meaning, values, purpose, and significance). However, ethical considerations are at the very heart of leadership. The readings in Section VI attempt to combine the rational approach to leadership in Sections I through V with ethical concerns.

Virtually every survey of the qualities most desired in a leader reports that honesty and integrity are the most important leadership attributes (Kouzes and Posner, 2002). An organization's leadership is responsible for the cultures and systems that can lead to ethical lapses. When people working within organizations are convinced that ethical values play a key role in their leaders' decisions and activities, then everyone in the organization is more likely to commit to making ethics part of their everyday behavior.

Moral leadership involves distinguishing between right and wrong and then doing what is right. Moral leadership enhances the lives of others, while immoral leadership takes away from others in order to enhance the self.

In the first reading found in Section VI, Plato suggests that people would violate justice if there were nothing to hinder them, yet in the next reading, Jesus Christ suggests that people would want do good just to please God. Nevertheless, in the third reading Machiavelli suggests that it is more important to appear just and good than to be just and good.

In the fourth reading, McCoy (1983), like Jesus Christ in the Book of Matthew, uses the form of a parable to express his views. In the "Parable of the Sadhu," McCoy asks us to consider our ethical responsibility to those in need especially when their serious situations conflict with our own self-interests. Similarly, the next writer, Robert Greenleaf (1977), writes of a servant leadership that is humble and asks of followers, "How can I be of service to you?"

In *People of the Lie*, psychiatrist, M. Scott Peck (1983) explores the existence of human evil and why it is important for therapists, victims, and people in general to recognize that evil exists and to know what it looks like. Craig Johnson (2001), writer of the next reading, suggests a global ethic to be shared by all people—a platinum rule that is an even higher standard than the widely accepted Golden Rule. Kanungo and Mendonca (1996), writers of the next selection, suggest how both ethical individuals and environments can be developed. Finally, Russ Moxley (2000) explains how the leader can be helped to develop an inner life that enables him/her to reconcile the light of good and the shadow of evil.

Source:

Kouzes, J. M. & Posner, B. Z. (2002). *Leadership challenge* (3rd ed.). San Francisco: Jossey-Bass.

PLATO

(427-347 B.C.E.)

The Republic of Plato

(*ca* 360 B.C.E.)

Plato, famous student of Socrates, was the son of wealthy and influential Athenians. Plato begins his masterpiece, *The Republic*, with a Socratic conversation about justice, wisdom, courage, and moderation as applied to both individuals and society. In another reading excerpted from *The Republic* (found in Section I), Plato looked at the requirements for the ideal leader of the ideal state (the philosopher king). In this reading in Section VI, Plato confronts the possibility that people and leaders would not be just if they thought they could get away with transgression. What does Plato appear to think about human nature and its corruption? If you were an organizational specialist, how would you compensate for this apparent shortcoming in human nature?

Selection from:

Plato. (1935). *The republic of Plato.* Book II. (J. L. Davis & D. J. Vaughan, Trans.) (pp. 41-43.) London: Macmillan. (Original work written *ca.* 360 B.C.E.)

[***]

Admirably spoken! So now listen to me while I speak on my first theme, the nature and the origin of justice.

To commit injustice is, they say, in its nature, a good thing, and to suffer it is an evil thing; but the evil of the latter exceeds the good of the former; and so, after the two-fold experience of both doing and suffering injustice, those who cannot avoid the latter and compass the former find it expedient to make a compact of mutual abstinence from injustice. Hence arose legislation and contrails between man and man, and hence it became the custom to call that which the law enjoined just, as well as lawful. Such, they tell us, is justice, and so it came into being; and it stands midway between that which is best, to commit injustice with impunity, and that which is worst, to suffer injustice without any power of retaliating. And being a mean between these two extremes, the principle of justice is regarded with satisfaction, not as a positive good, but because the inability to commit injustice has rendered it valuable; for they say that one who had it in his power to be unjust, and who deserved the name of a man, would never be so weak as to contract with any one that both the parties should abstain from injustice. Such is the current account, Socrates, of the nature of justice, and of the circumstances in which it originated.

The truth of my second statement—that men practise justice unwillingly, and because they lack the power to violate it, will be most readily perceived, if we make a supposition like the following. Let us give full liberty to the just man and to the unjust alike, to do whatever they please, and then let us follow them, and see whither the inclination of each will lead him. In that case we shall surprise the just man in the act of travelling in the same direction as the unjust, owing to that covetous desire, the gratification of which every creature naturally pursues as a good, only that it is forced out of its path by law, and constrained to respect the principle of equality. That full liberty of action would, perhaps, be most effectually realized if they were invested with a power which they say was in old time possessed by the ancestor of Gyges the Lydian. He was a shepherd, so the story runs, in the service of the reigning sovereign of Lydia, when one day a violent storm of rain fell, the ground was rent asunder by an earthquake, and a yawning gulf appeared on the spot where he was feeding his flocks. Seeing what had happened, and wondering at it, he went down into the gulf, and among other marvellous objects he saw, as the legend relates, a hollow brazen horse, with windows in its sides, through which he looked, and beheld in the interior a corpse, apparently of superhuman size; from which he took nothing but a golden ring off the hand, and therewith made his way out. Now when the usual meeting of the shepherds occurred, for the purpose of sending to the king their monthly report of the state of his flocks, this shepherd came with the rest, wearing the ring. And, as he was seated with the company, he happened to turn the hoop of the ring round towards himself, till it came to the inside of his hand. Whereupon he became invisible to his neighbours, who fell to talking about him as if he were gone away. While he was marvelling at this, he again began playing with the ring, and turned the hoop to the outside, upon which he became once more visible. Having noticed this effect, he made experiments with the ring, to see whether it possessed this virtue; and so it was, that when he turned the hoop inwards he became invisible, and when he turned it outwards he was again visible. After this discovery, he immediately contrived to be appointed one of the messengers to carry the report to the king; and upon his arrival he seduced the queen, and, conspiring with her, slew the king, and took possession of the throne.

If then there were two such rings in existence, and if the just and the unjust man were each to put on one, it is to be thought that no one would be so steeled against temptation as to abide in the practice of justice, and resolutely to abstain from touching the property of his neighbours, when he had it in his power to help himself without fear to any thing he pleased in the market, or to go into private houses and have intercourse with whom he would, or to kill and release from prison according to his own pleasure, and in every thing else to act among men with the power of a god. And in thus following out his desires the just man will be doing precisely what the unjust man would do; and so they would both be pursuing the same path. Surely this will be allowed to be strong evidence that none are just willingly, but only by compulsion, because to be just is not a good to the individual; for all violate justice whenever they imagine that there is nothing to hinder them. And they do so because every one thinks that, in the individual case, injustice is much more profitable than justice; and they are right in so thinking, as the advocate of this doctrine will maintain. For if any one having this licence within his grasp were to refuse to do any injustice, or to touch the property of others, all who were aware of it would think him a most pitiful and irrational creature, though they would praise him before each other's faces, to impose on one another, through their fear of being treated with injustice. And so much for this topic.

The Gospel According to Matthew
ca. AD 70

Jesus' Sermon on the Mount, according to chapters five through seven of the Gospel of Matthew, was a sermon given by Jesus of Nazareth around AD 30 on a mountainside west of the Sea of Galilee to his disciples and a large crowd. The best known parts of this sermon are the Beatitudes and the Lord's Prayer. The Sermon on the Mount contains the chief tenets of the Christian faith. Jesus' Sermon on the Mount enables the leadership and ethics student to study the moral character of leaders via an examination of underlying motives and values. The Beatitudes (Matthew 5:1-12) specifically describe the ideal Christian character. According to Christ, what is the relationship between leadership, ethics, and character?

Selection from:

Matthew 5:1-48; 6:1-34; 7:1-29 (Revised Standard Version)

Matt. 5

1   Seeing the crowds, he went up on the mountain, and when he sat down his disciples came to him. ² And he opened his mouth and taught them, saying:
3   "Blessed are the poor in spirit, for theirs is the kingdom of heaven.
4   "Blessed are those who mourn, for they shall be comforted.
5   "Blessed are the meek, for they shall inherit the earth.
6   "Blessed are those who hunger and thirst for righteousness, for they shall be satisfied.
7   "Blessed are the merciful, for they shall obtain mercy.
8   "Blessed are the pure in heart, for they shall see God.
9   "Blessed are the peacemakers, for they shall be called sons of God.

10 "Blessed are those who are persecuted for righteousness' sake, for theirs is the kingdom of heaven.

11 "Blessed are you when men revile you and persecute you and utter all kinds of evil against you falsely on my account. 12 Rejoice and be glad, for your reward is great in heaven, for so men persecuted the prophets who were before you.

13 "You are the salt of the earth; but if salt has lost its taste, how shall its saltness be restored? It is no longer good for anything except to be thrown out and trodden under foot by men.

14 "You are the light of the world. A city set on a hill cannot be hid. 15 Nor do men light a lamp and put it under a bushel, but on a stand, and it gives light to all in the house. 16 Let your light so shine before men, that they may see your good works and give glory to your Father who is in heaven.

17 "Think not that I have come to abolish the law and the prophets; I have come not to abolish them but to fulfil them. 18 For truly, I say to you, till heaven and earth pass away, not an iota, not a dot, will pass from the law until all is accomplished. 19 Whoever then relaxes one of the least of these commandments and teaches men so, shall be called least in the kingdom of heaven; but he who does them and teaches them shall be called great in the kingdom of heaven. 20 For I tell you, unless your righteousness exceeds that of the scribes and Pharisees, you will never enter the kingdom of heaven.

21 "You have heard that it was said to the men of old, `You shall not kill; and whoever kills shall be liable to judgment.' 22 But I say to you that every one who is angry with his brother shall be liable to judgment; whoever insults his brother shall be liable to the council, and whoever says, `You fool!' shall be liable to the hell of fire. 23 So if you are offering your gift at the altar, and there remember that your brother has something against you, 24 leave your gift there before the altar and go; first be reconciled to your brother, and then come and offer your gift. 25 Make friends quickly with your

accuser, while you are going with him to court, lest your accuser hand you over to the judge, and the judge to the guard, and you be put in prison; ²⁶ truly, I say to you, you will never get out till you have paid the last penny.

²⁷ "You have heard that it was said, `You shall not commit adultery.' ²⁸ But I say to you that every one who looks at a woman lustfully has already committed adultery with her in his heart. ²⁹ If your right eye causes you to sin, pluck it out and throw it away; it is better that you lose one of your members than that your whole body be thrown into hell. ³⁰ And if your right hand causes you to sin, cut it off and throw it away; it is better that you lose one of your members than that your whole body go into hell.

³¹ "It was also said, `Whoever divorces his wife, let him give her a certificate of divorce.' ³² But I say to you that every one who divorces his wife, except on the ground of unchastity, makes her an adulteress; and whoever marries a divorced woman commits adultery.

³³ "Again you have heard that it was said to the men of old, `You shall not swear falsely, but shall perform to the Lord what you have sworn.' ³⁴ But I say to you, Do not swear at all, either by heaven, for it is the throne of God, ³⁵ or by the earth, for it is his footstool, or by Jerusalem, for it is the city of the great King. ³⁶ And do not swear by your head, for you cannot make one hair white or black. ³⁷ Let what you say be simply `Yes' or `No'; anything more than this comes from evil.

³⁸ "You have heard that it was said, `An eye for an eye and a tooth for a tooth.' ³⁹ But I say to you, Do not resist one who is evil. But if any one strikes you on the right cheek, turn to him the other also; ⁴⁰ and if any one would sue you and take your coat, let him have your cloak as well;

⁴¹ and if any one forces you to go one mile, go with him two miles. ⁴² Give to him who begs from you, and do not refuse him who would borrow from you.

⁴³ "You have heard that it was said, `You shall love your neighbor and hate your enemy.' ⁴⁴ But I say to you, Love

your enemies and pray for those who persecute you, [45] so that you may be sons of your Father who is in heaven; for he makes his sun rise on the evil and on the good, and sends rain on the just and on the unjust. [46] For if you love those who love you, what reward have you? Do not even the tax collectors do the same? [47] And if you salute only your brethren, what more are you doing than others? Do not even the Gentiles do the same? [48] You, therefore, must be perfect, as your heavenly Father is perfect.

Matt. 6

[1] "Beware of practicing your piety before men in order to be seen by them; for then you will have no reward from your Father who is in heaven.

[2] "Thus, when you give alms, sound no trumpet before you, as the hypocrites do in the synagogues and in the streets, that they may be praised by men. Truly, I say to you, they have received their reward. [3] But when you give alms, do not let your left hand know what your right hand is doing, [4] so that your alms may be in secret; and your Father who sees in secret will reward you.

[5] "And when you pray, you must not be like the hypocrites; for they love to stand and pray in the synagogues and at the street corners, that they may be seen by men. Truly, I say to you, they have received their reward. [6] But when you pray, go into your room and shut the door and pray to your Father who is in secret; and your Father who sees in secret will reward you.

[7] "And in praying do not heap up empty phrases as the Gentiles do; for they think that they will be heard for their many words. [8] Do not be like them, for your Father knows what you need before you ask him. [9] Pray then like this: Our Father who art in heaven, Hallowed be thy name.

[10] Thy kingdom come.
Thy will be done,

On earth as it is in heaven.

11 Give us this day our daily bread;

12 And forgive us our debts,
As we also have forgiven our debtors;

13 And lead us not into temptation,
But deliver us from evil.

14 For if you forgive men their trespasses, your heavenly Father also will forgive you; 15 but if you do not forgive men their trespasses, neither will your Father forgive your trespasses.

16 "And when you fast, do not look dismal, like the hypocrites, for they disfigure their faces that their fasting may be seen by men. Truly, I say to you, they have received their reward. 17 But when you fast, anoint your head and wash your face, 18 that your fasting may not be seen by men but by your Father who is in secret; and your Father who sees in secret will reward you.

19 "Do not lay up for yourselves treasures on earth, where moth and rust consume and where thieves break in and steal, 20 but lay up for yourselves treasures in heaven, where neither moth nor rust consumes and where thieves do not break in and steal. 21 For where your treasure is, there will your heart be also.

22 "The eye is the lamp of the body. So, if your eye is sound, your whole body will be full of light; 23 but if your eye is not sound, your whole body will be full of darkness. If then the light in you is darkness, how great is the darkness!

24 "No one can serve two masters; for either he will hate the one and love the other, or he will be devoted to the one and despise the other. You cannot serve God and mammon.

25 "Therefore I tell you, do not be anxious about your life, what you shall eat or what you shall drink, nor about your body, what you shall put on. Is not life more than food, and the body more than clothing? 26 Look at the birds of the air: they neither sow nor reap nor gather into barns, and yet your heavenly Father feeds them. Are you not of more value than they? 27 And which of you by being anxious

can add one cubit to his span of life? [28] And why are you anxious about clothing? Consider the lilies of the field, how they grow; they neither toil nor spin; [29] yet I tell you, even Solomon in all his glory was not arrayed like one of these. [30] But if God so clothes the grass of the field, which today is alive and tomorrow is thrown into the oven, will he not much more clothe you, O men of little faith? [31] Therefore do not be anxious, saying, `What shall we eat?' or `What shall we drink?' or `What shall we wear?' [32] For the Gentiles seek all these things; and your heavenly Father knows that you need them all. [33] But seek first his kingdom and his righteousness, and all these things shall be yours as well.

[34] "Therefore do not be anxious about tomorrow, for tomorrow will be anxious for itself. Let the day's own trouble be sufficient for the day.

Matt. 7

[1] "Judge not, that you be not judged. [2] For with the judgment you pronounce you will be judged, and the measure you give will be the measure you get. [3] Why do you see the speck that is in your brother's eye, but do not notice the log that is in your own eye? [4] Or how can you say to your brother, `Let me take the speck out of your eye,' when there is the log in your own eye? [5] You hypocrite, first take the log out of your own eye, and then you will see clearly to take the speck out of your brother's eye.

[6] "Do not give dogs what is holy; and do not throw your pearls before swine, lest they trample them under foot and turn to attack you.

[7] "Ask, and it will be given you; seek, and you will find; knock, and it will be opened to you. [8] For every one who asks receives, and he who seeks finds, and to him who knocks it will be opened. [9] Or what man of you, if his son asks him for bread, will give him a stone? [10] Or if he asks for a fish, will give him a serpent? [11] If you then, who are

evil, know how to give good gifts to your children, how much more will your Father who is in heaven give good things to those who ask him! [12] So whatever you wish that men would do to you, do so to them; for this is the law and the prophets.

[13] "Enter by the narrow gate; for the gate is wide and the way is easy, that leads to destruction, and those who enter by it are many. [14] For the gate is narrow and the way is hard, that leads to life, and those who find it are few.

[15] "Beware of false prophets, who come to you in sheep's clothing but inwardly are ravenous wolves. [16] You will know them by their fruits. Are grapes gathered from thorns, or figs from thistles? [17] So, every sound tree bears good fruit, but the bad tree bears evil fruit. [18] A sound tree cannot bear evil fruit, nor can a bad tree bear good fruit. [19] Every tree that does not bear good fruit is cut down and thrown into the fire. [20] Thus you will know them by their fruits.

[21] "Not every one who says to me, `Lord, Lord,' shall enter the kingdom of heaven, but he who does the will of my Father who is in heaven. [22] On that day many will say to me, `Lord, Lord, did we not prophesy in your name, and cast out demons in your name, and do many mighty works in your name?' [23] And then will I declare to them, `I never knew you; depart from me, you evildoers.'

[24] "Every one then who hears these words of mine and does them will be like a wise man who built his house upon the rock; [25] and the rain fell, and the floods came, and the winds blew and beat upon that house, but it did not fall, because it had been founded on the rock. [26] And every one who hears these words of mine and does not do them will be like a foolish man who built his house upon the sand; [27] and the rain fell, and the floods came, and the winds blew and beat against that house, and it fell; and great was the fall of it."

[28] And when Jesus finished these sayings, the crowds were astonished at his teaching, [29] for he taught them as one who had authority, and not as their scribes.

NICCOLÒ MACHIAVELLI

1469-1527

The Prince

1513

Niccolò Machiavelli was born in 1469 in Florence, Italy. He was an active politician and Italian diplomat in the city-state of Florence. He wrote *Principe* (*The Prince*) in 1513 to secure favor with the ruling Medici family. *The Prince* is a pragmatic guide on the use of raw political power by any means. Machiavelli maintains that only success and glory matter, whatever the form of government.

Machiavelli's works have had a widespread and lasting effect in the realms of ethics, psychology, and politics in particular. What does it mean to be called a Machiavellian? Machiavelli (1950) also challenges the reader to think about leadership and the degree to which it can be taught: "The leader should think how to avoid those things that make him hateful and contemptible . . . What makes him contemptible is to be held variable, light, effeminate, pusillanimous, irresolute, from which a prince should guard himself from a shoal. He should contrive that greatness, spiritedness, gravity, and strength are recognized in his actions, and he should insist that his judgments in the private converse of his subjects be irrevocable. And he should maintain such an opinion of himself that no one thinks either of deceiving him or of getting around him" (pp. 66-67).

Sources:

Machiavelli, N. (1950). *The prince and the discourses.* New York: The Modern Library. Random House. (Original work written 1513.)

Niccolo Machiavelli. *Stanford Encyclopedia of Philosophy.* Retrieved from http://plato.stanford.edu/entries/machiavelli

Selection from:

Machiavelli, N. (1950). *The prince and the discourses.* (pp. 60-63, 126). New York: The Modern Library. Random House. (Original work written 1513.)

CHAPTER XVII
Of Cruelty and Clemency, And Whether It Is Better To Be Loved Than Feared

Proceeding to the other qualities mentioned above, I say that every prince ought to desire to be considered merciful and not cruel. He must take care not to misuse this mercifulness. Cesare Borgia was considered cruel, but his cruelty had brought order to the Romagna, united it, and reduced it to peace and fealty. If this is considered well, it will be seen that he was much more merciful than the Florentine people, who, to avoid the name of cruelty, allowed Pistoia to be destroyed. A prince, therefore, must not mind incurring the charge of cruelty for the purpose of keeping his subjects united and faithful; for, with a very few examples, he will be more merciful than those who, from excess of tenderness, allow disorders to arise, from whence spring bloodshed and rapine; for these as a rule injure the whole community, while the executions carried out by the prince injure only individuals. And of all princes, it is impossible for a new prince to escape the imputation of cruelty, new states being always full of dangers. Wherefore Virgil through the mouth of Dido, says:

Res dura, et regni novitas me talia cogunt
Moliri, et late fines custode tueri.[1]

Nevertheless he must be cautious in believing and acting, and must be afraid of his own shadow, and must proceed in a temperate manner with prudence and humanity, so that too much confidence may not render him incautious, and too much diffidence does not render him intolerant.

From this arises the question whether it is better to be loved more than feared, or feared than loved. The reply is, that one ought to be both feared and loved, but, as it is difficult for the two to go together, it is much safer to be feared than loved, if one of the two has to be wanting. For it may be said of men in general that they are ungrateful, voluble, dissemblers, anxious to avoid danger, covetous of gain; as long as you benefit them, they are entirely yours; they offer you their blood, their goods, their life, and their children, as I have before said, when the necessity is remote; but when it approaches they revolt. And that prince who has relied solely on their words, without making other preparations, is ruined; for the friendship which is gained by purchase and not through grandeur and nobility of spirit is bought but not secured, and at a pinch is not to be expended in your service. And men have less scruple in offending one who makes himself loved than one who makes himself feared; for love is held by a chain of obligation which, men being selfish, is broken whenever it serves their purpose; but fear is maintained by a dread of punishment which never fails.

---

[1]   A difficult situation and the newness of rule compel me to undertake such things and to guard the borders widely. [Dr. E. Tiner, Trans.]

Still, a prince should make himself feared in such a way that if he does not gain love, he at any rate avoids hatred; for fear and the absence of hatred may well go together, and will be always attained by one who abstains from interfering with the property of his citizens and subjects or with their women. And when he is obliged to take the life of any one, let him do so when there is a proper justification and manifest reason for it; but above all he must abstain from taking the property of others, for men forget more easily the death of their father than the loss of their patrimony. Then also pretexts for seizing property are never wanting, and one who begins to live by rapine will always find some reason for taking the goods of others, whereas causes for taking life are rarer and more fleeting.

But when the prince is with his army and has a large number of soldiers under his control, then it is extremely necessary that he should not mind being thought cruel; for without this reputation he could not keep an army united or disposed to any duty. Among the noteworthy actions of Hannibal is numbered this, that although he had an enormous army, composed of men of all nations and fighting in foreign countries, there never arose any dissension either among them or against the prince, either in good fortune or in bad. This could not be due to anything but his inhuman cruelty, which together with his infinite other virtues, made him always venerated and terrible in the sight of his soldiers, and without it his other virtues would not have sufficed to produce that effect. Thoughtless writers admire on the one hand his actions, and on the other blame the principal cause of them.

And that it is true that his other virtues would not have sufficed may be seen from the case of Scipio (famous not only in regard to his own times, but all times of which memory remains), whose armies rebelled against him in Spain, which arose from nothing but his excessive kindness, which allowed more licence to the soldiers than was consonant with military discipline. He was reproached with this in the senate by Fabius Maximus, who called him a corrupter of the Roman militia.

Locri having been destroyed by one of Scipio's officers was not revenged by him, nor was the insolence of that officer punished, simply by reason of his easy nature; so much so, that some one wishing to excuse him in the senate, said that there were many men who knew rather how not to err, than how to correct the errors of others. This disposition would in time have tarnished that fame and glory of Scipio had he persevered in it under the empire, but living under the rule of the senate this harmful quality was not only concealed but became a glory to him.

I conclude, therefore, with regard to being feared and loved, that men love at their own free will, but fear at the will of the prince, and that a wise prince must rely on what is in his power and not on what is in the power of others, and he must only contrive to avoid incurring hatred, as has been explained.

Chapter XLII
HOW EASILY MEN MAY BE CORRUPTED

In connection with this matter of the Decemvirate, we should notice also how easily men are corrupted and become wicked, although originally good and well educated. This may be observed in those young nobles whom Appius had chosen for his followers, and who, for the small advantages they derived from it, became supporters of his tyranny; also in Quintus Fabius, one of the second Decemvirate, who, having been one of the best of men, but blinded by a little ambition and seduced by the villany of Appius, changed his good habits into the worst, and became like Appius himself. All this, if carefully studied by the legislators of republics and monarchies, will make them more prompt in restraining the passions of men, and depriving them of all hopes of being able to do wrong with impunity.

BOWEN H. MCCOY

1925-

The Parable of the Sadhu

1983

Bowen H. McCoy has taught graduate students in a number of business schools, such as UCLA, USC, Notre Dame, and Stanford. He graduated from Stanford University with a B.S. in Economics and from Harvard Business School with an M.B.A. He has been a real estate and business counselor with McCoy Associates, Inc. since 1990. The following reading provides a parable of an Indian holy man (sadhu) who was discovered almost dead near a high Himalayan mountain pass. What would the average person have done in the circumstances developed below? Why? How could this parable relate to the ethical consciousness of a leader?

Source:

McCoy, B. H. (1983, September-October). The parable of the sadhu. *Harvard Business Review,* 103-108.

Selection from:

McCoy, B. H. (1983, September-October). The parable of the sadhu. *Harvard Business Review,* 103-108.

After encountering a dying pilgrim on a climbing trip in the Himalayas, a businessman ponders the differences between individual and corporate ethics.

It was early in the morning before the sun rose, which gave them time to climb the treacherous slope to the pass at 18,000 feet before the ice steps melted. They were also concerned about their stamina and altitude sickness and felt the need to press on. Into this chance collection of climbers on that Himalayan slope an ethical dilemma arose in the guise of an unconscious, almost naked sadhu, an Indian holy man. Each climber gave the sadhu help but none made sure he would be safe. Should somebody have stopped to help the sadhu to safety? Would it have done any good? Was the group responsible? Since leaving the sadhu on the mountain slope, the author, who was one of the climbers, has pondered these issues. He sees many parallels for business people as they face ethical decisions at work. Mr. McCoy is a managing director of Morgan Stanley & Co., Inc., and president of Morgan Stanley Realty Inc. He is also an ordained ruling elder of the United Presbyterian Church.

Last year, as the first participant in the new six-month sabbatical program that Morgan Stanley has adopted, I enjoyed a rare opportunity to collect my thoughts as well as do some traveling. I spent the first three months in Nepal, walking 600 miles through 200 villages in the Himalayas and climbing some 120,000 vertical feet. On the trip my sole Western companion was an anthropologist who shed light on the cultural patterns of the villages we passed through.

During the Nepal hike, something occurred that has had a powerful impact on my thinking about corporate ethics. Although some might argue that the experience has no relevance to business, it was a situation in which a basic ethical dilemma suddenly intruded into the lives of a group of individuals. How the group responded I think holds a lesson for all organizations no matter how defined.

The sadhu

The Nepal experience was more rugged and adventuresome than I had anticipated. Most commercial treks last two or three weeks and cover a quarter of the distance we traveled.

My friend Stephen, the anthropologist, and I were halfway through the 60-day Himalayan part of the trip when we reached the high point, an 18,000-foot pass over a crest that we'd have to traverse to reach to the village of Muklinath, an ancient holy place for pilgrims.

Six years earlier I had suffered pulmonary edema, an acute form of altitude sickness, at 16,500 feet in the vicinity of Everest base camp, so we were understandably concerned about what would happen at 18,000 feet. Moreover, the Himalayas were having their wettest spring in 20 years; hip-deep powder and ice had already driven us off one ridge. If we failed to cross the pass, I feared that the last half of our "once in a lifetime" trip would be ruined.

The night before we would try the pass, we camped at a hut at 14,500 feet. In the photos taken at that camp, my face appears wan. The last village we'd passed through was a sturdy two-day walk below us, and I was tired.

During the late afternoon, four backpackers from New Zealand joined us, and we spent most of the night awake, anticipating the climb. Below we could see the fires of two other parties, which turned out to be two Swiss couples and a Japanese hiking club.

To get over the steep part of the climb before the sun melted the steps cut in the ice, we departed at 3:30 A.M. The New Zealanders left first, followed by Stephen and myself, our porters and Sherpas, and then the Swiss. The Japanese lingered in their camp. The sky was clear, and we were confident that no spring storm would erupt that day to close the pass.

At 15,500 feet, it looked to me as if Stephen were shuffling and staggering a bit, which are symptoms of altitude sickness.

(The initial stage of altitude sickness brings a headache and nausea. As the condition worsens, a climber may encounter difficult breathing, disorientation, aphasia, and paralysis.) I felt strong, my adrenaline was flowing, but I was very concerned about my ultimate ability to get across. A couple of our porters were also suffering from the height, and Pasang, our Sherpa sirdar (leader), was worried.

Just after daybreak, while we rested at 15,500 feet, one of the New Zealanders, who had gone ahead, came staggering down toward us with a body slung across his shoulders. He dumped the almost naked, barefoot body of an Indian holy man—a sadhu—at my feet. He had found the pilgrim lying on the ice, shivering and suffering from hypothermia. I cradled the sadhu's head and laid him out on the rocks. The New Zealander was angry. He wanted to get across the pass before the bright sun melted the snow. He said, "Look, I've done what I can. You have porters and Sherpa guides. You care for him. We're going on!" He turned and went back up the mountain to join his friends.

I took a carotid pulse and found that the sadhu was still alive. We figured he had probably visited the holy shrines at Muklinath and was on his way home. It was fruitless to question why he had chosen this desperately high route instead of the safe, heavily traveled caravan route through the Kali Gandaki gorge. Or why he was almost naked and with no shoes, or how long he had been lying in the pass. The answers weren't going to solve our problem.

Stephen and the four Swiss began stripping off outer clothing and opening their packs. The sadhu was soon clothed from head to foot. He was not able to walk, but he was very much alive. I looked down the mountain and spotted below the Japanese climbers marching up with a horse.

Without a great deal of thought, I told Stephen and Pasang that I was concerned about withstanding the heights to come and wanted to get over the pass. I took off after several of our porters who had gone ahead.

On the steep part of the ascent where, if the ice steps had given way, I would have slid down about 3,000 feet, I felt vertigo. I stopped for a breather, allowing the Swiss to catch up with me. I inquired about the sadhu and Stephen. They said that the sadhu was fine and that Stephen was just behind. I set off again for the summit.

Stephen arrived at the summit an hour after I did. Still exhilarated by victory I ran down the snow slope to congratulate him. He was suffering from altitude sickness, walking 15 steps, then stopping, walking 15 steps, then stopping. Pasang accompanied him all the way up. When I reached them, Stephen glared at me and said: "How do you feel about contributing to the death of a fellow man?"

I did not fully comprehend what he meant.

"Is the sadhu dead?" I inquired.

"No," replied Stephen, "but he surely will be!"

After I had gone, and the Swiss had departed not long after, Stephen had remained with the sadhu. When the Japanese had arrived, Stephen had asked to use their horse to transport the sadhu down to the hut. They had refused. He had then asked Pasang to have a group of our porters carry the sadhu. Pasang had resisted the idea, saying that the porters would have to exert all their energy to get themselves over the pass. He had thought they could not carry a man down 1,000 feet to the hut, reclimb the slope, and get across safely before the snow melted. Pasang had pressed Stephen not to delay any longer.

The Sherpas had carried the sadhu down to a rock in the sun at about 15,000 feet and had pointed out the hut another 500 feet below. The Japanese had given him food and drink. When they had last seen him he was listlessly throwing rocks at the Japanese party's dog, which had frightened him.

We do not know if the sadhu lived or died.

For many of the following days and evenings Stephen and I discussed and debated our behavior toward the sadhu. Stephen is a committed Quaker with deep moral vision. He said, "I feel that what happened with the sadhu is a good example of the breakdown between the individual ethic and the corporate ethic. No one person was willing to assume ultimate responsibility for the sadhu. Each was willing to do his bit just so long as it was not too inconvenient. When it got to be a bother, everyone just passed the buck to someone else and took off. Jesus was relevant to a more individualistic stage of society, but how do we interpret his teaching today in a world filled with large, impersonal organizations and groups?"

I defended the larger group, saying, "Look, we all cared. We all stopped and gave aid and comfort. Everyone did his bit. The New Zealander carried him down below the snow line. I took his pulse and suggested we treat him for hypothermia. You and the Swiss gave him clothing and got him warmed up. The Japanese gave him food and water. The Sherpas carried him down to the sun and pointed out the easy trail toward the hut. He was well enough to throw rocks at a dog. What more could we do?"

"You have just described the typical affluent Westerner's response to a problem. Throwing money—in this case food and sweaters—at it, but not solving the fundamentals!" Stephen retorted.

"What would satisfy you?" I said. "Here we are, a group of New Zealanders, Swiss, Americans, and Japanese who have never met before and who are at the apex of one of the most powerful experiences of our lives. Some years the pass is so bad no one gets over it. What right does an almost naked pilgrim who chooses the wrong trail have to disrupt our lives? Even the Sherpas had no interest in risking the trip to help him beyond a certain point."

Stephen calmly rebutted, "I wonder what the Sherpas would have done if the sadhu had been a well-dressed Nepali, or what the Japanese would have done if the sadhu had been a well-dressed Asian, or what you would have done, Buzz, if the sadhu had been a well-dressed Western woman?"

"Where, in your opinion," I asked instead, "is the limit of our responsibility in a situation like this? We had our own well-being to worry about. Our Sherpa guides were unwilling to jeopardize us or the porters for the sadhu. No one else on the mountain was willing to commit himself beyond certain self-imposed limits."

Stephen said, "As individual Christians or people with a Western ethical tradition, we can fulfill our obligations in such a situation only if (1) the sadhu dies in our care, (2) the sadhu demonstrates to us that he could undertake the two-day walk down to the village, or (3) we carry the sadhu for two days down to the village and convince someone there to care for him."

"Leaving the sadhu in the sun with food and clothing, while he demonstrated hand-eye coordination by throwing a rock at a dog, comes close to fulfilling items one and two," I answered. "And it wouldn't have made sense to take him to the village where the people appeared to be far less caring than the Sherpas, so the third condition is impractical. Are you really saying that, no matter what the implications, we should, at the drop of a hat, have changed our entire plan?"

The individual vs. the group ethic

Despite my arguments, I felt and continue to feel guilt about the sadhu. I had literally walked through a classic moral dilemma without fully thinking through the consequences. My excuses for my actions include a high adrenaline flow, a super-ordinate goal, and a once-in-a-lifetime opportunity—factors in the usual corporate situation, especially when one is under stress.

Real moral dilemmas are ambiguous, and many of us hike right through them, unaware that they exist. When, usually after the fact, someone makes an issue of them, we tend to resent his or her bringing it up. Often, when the full import of what we have done (or not done) falls on us, we dig into a defensive position from which it is very difficult to emerge. In rare circumstances we may contemplate what we have done from inside a prison.

Had we mountaineers been free of physical and mental stress caused by the effort and the high altitude, we might have treated the sadhu differently. Yet isn't stress the real test of personal and corporate values? The instant decisions executives make under pressure reveal the most about personal and corporate character.

Among the many questions that occur to me when pondering my experience are: What are the practical limits of moral imagination and vision? Is there a collective or institutional ethic beyond the ethics of the individual? At what level of effort or commitment can one discharge one's ethical responsibilities?

Not every ethical dilemma has a right solution. Reasonable people often disagree; otherwise there would be no dilemma. In a business context, however, it is essential that managers agree on a process for dealing with dilemmas.

The sadhu experience offers an interesting parallel to business situations. An immediate response was mandatory. Failure to act was a decision in itself. Up on the mountain we could not resign and submit our resumes to a headhunter. In contrast to philosophy, business involves action and implementation—getting things done. Managers must come up with answers to problems based on what they see and what they allow to influence their decision-making processes. On the mountain, none of us but Stephen realized the true dimensions of the situation we were facing.

One of our problems was that as a group we had no process for developing a consensus. We had no sense of purpose or plan. The difficulties of dealing with the sadhu were so complex that no one person could handle it. Because it did not have a set of preconditions that could guide its action to an acceptable resolution, the group reacted instinctively as individuals. The cross-cultural nature of the group added a further layer of complexity. We had no leader with whom we could all identify and in whose purpose we believed. Only Stephen was willing to take charge, but he could not gain adequate support to care for the sadhu.

Some organizations do have a value system that transcends the personal values of the managers. Such values, which go beyond profitability, are usually revealed when the organization is under stress. People throughout the organization generally accept its values, which, because they are not presented as a rigid list of commandments, may be somewhat ambiguous. The stories people tell, rather than printed materials, transmit these conceptions of what is proper behavior.

For 20 years I have been exposed at senior levels to a variety of corporations and organizations. It is amazing how quickly an outsider can sense the tone and style of an organization and the degree of tolerated openness and freedom to challenge management.

Organizations that do not have a heritage of mutually accepted, shared values tend to become unhinged during stress, with each individual bailing out for himself. In the great takeover battles we have witnessed during past years, companies that had strong cultures drew the wagons around them and fought it out, while other companies saw executives supported by their golden parachutes, bail out of the struggles.

Because corporations and their members are interdependent, for the corporation to be strong the members need to share a preconceived notion of what is correct behavior, a "business ethic," and think of it as a positive force, not a constraint.

As an investment banker I am continually warned by well-meaning lawyers, clients, and associates to be wary of conflicts of interest. Yet if I were to run away from every difficult situation, I wouldn't be an effective investment banker. I have to feel my way through conflicts. An effective manager can't run from risk either; he or she has to confront and deal with risk. To feel "safe" in doing this, managers need the guidelines of an agreed-on process and set of values within the organization.

After my three months in Nepal, I spent three months as an executive-in-residence at both Stanford Business School and the Center for Ethics and Social Policy at the Graduate Theological Union at Berkeley. These six months away from my job gave me time to assimilate 20 years of business experience. My thoughts turned often to the meaning of the leadership role in any large organization. Students at the seminary thought of themselves as antibusiness. But when I questioned them they agreed that they distrusted all large organizations, including the church. They perceived all large organizations as impersonal and opposed to individual values and needs. Yet we all know of organizations where peoples' values and beliefs are respected and their expressions encouraged. What makes the difference? Can we identify the difference and, as a result, manage more effectively?

The word "ethics" turns off many and confuses more. Yet the notions of shared values and an agreed-on process for dealing with adversity and change—what many people mean when they talk about corporate culture—seem to be at the heart of the ethical issue. People who are in touch with their own core beliefs and the beliefs of others and are sustained by them can be more comfortable living on the cutting edge. At times, taking a tough line or a decisive stand in a muddle of ambiguity is the only ethical thing to do. If a manager is indecisive and spends time trying to figure out the "good" thing to do, the enterprise may be lost.

Business ethics, then, has to do with the authenticity and integrity of the enterprise. To be ethical is to follow the business as well as the cultural goals of the corporation, its owners, its employees, and its customers. Those who cannot serve the corporate vision are not authentic business people and, therefore, are not ethical in the business sense.

At this stage of my own business experience I have a strong interest in organizational behavior. Sociologists are keenly studying what they call corporate stories, legends, and heroes as a way organizations have of transmitting the value system.

Corporations such as Arco have even hired consultants to perform an audit of their corporate culture. In a company, the leader is the person who understands, interprets, and manages the corporate value system. Effective managers are then action-oriented people who resolve conflict, are tolerant of ambiguity, stress, and change, and have a strong sense of purpose for themselves and their organizations.

If all this is true, I wonder about the role of the professional manager who moves from company to company. How can he or she quickly absorb the values and culture of different organizations? Or is there, indeed, an art of management that is totally transportable? Assuming such fungible managers do exist, is it proper for them to manipulate the values of others?

What would have happened had Stephen and I carried the sadhu for two days back to the village and become involved with the villagers in his care? In four trips to Nepal my most interesting experiences occurred in 1975 when I lived in a Sherpa home in the Khumbu for five days recovering from altitude sickness. The high point of Stephen's trip was an invitation to participate in a family funeral ceremony in Manang. Neither experience had to do with climbing the high passes of the Himalayas. Why were we so reluctant to try the lower path, the ambiguous trail? Perhaps because we did not have a leader who could reveal the greater purpose of the trip to us.

Why didn't Stephen with his moral vision opt to take the sadhu under his personal care? The answer is because, in part, Stephen was hard-stressed physically himself, and because, in part, without some support system that involved our involuntary and episodic community on the mountain, it was beyond his individual capacity to do so.

I see the current interest in corporate culture and corporate value systems as a positive response to Stephen's pessimism about the decline of the role of the individual in large organizations. Individuals who operate from a thoughtful set of personal values provide the foundation for a corporate culture. A corporate tradition that encourages freedom of inquiry, supports personal values, and reinforces a focused sense of direction can fulfill the need for individuality along with the prosperity and success of the group. Without such corporate support, the individual is lost.

That is the lesson of the sadhu. In a complex corporate situation, the individual requires and deserves the support of the group. If people cannot find such support from their organization, they don't know how to act. If such support is forthcoming, a person has a stake in the success of the group, and can add much to the process of establishing and maintaining a corporate culture. It is management's challenge to be sensitive to individual needs, to shape them, and to direct and focus them for the benefit of the group as a whole.

For each of us the sadhu lives. Should we stop what we are doing and comfort him; or should we keep trudging up toward the high pass? Should I pause to help the derelict I pass on the street each night as I walk by the Yale Club en route to Grand Central Station? Am I his brother? What is the nature of our responsibility if we consider ourselves to be ethical persons? Perhaps it is to change the values of the group so that it can, with all its resources, take the other road.

ROBERT K. GREENLEAF

1904-1990

Servant Leadership:
A Journey into the Nature of Legitimate Power and Greatness

1977

Robert K. Greenleaf was born in Terre Haute, Indiana. He has been a philosopher and trusted consultant to key leaders in business, education, philanthropy, and religion. Greenleaf's work has had widespread influence in areas such as research in the field of leadership, the philosophies of corporations, approaches to trusteeship, and service learning programs. The excerpt below challenges leaders to rethink their identity from a lofty and powerful position to a humble and helpful one. Greenleaf challenges his readers to consider leadership opportunities from both exciting and discouraging points of view. Does Greenleaf make the leadership role look more or less appealing?

Selection from:

Greenleaf, R. K. (1977). *Servant leadership: A journey into the nature of legitimate power and greatness.* (pp. 7-14, 40-48). New York: Paulist Press.

I
The Servant as Leader

Servant and leader—can these two roles be fused in one real person, in all levels of status or calling? If so, can that person live and be productive in the real world of the present? My sense of the present leads me to say yes to both questions. This chapter is an attempt to explain why and to suggest how.

The idea of *The Servant as Leader* came out of reading Hermann Hesse's *Journey to the East.* In this story we see a band of men on a mythical journey, probably also Hesse's own journey. The central figure of the story is Leo who accompanies the party as the *servant* who does their menial chores, but who also sustains them with his spirit and his song. He is a person of extraordinary presence. All goes well until Leo disappears. Then the group falls into disarray and the journey is abandoned. They cannot make it without the servant Leo. The narrator, one of the party, after some years of wandering finds Leo and is taken into the Order that had sponsored the journey. There he discovers that Leo, whom he had known first as *servant,* was in fact the titular head of the Order, its guiding spirit, a great and noble *leader.*

One can muse on what Hesse was trying to say when he wrote this story. We know that most of his fiction was autobiographical, that he led a tortured life, and that *Journey to the East* suggests a turn toward the serenity he achieved in his old age. There has been much speculation by critics on Hesse's life and work, some of it centering on this story which they find the most puzzling. But to me, this story clearly says that *the great leader is seen as servant first,* and that simple fact is the key to his greatness. Leo was actually the leader all of the time, but he was servant first because that was what he was, *deep down inside.* Leadership was bestowed upon a man who was by nature a servant. It was something given, or assumed, that could be taken away. His servant nature was the real man, not bestowed, not assumed, and not to be taken away. He was servant first.

I mention Hesse and *Journey to the East* for two reasons. First, I want to acknowledge the source of the idea of *The Servant as Leader*. Then I want to use this reference as an introduction to a brief discussion of prophecy.

Fifteen years ago when I first read about Leo, if I had been listening to contemporary prophecy as intently as I do now, the first draft of this piece might have been written then. As it was, the idea lay dormant for eleven years until, four years ago, I concluded that we in this country were in a leadership crisis and that I should do what I could about it. I became painfully aware of how dull my sense of contemporary prophecy had been. And I have reflected much on why we do not hear and heed the prophetic voices in our midst (not a new question in our times, nor more critical than heretofore).

I now embrace the theory of prophecy which holds that prophetic voices of great clarity, and with a quality of insight equal to that of any age, are speaking cogently all of the time. Men and women of a stature equal to the greatest of the past are with us now addressing the problems of the day and pointing to a better way and to a personeity better able to live fully and serenely in these times.

The variable that marks some periods as barren and some as rich in prophetic vision is in the interest, the level of seeking, the responsiveness of the hearers. The variable is not in the presence or absence or the relative quality and force of the prophetic voices. Prophets grow in stature as people respond to their message. If their early attempts are ignored or spurned, their talent may wither away.

It is *seekers*, then, who make prophets, and the initiative of any one of us in searching for and responding to the voice of contemporary prophets may mark the turning point in their growth and service. But since we are the product of our own history, we see current prophecy within the context of past wisdom. We listen to as wide a range of contemporary thought as we can attend to. Then we *choose* those we elect to heed as prophets—*both old and new*—and meld their advice with our own leadings. This we test in real-life experiences to establish our own position.

Some who have difficulty with this theory assert that their faith rests on one or more of the prophets of old having given the "word" for all time and that the contemporary ones do not speak to their condition as the older ones do. But if one really believes that the "word" has been given for all time, how can one be a seeker? How can one hear the contemporary voice when one has decided not to live in the present and has turned that voice off?

Neither this hypothesis nor its opposite can be proved. But I submit that the one given here is the more hopeful choice, one that offers a significant role in prophecy to every individual. One cannot interact with and build strength in a dead prophet, but one can do it with a living one. "Faith," Dean Inge has said, "is the choice of the nobler hypothesis."

One does not, of course, ignore the great voices of the past. One does not awaken each morning with the compulsion to reinvent the wheel. But if one is *servant*, either leader or follower, one is always searching, listening, expecting that a better wheel for these times is in the making. It may emerge any day. Any one of us may find it out from personal experience. I am hopeful.

I am hopeful for these times, despite the tension and conflict, because more natural servants are trying to see clearly the world as it is and are listening carefully to prophetic voices that are speaking *now*. They are challenging the pervasive injustice with greater force and they are taking sharper issue with the wide disparity between the quality of society they know is reasonable and possible with available resources, and, on the other hand, the actual performance of the whole range of institutions that exist to serve society.

A fresh critical look is being taken at the issues of power and authority, and people are beginning to learn, however haltingly, to relate to one another in less coercive and more creatively supporting ways. A new moral principle is emerging which holds that the only authority deserving one's allegiance is that which is freely and knowingly granted by the led to the leader in response to, and in proportion to, the clearly evident servant stature of the leader. Those who choose to follow this principle will not casually accept the authority of existing institutions. *Rather, they will freely respond only to individuals who are chosen as leaders because they are proven and trusted as servants.* To the extent that this principle prevails in the future, the only truly viable institutions will be those that are predominantly servant-led.

I am mindful of the long road ahead before these trends, which I see so clearly, become a major society-shaping force. We are not there yet. But I see encouraging movement on the horizon.

What direction will the movement take? Much depends on whether those who stir the ferment will come to grips with the age-old problem of how to live in a human society. I say this because so many, having made their awesome decision for autonomy and independence from tradition, and having taken their firm stand against injustice and hypocrisy, find it hard to convert themselves into *affirmative builders* of a better society. How many of them will seek their personal fulfillment by making the hard choices, and by undertaking the rigorous preparation that building a better society requires? It all depends on what kind of leaders emerge and how they—we—respond to them.

My thesis, that more servants should emerge as leaders, or should follow only servant-leaders, is not a popular one. It is much more comfortable to go with a less demanding point of view about what is expected of one now. There are several undemanding, plausibly-argued alternatives to choose. One, since society seems corrupt, is to seek to avoid the center of it by retreating to an idyllic existence that minimizes involvement with the "system" (with the "system" that makes such withdrawal possible). Then there is the assumption that since the effort to reform existing institutions has not brought instant perfection, the remedy is to destroy them completely so that fresh new perfect ones can grow. Not much thought seems to be given to the problem of where the new seed will come from or who the gardener to tend them will be. The concept of the servant-leader stands in sharp contrast to this kind of thinking.

Yet it is understandable that the easier alternatives would be chosen, especially by young people. By extending education for so many so far into the adult years, the normal participation in society is effectively denied when young people are ready for it. With education that is preponderantly abstract and analytical it is no wonder that there is a preoccupation with criticism and that not much thought is given to "What can *I* do about it?"

Criticism has its place, but as a total preoccupation it is sterile. In a time of crisis, like the leadership crisis we are now in, if too many potential builders are taken in by a complete absorption with dissecting the wrong and by a zeal for instant perfection, then the movement so many of us want to see will be set back. The danger, perhaps, is to hear the analyst too much and the artist too little.

Albert Camus stands apart from other great artists of his time, in my view, and deserves the title of *prophet*, because of his unrelenting demand that each of us confront the exacting terms of our own existence, and, like Sisyphus, *accept our rock and find our happiness in dealing with it*. Camus sums up the relevance of his position to our concern for the servant as leader in the last paragraph of his last published lecture, entitled *Create Dangerously*:

> One may long, as I do, for a gentler flame, a respite, a pause for musing. But perhaps there is no other peace for the artist than what he finds in the heat of combat. "Every wall is a door," Emerson correctly said. Let us not look for the door, and the way out, anywhere but in the wall against which we are living.

Instead, let us seek the respite where it is—in the very thick of battle. For in my opinion, and this is where I shall close, it *is* there. Great ideas, it has been said, come into the world as gently as doves. Perhaps, then, if we listen attentively, we shall hear, amid the uproar of empires and nations, a faint flutter of wings, the gentle stirring of life and hope. Some will say that this hope lies in a nation, others, in a man. I believe rather that it is awakened, revived, nourished by millions of solitary individuals whose deeds and works every day negate frontiers and the crudest implications of history. As a result, there shines forth fleetingly the ever-threatened truth that each and every man, on the foundations of his own sufferings and joys, builds for them all.

One is asked, then, to accept the human condition, its sufferings and its joys, and to work with its imperfections as the foundation upon which the individual will build wholeness through adventurous creative achievement. For the person with creative potential there is no wholeness except in using it. And, as Camus explained, the going is rough and the respite is brief. It is significant that he would title his last university lecture *Create Dangerously*. And, as I ponder the fusing of servant and leader, it seems a dangerous creation: dangerous for the natural servant to become a leader, dangerous for the leader to be servant first, and dangerous for a follower to insist on being led by a servant. There are safer and easier alternatives available to all three. But why take them?

As I respond to the challenge of dealing with this question in the ensuing discourse I am faced with two problems.

First, I did not get the notion of the servant as leader from conscious logic. Rather it came to me as an intuitive insight as I contemplated Leo. And I do not see what is relevant from my own searching and experience in terms of a logical progression from premise to conclusion. Rather I see it as fragments of data to be fed into my internal computer from which intuitive insights come. Serving and leading are still mostly intuition-based concepts in my thinking.

The second problem, and related to the first, is that, just as there may be a real contradiction in the servant as leader, so my perceptual world is full of contradictions. Some examples: I believe in order, and I want creation out of chaos. My good society will have strong individualism amidst community. It will have elitism along with populism. I listen to the old and to the young and find myself baffled and heartened by both. Reason and intuition, each in its own way, both comfort and dismay me. There are many more. Yet, with all of this, I believe that I live with as much serenity as do my contemporaries who venture into controversy as freely as I do but whose natural bent is to tie up the essentials of life in neat bundles of logic and consistency. But I am deeply grateful to the people who are logical and consistent because some of them, out of their natures, render invaluable services for which I am not capable.

My resolution of these two problems is to offer the relevant gleanings of my experience in the form of a series of unconnected little essays, some developed more fully than others, with the suggestion that they be read and pondered on separately within the context of this opening section.

Who Is the Servant-Leader?

The servant-leader *is* servant first—as Leo was portrayed. It begins with the natural feeling that one wants to serve, to serve *first*. Then conscious choice brings one to aspire to lead. That person is sharply different from one who is *leader* first, perhaps because of the need to assuage an unusual power drive or to acquire material possessions. For such it will be a later choice to serve—after leadership is established. The leader-first and the servant-first are two extreme types. Between them there are shadings and blends that are part of the infinite variety of human nature.

The difference manifests itself in the care taken by the servant-first to make sure that other people's highest priority needs are being served. The best test, and difficult to administer, is: Do those served grow as persons? Do they, *while being served*, become healthier, wiser, freer, more autonomous, more likely themselves to become servants? *And*, what is the effect on the least privileged in society; will they benefit, or, at least, not be further deprived?

As one sets out to serve, how can one know that this will be the result? This is part of the human dilemma; one cannot know for sure. One must, after some study and experience, hypothesize—but leave the hypothesis under a shadow of doubt. Then one acts on the hypothesis and examines the result. One continues to study and learn and periodically one re-examines the hypothesis itself.

Finally, one chooses again. Perhaps one chooses the same hypothesis again and again. But it is always a fresh open choice. And it is always an hypothesis under a shadow of doubt. "Faith is the choice of the nobler hypothesis." Not the *noblest*; one never knows what that is. But the *nobler*, the best one can see when the choice is made. Since the test of results of one's actions is usually long delayed, the faith that sustains the choice of the nobler hypothesis is psychological self-insight. This is the most dependable part of the true servant.

The natural servant, the person who is *servant first*, is more likely to persevere and refine a particular hypothesis on what serves another's highest priority needs than is the person who is *leader first* and who later serves out of promptings of conscience or in conformity with normative expectations.

My hope for the future rests in part on my belief that among the legions of deprived and unsophisticated people are many true servants who will lead, and that most of them can learn to discriminate among those who presume to serve them and identify the true servants whom they will follow.

[***]

Trustees

Institutions need two kinds of leaders: those who are inside and carry the active day-to-day roles, and those who stand outside but are intimately concerned, and who, with the benefit of some detachment, oversee the active leaders. These are the *trustees*.

Trustees are what their title implies, persons in whom ultimate trust is placed. Because institutions inevitably harbor conflict, trustees are the court of last resort if an issue arises that cannot be resolved by the active parties. If tangible assets are involved, trustees legally hold them and are responsible to all interested parties for their good use. They have a prime concern for goals and for progress toward goals. They make their influence felt more by knowing and asking questions than by authority, although they usually have authority and can use it if need be. If, as is usual, there are several trustees, their chairman has a special obligation to see that the trustees as a group sustain a common purpose and are influential in helping the institution maintain consistent high-level performance toward its goals. The chairman is not simply the presider over meetings, but also must serve and lead the trustees as a group and act as their major contact with the active inside leadership. Although trustees usually leave the "making of news" to active persons in the enterprise, theirs is an important leadership opportunity.

So conceived, the role of trustees provides a great opportunity for those who would serve and lead. And no one step will more quickly raise the quality of the total society than a radical reconstruction of trustee bodies so that they are predominantly manned by able, dedicated servant-leaders. Two disturbing questions: Is there now enough discerning toughness strategically placed to see that this change takes place, in the event that able, dedicated servant-leaders become available in sufficient numbers to do it? And are enough able people now preparing themselves for these roles so that this change *can* be made in the event that it is possible to make it? (For a fuller discussion of the trustee role, see the following two chapters, "The Institution as Servant" and "Trustees as Servants.")

Power and Authority—
The Strength and the Weakness

In a complex institution-centered society, which ours is likely to be into the indefinite future, there will be large and small concentrations of power. Sometimes it will be a servant's power of persuasion and example. Sometimes it will be coercive power used to dominate and manipulate people. The difference is that, in the former, power is used to create opportunity and alternatives so that individuals may choose and build autonomy. In the latter, individuals are coerced into a predetermined path. Even if it is "good" for them, if they experience nothing else, ultimately their autonomy will be diminished.

Some coercive power is overt and brutal. Some is covert and subtly manipulative. The former is open and acknowledged, the latter is insidious and hard to detect. Most of us are more coerced than we know. We need to be more alert in order to know, and we also need to acknowledge that, in an imperfect world, authority backed up by power is still necessary because we just don't know a better way. We may one day find one. It is worth searching for. Part of our dilemma is that all leadership is, to some extent, manipulative. Those who follow must be strong!

The trouble with coercive power is that it only strengthens resistance. And, if successful, its controlling effect lasts only as long as the force is strong. It is not organic. Only persuasion and the consequent voluntary acceptance are organic.

Since both kinds of power have been around for a long time, an individual will be better off by at some point being close enough to raw coercion to know what it is. One must be close to both the bitterness and goodness of life to be fully human.

Servants, by definition, are fully human. Servant-leaders are functionally superior because they are closer to the ground—they hear things, see things, know things, and their intuitive insight is exceptional. Because of this they are dependable and trusted, they know the meaning of that line from Shakespeare's sonnet: "They that have power to hurt and will do none . . ."

How Does One Know the Servant?

For those who follow—and this is everyone, including those who lead—the really critical question is: Who is this moral individual we would see as leader? Who is the servant? How does one tell a truly giving, enriching servant from the neutral person or the one whose net influence is to take away from or diminish other people?

Rabbi Heschel had just concluded a lecture on the Old Testament prophets in which he had spoken of true prophets and false prophets. A questioner asked him how one tells the difference between the true and the false prophets. The rabbi's answer was succinct and to the point. "There is no *way!*" he said. Then he elaborated, "If there were a *way*, if one had a gauge to slip over the head of the prophet and establish without question that he is or he isn't a true prophet, there would be no human dilemma and life would have no meaning."

So it is with the servant issue. If there were a dependable *way* that would tell us, "These people enrich by their presence, they are neutral, or they take away," life would be without challenge. Yet it is terribly important that one *know*, both about oneself and about others, whether the net effect of one's influence on others enriches, is neutral, or diminishes and depletes.

Since there is no certain way to know this, one must turn to the artists for illumination. Such an illumination is in Hermann Hesse's idealized portrayal of the servant Leo whose servanthood comes through in his leadership. In stark modern terms it can also be found in the brutal reality of the mental hospital where Ken Kesey (in *One Flew Over the Cuckoo's Nest*) gives us Big Nurse —strong, able, dedicated, dominating, authority-ridden, manipulative, exploitative—the net effect of whose influence diminished other people, literally destroyed them. In the story she is pitted in a contest with tough, gutter-bred MacMurphy, a patient, the net effect of whose influence is to build up people and make both patients and the doctor in charge of the ward grow larger as persons, stronger, healthier—an effort that ultimately costs MacMurphy his life. If one will study the two characters, Leo and MacMurphy, one will get a measure of the range of possibilities in the role of servant as leader.

In Here, Not Out There

A king once asked Confucius' advice on what to do about the large number of thieves. Confucius answered, "If you, sir, were not covetous, although you should reward them to do it, they would not steal." This advice places an enormous burden on those who are favored by the rules, and it establishes how old is the notion that the servant views any problem in the world as *in here*, inside oneself, not *out there*. And if a flaw in the world is to be remedied, to the servant the process of change starts *in here*, in the servant, not *out there*. This is a difficult concept for that busybody, modern man.

So it is with joy. Joy is inward, it is generated inside. It is not found outside and brought in. It is for those who accept the world as it is, part good, part bad, and who identify with the good by adding a little island of serenity to it.

Hermann Hesse dramatized it in the powerful leadership exerted by Leo who ostensibly served only in menial ways but who, by the quality of his inner life that was manifest in his presence, lifted men up and made the journey possible. Camus, in his final testament quoted earlier, leaves us with: "Each and every man, on the foundations of his own sufferings and joys, builds for them all."

Who Is the Enemy?

Who is the enemy? Who is holding back more rapid movement to the better society that is reasonable and possible with available resources? Who is responsible for the mediocre performance of so many of our institutions? Who is standing in the way of a larger consensus on the definition of the better society and paths to reaching it?

Not evil people. Not stupid people. Not apathetic people. Not the "system." Not the protesters, the disrupters, the revolutionaries, the reactionaries.

Granting that fewer evil, stupid, or apathetic people or a better "system" might make the job easier, their removal would not change matters, not for long. The better society will come, if it comes, with plenty of evil, stupid, apathetic people around and with an imperfect, ponderous, inertia-charged "system" as the vehicle for change. Liquidate the offending people, radically alter or destroy the system, and in less than a generation they will all be back. It is not in the nature of things that a society can be cleaned up once and for all according to an ideal plan. And even if it were possible, who would want to live in an aseptic world? Evil, stupidity, apathy, the "system" are not the enemy even though society building forces will be contending with them all the time. The healthy society, like the healthy body, is not the one that has taken the most medicine. It is the one in which the internal health building forces are in the best shape.

The real enemy is fuzzy thinking on the part of good, intelligent, vital people, and their failure to lead, and to follow servants as leaders. Too many settle for being critics and experts. There is too much intellectual wheel spinning, too much retreating into "research," too little preparation for and willingness to undertake the hard and high risk tasks of building better institutions in an imperfect world, too little disposition to see "the problem" as residing *in here* and not *out there.*

In short, the enemy is strong natural servants who have the potential to lead but do not lead, or who choose to follow a nonservant. They suffer. Society suffers. And so it may be in the future.

Implications

The future society may be just as mediocre as this one. It may be worse. And no amount of restructuring or changing the system or tearing it down in the hope that something better will grow will change this. There may be a better system than the one we now have. It is hard to know. But, whatever it is, if the people to lead it well are not there, a better system will not produce a better society.

Many people finding their wholeness through many and varied contributions make a good society. Here we are concerned with but one facet: *able servants with potential to lead will lead, and, where appropriate, they will follow only servant-leaders.* Not much else counts if this does not happen.

This brings us to that critical aspect of realism that confronts the servant-leader, that of *order.* There must be some order because we know for certain that the great majority of people will choose some kind of order over chaos even if it is delivered by a brutal non-servant and even if, in the process, they lose much of their freedom. Therefore the servant-leader will beware of pursuing an idealistic path regardless of its impact on order. The big question is: What kind of order? This is the great challenge to the emerging generation of leaders: Can they build better order?

Older people who grew up in a period when values were more settled and the future seemed more secure will be disturbed by much they find today. But one firm note of hope comes through—loud and clear; we are at a turn of history in which people are growing up faster and some extraordinarily able, mature, servant-disposed men and women are emerging in their early and middle twenties. The percentage may be small, and, again, it may be larger than we think. Moreover, it is not an elite; it is all sorts of exceptional people. Most of them could be ready for some large society-shaping responsibility by the time they are thirty *if* they are encouraged to prepare for leadership as soon as their potential as builders is identified, which is possible for many of them by age eighteen or twenty. Preparation to lead need not be at the complete expense of vocational or scholarly preparation, but it must be the *first priority.* And it may take some difficult bending of resources and some unusual initiatives to accomplish all that should be accomplished in these critical years *and* give leadership preparation first priority. But whatever it takes, it must be done. For a while at least, until a better led society is assured, some other important goals should take a subordinate place.

All of this rests on the assumption that the only way to change a society (or just make it go) is to produce people, enough people, who will change it (or make it go). The urgent problems of our day—the disposition to venture into immoral and senseless wars, destruction of the environment, poverty, alienation, discrimination, overpopulation—are here because of human failures, individual failures, one person at a time, one action at a time failures.

If we make it out of all of this (and this is written in the belief that we will make it), the "system" will be whatever works best. The builders will find the useful pieces wherever they are, and invent new ones when needed, all without reference to ideological coloration. "How do we get the right things done?" will be the watchword of the day, every day. And the context of those who bring it off will be: all men and women who are touched by the effort grow taller, and become healthier, stronger, more autonomous, *and* more disposed to serve.

Leo the *servant,* and the exemplar of the *servant-leader,* has one further portent for us. If we may assume that Hermann Hesse is the narrator in *Journey to the East* (not a difficult assumption to make), at the end of the story he establishes his identity. His final confrontation at the close of his initiation into the Order is with a small transparent sculpture two figures joined together. One is Leo, the other is the narrator. The narrator notes that a movement of substance is taking place within the transparent sculpture.

I perceived that my image was in the process of adding to and flowing into Leo's, nourishing and strengthening it. It seemed that, in time . . . only one would remain: Leo. He must grow, I must disappear.

As I stood there and looked and tried to understand what I saw, I recalled a short conversation that I had once had with Leo during the festive days at Bremgarten. We had talked about the creations of poetry being more vivid and real than the poets themselves.

What Hesse may be telling us here is that Leo is the symbolic personification of Hesse's aspiration to serve through his literary creations, creations that are greater than Hesse himself; and that his work, for which he was but the channel, will carry on and serve and lead in a way that he, a twisted and tormented man, could not—except as he created.

Does not Hesse dramatize, in extreme form, the dilemma of us all? Except as we venture to create, we cannot project ourselves beyond ourselves to serve and lead.

To which Camus would add: *Create dangerously!*

M. SCOTT PECK, M.D.

1936-2005

People of the Lie: The Hope for Healing Human Evil

1983

Dr. Scott Peck graduated with a B.A. degree from Harvard College and a M.D. degree from the Case Western Reserve University School of Medicine. He served in the United States Army as head of Psychiatry and resigned with the rank of Lieutenant Colonel. He worked in the private practice of psychiatry in Litchfield County, Connecticut, for a number of years. Peck became a nationally recognized authority on the relationship between religion and science, and on the role of psychology in that relationship. His first and best known book was *The Road Less Traveled* (1978). In *People of the Lie* (1980), Peck asserts that an evil person is one who: a.) projects his or her evils and sins onto others; b.) usually maintains a high level of respectability; c.) lies constantly in order to remain respectable; d.) is consistent in evil-doing, and e.) cannot take the point of view of others. An evil person simply lacks empathy. Peck worked to develop caring communities, and for his lifetime achievements, he received the 1984 Kaleidoscope Award for Peacemaking, the 1994 Temple International Peace Prize, and the 1996 Learning, Faith, and Freedom Medal from Georgetown University.

This reading can serve as a source of insight and healing for those who have been exposed to human evil. How is this knowledge useful to the leader and to followers?

Source:

MacMillan Interactive Communications. (2001). *M. Scott Peck, Author of the Road Less Traveled.* Retrieved from http://www. mscottpeck.com/html/biography.html

Selection from:

Peck, M. S. (1983). Mylai: An examination of group evil. In *People of the lie: The hope for healing human evil.* (pp. 243-250). New York: Simon and Schuster.

HUMAN KILLING

We must remind ourselves in this consideration that America is itself merely a group and not the whole. Specifically, it is one of the many political subgroups of the human race which we call nation states. And, of course, the human race itself is but one of the enormous number of different life forms of the planet. (That we need remind ourselves of this at all is another reflection of our human narcissistic propensity to think only in terms of our own species.)

We must also remind ourselves that evil has to do with killing—that evil is live spelled backward. We have been considering MyLai as an example of group evil because of the particular kind of killing that occurred there. But that brand of killing was only a misstep in the ritualistic dance of death we call war. War is a form of large-scale killing that we humans consider an acceptable instrument of national policy. It is necessary for us now to examine the subject of killing in general and human killing specifically.

All animals kill, and not necessarily just for food or self-defense. Our two well-fed cats, for instance, routinely horrify us by bringing into the house the shattered corpses of chipmunks they have murdered for the joy of the hunt. But there is something unique about human killing. Human killing is not instinctual. One manifestation of the noninstinctual nature of human beings is the extraordinary variability of their behavior. Some are hawks and some are doves. In regard to a form of killing, some love to hunt and others abhor hunting, while still others are indifferent on the matter. Not so with cats. All cats will hunt chipmunks, given the opportunity.

The almost total lack of instincts—elaborate, predetermined, stereotypic behavior patterns—is the most significant aspect of human nature. It is our lack of instincts that is responsible for the extraordinary variability and mutability of our nature and our behavior. What replaces species-wide instincts in human beings is learned individual choice. Each of us is ultimately free to choose how we are going to behave. We are even free to reject what we have been taught and what is normal for our society. We may even reject the few instincts we have, as do those who rationally choose celibacy or submit themselves to death by martyrdom. Free will is the ultimate human reality.

Let us remember what so many theologians have said: Evil is the inevitable concomitant of free will, the price we pay for our unique human power of choice. Since ours is the power to choose, we are free to choose wisely or stupidly, to choose well or badly, to choose for evil or for good. Since we have this enormous—almost incredible—freedom, it is no wonder that we so often abuse it and that human behavior, in comparison to that of the "lower" animals, so often seems to get out of whack. Many animals may kill to protect their territory. But only a human could direct mass killing of his own species so as to protect his "interests" in a far distant land he has never set eyes upon.

So our human killing is a matter of choice. In order to survive, we cannot not kill. But we can choose how, when, where, and what we will kill. The moral complexities of such choices are enormous and often quite paradoxical. A person may become a vegetarian as an ethical choice in order to refrain from even the indirect responsibility for killing, yet to survive, he or she must still bear the responsibility for hacking living plants off at the roots and roasting the corpses thereof in ovens. Should the vegetarian, one wonders, eat eggs (the potentially unborn children of beautiful birds) or drink milk (taken from cows whose calves have been slaughtered for veal)? Then there are such matters as the issue of abortion. Does a woman have the right to bear to full viability an infant whom she neither wants nor has the capacity to care for? But does she have the right to kill that same potentially holy fetus? Is it not strange that many pacifists are advocates of abortion? Or that those who would seek to deprive others of their choice to abort on the grounds that life is sacred are so often those who champion capital punishment? And for that matter, what ethical sense does it make to kill a murderer as an example to convince others that killing is morally wrong?

Complex though the ethics of our choices to kill or not to kill may be, there is clearly one factor that contributes to unnecessary and obviously immoral killing: narcissism. Once again, narcissism. One manifestation of our narcissism is that we are far more likely to kill that which is different from us than that which resembles us. The vegetarian feels guilty killing other animal life forms but not plant life forms. There are specialized vegetarians who will eat fish but not meat; others who will eat chicken but not mammalian flesh. There are fishermen who abhor the idea of hunting and hunters who shoot birds but would shudder at killing a deer with its all-too-human eyes. The same principle applies when humans kill other humans. Those of us who are Caucasians seem to have fewer compunctions about killing blacks or Indians or Orientals than we do in killing our fellow white men. It's easier for a white man to lynch a "nigger" than a "redneck." I also suspect it's probably easier for an Oriental to kill a Caucasian than a fellow Oriental. But I do not know for sure. The matter of the racial aspects of intraspecies killing is yet another one deserving significant scientific investigation.[1]

War today is at least as much a matter of national pride as of racial pride. What we call nationalism is more frequently a malignant national narcissism than it is a healthy satisfaction in the accomplishments of one's culture. In fact, to a large extent it is nationalism that preserves the nation-state system. A century ago, when it required weeks for a message to get from the United States to France, and months to get to China, the nation-state system made sense. In our current age of instant global communication as well as instant holocaust, much of the international political system has become obsolete. It is our national narcissism, however, that clings to our outmoded notions of sovereignty and prevents the development of effective international peacekeeping machinery.

Wittingly or unwittingly, we actually teach our children national narcissism. The linear map of the world that stretches above our countless schoolroom blackboards shows that the United States is more or less at the center of that map. And on the maps of little Russian schoolchildren it is the USSR that is more or less at the center. The results of this kind of teaching can sometimes be ridiculous.

As we were driving along one of the back roads of Okinawa one day a small child ran out directly in front of the car. We screeched to a stop, barely missing him. We trembled with anxiety and horror at the terrible injury we had almost caused. The boy's mother, a young Okinawan woman, standing by the side of the road, looked at us and giggled. Smiling and giggling still, she went out on the road and collected her son.

---

[1] There are subtleties involved in the matter of interracial killing that not only deserve to be investigated but that are also extremely fascinating. One of the group of proposals (rejected *in toto*) made to the Chief of Staff of the Army in relation to the psychological aspects of MyLai was that research should be conducted on interracial and intercultural differences in nonverbal behavior.

We experienced a wave of the most intense fury at her. Here we were, trembling at what we might have done to her child, and she was giggling as if she didn't even care. How could she be so callous? Goddamn Orientals, they don't care about human life, even that of their own children. We'd like to smash her with the car and see how she feels about it!

It was only after we had driven away a few miles down the road that we became calm enough to reflect on the fact that when they are embarrassed or frightened, Okinawans invariably smile and giggle. The woman had been just as frightened as we were, but we had misinterpreted her behavior. One wonders what the nonverbal behavior of the Vietnamese civilians was when they were herded at gunpoint at MyLai. Did they fall down on their knees, weeping and begging in the supplicant posture that we Caucasians would likely take in a similar situation and that might have stirred the troops' hearts to pity? Or did they, perhaps like the Okinawan woman, smile and giggle in terror, thereby possibly infuriating the Americans, who might have felt that they were being laughed at in derision? We do not know. But we need to know such things.

I am reminded of May 1, 1964, when my wife was awarded her citizenship along with two hundred other new citizens at a celebration attended by their families and assorted dignitaries and officials in downtown Honolulu. The festivities began with a parade. Three companies of spit-polished soldiers with rifles gleaming marched around the field and then took their formation behind seven howitzers. The cannon were then used to offer a roaring twenty-one-gun salute to the occasion. At this point the governor of Hawaii stepped to the podium, just in front of the still-smoking howitzers. "Today is referred to as May Day," he began, "but our nation has designated it as Law Day. Here in Hawaii," he quipped, "we might call it Lei Day. Anyway, the point is that here we are celebrating this day with flowers, while in the Communist countries they are having military demonstrations."

No one laughed. It was as if the absurdity—the insanity—went unnoticed: this undoubtedly intelligent, certainly dignified man, with three companies of soldiers standing at attention behind him while the smoke of seven cannon encircled his head, chastising the Russians for the military nature of *their* festivities.

Organized, group, intraspecies mass killing—war—is a uniquely human form of behavior. Because this behavior has characterized essentially all cultures since the dawn of history, many have proposed that humans have an instinct for war—that war behavior is an immutable fact of human nature. It is, I suppose, why the hawks always refer to themselves as realists and to the doves as fuzzy-headed idealists. Idealists are people who believe in the potential of human nature for transformation. But I have already stated that the most essential attribute of human nature is its mutability and freedom from instinct—that it is always within our power to change our nature. So it is actually the idealists who are on the mark and the realists who are off base. Anyone who argues that waging war is something other than a choice ignores both the reality of evil and the evidence of human psychology. To wage war may not be always necessarily evil, but it is always a choice.

It is personally extremely tempting for me to think simplistically about war. I would like to take the Sixth Commandment literally, to believe that "Thou shalt not kill" means just that—at least, Thou shalt not kill other human beings. And it is similarly tempting for me to believe in the utter universality of that greatest of all ethical principles: the end does not justify the means. But thus far I cannot escape the conclusion that in rare previous moments of human history it has been necessary and morally right to kill in order to prevent even greater killing. I am profoundly uncomfortable with this position.

Not all, however, is ambiguity. I do remain sufficiently simplistic to believe that whenever war is waged, some human beings have lost their moorings and that some (more likely many) have succumbed to evil. Whenever there is war, someone is at fault. One side or both are to blame. A wrong choice has been made somewhere.

It is important to bear this in mind, because it is customary these days for both sides in a war to proclaim themselves victims. In days of old, when human beings were not so scrupulous, one tribe would not hesitate to kill another with the frankly avowed motive of conquest. But nowadays there is always the pretense of blamelessness. Even Hitler concocted pretenses for his invasions. It is likely that he and the majority of Germans even believed their own pretense. And so it has been since. Each side believes the other is the aggressor and itself the victim. In the face of this bilateral rhetoric and the complexities of international relations we tend to throw up our hands and think that maybe war really is no one's fault, that no one really is the aggressor, that no one made the wrong choice—that war somehow just happens, like spontaneous combustion.

I denounce this position of ethical hopelessness, this abrogation of our capacity for moral judgment. I can think of nothing that would fill Satan with greater glee or better signify the ultimate success of its conquest of the human race than an attitude on the part of humans that it is impossible to identify evil.

The war in Vietnam did not just happen. It was initiated by the British in 1945.[2] It was sustained by the French until their

---

[2]   Britain, assigned by the terms of the Yalta agreement the task of "disarming and repatriating the Japanese and restoring order" in Southern Indochina at the end of World War II, chose to interpret its task as the reestablishment of the French colonial regime (despite the fact that this had been a Vichy regime, cooperating with the Japanese occupation). British troops found the Japanese already disarmed and a unified Vietnam under the control of the Vietminh. They proceeded to rearm the Japanese and use them to reinforce their own troops in forcefully wresting control of Saigon from Ho Chi Minh's forces. They then by force of arms maintained their occupation of Saigon until masses of troops began arriving from France three months later. Handing Saigon over to the French, they then withdrew. The French Indochina War had begun.

defeat in 1954. Then, with peace in sight, it was reinitiated and sustained by the Americans for the next eighteen years: Although there are many who still debate the issue, it is my judgment—and I am convinced it will be the judgment of history—that America was the aggressor in that war during those years. Ours were the choices that were most morally reprehensible. We were the villains.

But how could we—we Americans—be villains? The Germans and the Japanese in 1941, certainly. The Russians, yes. But the Americans? Surely we are not a villainous people. If we were villains, we must have been unwitting ones. This I concede; we were largely unwitting. But how does it come about that a person or a group or an entire nation is an unwitting villain? This is the crucial question. I have already addressed myself to this question at various levels. Let me return to it and discuss once again the issues of narcissism and laziness at this broadest level.

The term "unwitting villain" is particularly appropriate because our villainy lay in our unwittingness. We became villains precisely because we did not have our wits about us. The word "wit" in this regard refers to knowledge. We were villains out of ignorance. Just as what went on at MyLai was covered up for a year primarily because the troops of Task Force Barker did not know they had done something radically wrong, so America waged the war because it did not know that what it was doing was villainous.

I used to ask the troops on their way to battle in Vietnam what they knew about the war and its relationship to Vietnamese history. The enlisted men knew nothing. Ninety percent of the junior officers knew nothing. What little the senior officers and few junior officers did know was generally solely what they had been taught in the highly biased programs of their military schools. It was astounding. At least 95 percent of the men going off to risk their very lives did not even have the slightest knowledge of what the war was about. I also talked to Department of Defense civilians who directed the war and discovered a similar atrocious ignorance of Vietnamese history. The fact of the matter is that as a nation we did not even know why we were waging the war.

How could this have been? How could a whole people have gone to war not knowing why? The answer is simple. As a people we were too lazy to learn and too arrogant to think we needed to learn. We felt that whatever way we happened to perceive things was the right way without any further study. And that whatever we did was the right thing to do without reflection. We were so wrong because we never seriously considered that we might not be right. With our laziness and narcissism feeding each other, we marched off to impose our will on the Vietnamese people by bloodshed with practically no idea of what was involved. Only when we—the mightiest nation on earth—consistently suffered defeat at the hands of the Vietnamese did we in significant numbers begin to take the trouble to learn what we had done.

So it is that our "Christian" nation became a nation of villains. So it has been with other nations in the, past, and so it will be with other nations—including our own once again—in the future. As a nation and as a race, we shall not be immune to war until such a time as we have made much further progress toward eradicating from our human nature the twin progenitors of evil: laziness and narcissism.

CRAIG E. JOHNSON

1952-

Meeting the Ethical Challenges of Leadership

2001

Craig E. Johnson teaches leadership studies in the School of Management and directs the Doctor of Management program at George Fox University. He formerly headed the university's Communication Arts department for many years. His teaching responsibilities now include graduate and undergraduate courses in leadership, management, ethics, and communication. Johnson is the author of *Meeting the Ethical Challenges of Leadership: Casting Light or Shadow* and the co-author, with Michael Z. Hackman, of *Leadership: A Communication Perspective*. In the work excerpted here, Johnson lays the framework for a global ethic that can permit people the world around to speak on common ground about ethical matters.

Sources:

Sage Publications. (2009). *Craig E. Johnson*. Retrieved from http://www.sagepub.com/authorDetails.nav?contribId=530219

George Fox University, School of Business. (2009). *Craig Johnson*. Retrieved from http://www.georgefox.edu/som/faculty/johnsonc.html

Selection from:

Johnson, C. E. (2001). Standing on moral common ground. In *Meeting the ethical challenges of leadership: Casting light or shadow.* (pp. 232-237). Thousand Oaks: Sage.

Standing on Moral Common Ground

Confronted with a wide range of ethical values and standards, a number of philosophers, business leaders, anthropologists, and others opt for ethical relativism. In ethical relativism, there are no universal moral codes or standards. Each group or society is unique. Therefore, members of one culture can't pass moral judgment on members of another group.

I'll admit that at first glance, ethical relativism is appealing. It avoids the problem of ethnocentrism while simplifying the decision-making process. We can concentrate on fitting in with the prevailing culture and never have to pass judgment. On closer examination, however, the difficulties of ethical relativism become all too apparent. Without shared standards, there's little hope that the peoples of the world can work together to address global problems. There may be no basis on which to condemn the evil of notorious leaders who are popular in their own countries. Further, the standard of cultural relativism obligates us to follow (or at least not to protest against) abhorrent local practices such as female circumcision or the killing of brides by their in-laws in the rural villages of Pakistan. Without universal rights and wrongs, we have no basis on which to protest such practices.

I believe that there is ethical common ground. The existence of universal standards has enabled members of the world community to punish crimes against humanity and to create the United Nations and its Declaration of Human Rights. Responsible multinational corporations such as Merck, the Body Shop, and Levi-Strauss adhere to widely held moral principles as they conduct business in a variety of cultural settings. In this final section, I'll describe several approaches to universal ethics, any one of which could serve as a worldwide standard. As you read each description, look for commonalties. Then decide for yourself which approach or combinations of approaches best capture the foundational values of humankind (see exercise 6 in the section "For Further Exploration, Challenge, and Self-Assessment").

A Global Ethic

Many of the world's conflicts center on religious differences: Hindu versus Moslem, Protestant versus Catholic, Moslem versus Jew. These hostilities, however, did not prevent 6,500 representatives from a wide range of religious faiths from reaching agreement on a global ethic.[1] A council of former heads of state and prime ministers then ratified this statement. Delegates of both groups agreed on two universal principles. First, every person must be treated humanely regardless of language, skin color, mental ability, political beliefs, and national or social origin. Second, every person and group, no matter how powerful, must respect the dignity of others. These two foundational principles, in turn, led to these ethical directives or imperatives:

- ☐ Commitment to a culture of nonviolence and respect for all life
- ☐ Commitment to a culture of solidarity and a just economic order (do not steal, deal fairly and honestly with others)
- ☐ Commitment to a culture of tolerance and truthfulness

---

[1]   Kung, H. (1998). *A global ethic for global politics and economics*. New York: Oxford University Press; Kung, H. (1999). A global ethic in an age of globalization. In G. Enderle (Ed.) *International business ethics: Challenges and approaches* (pp. 109-127). Notre Dame, IN: University of Notre Dame Press.

☐ Commitment to a culture of equal rights and partnership between men and women (avoid immorality; respect and love members of both genders)

The Platinum Rule

A number of ethicists believe that the Golden Rule ("Do unto others as you would have others do unto you") can serve as a universal ethical standard. Mass communication professor Milton Bennett disagrees. He argues that the Golden Rule is based on the mistaken assumption that all people are essentially alike and therefore want the same things we do. This presumption of similarity encourages ethnocentric thinking. In Bennett's words,

> Treating other people the way we would like to be treated assumes one very important thing—that the other person wants to be treated in the same way as we would like. And under this assumption lies another, more pernicious belief: that all people are basically the same, and thus they really do want the same treatment (whether they admit it or not).[2]

Bennett argues that cross-cultural communicators must recognize both the essential differences between individuals of various cultures and the presence of multiple realities. In place of the Golden Rule, we need to follow the "Platinum Rule." The Platinum Rule is "Do unto others as they themselves would have done to them." To follow this standard, we need to replace sympathy with empathy. Feeling sympathetic means placing ourselves in the position of the other person and imagining how we would respond in this situation. Feeling empathetic,

---

[2]   Bennett, M.J. (1979). Overcoming the Golden Rule: Sympathy and empathy. In D. Nimmo (Ed.). *Communication yearbook 3* (pp. 407-422). New Brunswick, NJ: Transaction Books, p. 407.

in contrast, means putting ourselves in the position of another individual and trying to understand what *they* are thinking and feeling. Sympathy originates from our perspective, but empathy comes from what we imagine to be the perspective of the other person.

The Golden Rule calls for sympathy because it is based on the assumption that people are basically identical. The Platinum Rule requires empathy because it assumes differences and requires us to see the world from another's point of view. To establish empathy, we need to start with a solid sense of who we are and then set this identity aside to imagine how the other person might respond. Empathetic experiences are always temporary. We reestablish our personal identities after we've made empathetic connection.

Eight Global Values

Ethicist Rushworth Kidder and his colleagues at the Institute for Global Ethics identify eight core values that appear to be shared the world over. They isolated these values after conducting interviews with 24 international "ethical thought leaders."[3] Kidder's sample included United Nations officials, heads of states, university presidents, writers, and religious figures drawn from such nations as the United States, Vietnam, Mozambique, New Zealand, Bangladesh, Britain, China, Sri Lanka, Costa Rica, and Lebanon. Each interview ran from 1 to 3 hours and began with this question: "If you could help create a global code of ethics, what would be on it?" These global standards emerged:

1. *Love:* spontaneous concern for others; compassion that transcends political and ethnic differences

---

[3] Kidder, R.M. (1994). *Shared values for a troubled world: Conversations with men and women of conscience.* San Francisco: Jossey-Bass.

2. *Truthfulness*: achieving goals through honest means; keeping promises, being worthy of the trust of others
3. *Fairness (justice)*: fair play, evenhandedness, equality
4. *Freedom*: the pursuit of liberty; right of free expression and action and accountability
5. *Unity*: seeking the common good; cooperation, community, solidarity
6. *Tolerance*: respect for others and their ideas; empathy; appreciation for variety
7. *Responsibility*: care for self, the sick, and needy, the community, and future generations; responsible use of force
8. *Respect for life*: reluctance to kill through war and other means

Kidder and his fellow researchers don't claim to have discovered the one and only set of universal values, but they do believe that they have established ethical common ground. Kidder admits that the eight values are ordinary rather than unique. Yet that the list contains few surprises is evidence these standards are widely shared.

The Peace Ethic

Communication professor David Kale argues that peace ought to be the ultimate goal of all intercultural contact because living in peace protects the worth and dignity of the human spirit.[4] Conflicts are inevitable. Nevertheless, with the help of those in leadership roles, peoples and nations can learn to value the goals of other parties even in the midst of their differences. The four principles of the Peace Ethic are as follows:

---

[4] Kale, D.W. (1994). Peace as an ethic for intercultural communication. In L.A. Samover & R.E. Porter (Eds.), *Intercultural communication: A reader* (7th ed., pp. 435-440). Belmont, CA: Wadsworth.

Principle 1: Ethical communicators address people of other cultures with the same respect they desire themselves. Verbal and psychological violence, like physical violence, damages the human spirit. Demeaning or belittling others makes it hard for individuals to live at peace with themselves or their cultural heritage.

Principle 2: Ethical communicators describe the world as they see it as accurately as possible. Perceptions of what is truth vary from culture to culture, but all individuals, regardless of their cultural background, should be true to the truth as they perceive it. Lying undermines trust that lays the foundation for peace.

Principle 3: Ethical communicators encourage people of other cultures to express their cultural uniqueness. Individuals and nations have the right to hold and to express different values and beliefs, a principle enshrined in the United Nations Universal Declaration of Human Rights. As leaders, we shouldn't force others to adopt our standards before allowing them to engage in dialogue.

Principle 4: Ethical communicators strive for identification with people of other cultures. Whenever possible, we should seek mutual understanding and common ethical ground. Incidents of racial harassment at colleges and universities are unethical, according to this principle, because they lead to division, rather than peace.

International Rights

Philosopher Thomas Donaldson believes that multinational corporations should recognize that citizens of every culture have the 10 fundamental rights listed below.[5] Each of these

---

5   Donaldson, T. (1989). *The ethics of international business.* New York: Oxford University Press.

rights protects something of great value that can be taken away from individuals.

1. The right to freedom of physical movement
2. The right to ownership of property
3. The right to freedom from torture
4. The right to a fair trial
5. The right to nondiscriminatory treatment (freedom from discrimination on the basis of race or sex or other characteristics)
6. The right to physical security
7. The right to freedom of speech and association
8. The right to minimal education
9. The right to political participation
10. The right to subsistence

Honoring these 10 rights imposes certain duties or responsibilities. At the least, business leaders have a responsibility to do no harm. They shouldn't enslave or deliberately injure workers. Leaders of corporations and other international organizations may need to take a more active stance, however, by actively protecting fundamental rights. This might mean

- Establishing nondiscriminatory policies in cultures that discriminate according to caste, sex, age, or some other factor
- Maintaining the highest safety standards for all employees in every nation
- Refusing to hire children if this prevents them from learning how to read or write
- Paying a decent wage even if not required by a country's laws
- Protesting government attempts to take away the rights of free speech and association

Implications and Applications

☐ Cultural differences make ethical decisions more difficult. Resist the temptation, however, to revert to your old ways of thinking or to blindly follow local customs. Try instead to expand your capacity to act ethically in multicultural situations.

☐ Ethnocentrism and prejudice lead to a great many moral abuses. You can avoid casting cross-cultural shadows if you commit yourself to mindfulness, human dignity, and moral inclusiveness.

☐ Understanding the relationship between cultural differences and ethical values can help you predict how members of that group will respond to moral questions. Two popular cultural values classification systems are (a) programmed values (power distance, individualism-collectivism, masculinity-femininity, uncertainty avoidance) and (b) capitalistic values (universalism vs. particularism, individualism vs. communitarianism, analyzing vs. integrating, inner-directed vs. outer-directed, achieved vs. ascribed status, time as sequence vs. time as synchronization, equality vs. hierarchy).

☐ No culture has a monopoly on the truth. In your role as a leader, you can learn from the strengths of other cultures and help others do the same.

☐ Strive for cultural-ethical synergy, combining insights from a variety of cultures to create better than expected ethical solutions.

☐ Universal standards can help you establish common ground with diverse followers. These shared standards can take the form of religious commitments, empathy, global values, a commitment to peace, or international rights.

Rabindra N. Kanungo

1935-

Manuel Mendonca

1932-

Preparing for Ethical Leadership

1996

Dr. Rabi Kanungo is professor emeritus of McGill's Faculty of Management, having been a member of that faculty since 1969. Before that, he taught at Dalhousie University and at several notable institutions in India, including the Indian Institute of Technology in Bombay and the Indian Institute of Management in Calcutta and Ahmedabad. Dr. Kanungo's areas of expertise include comparative studies of work attitudes, work motivation and alienation, and leadership. He has authored, co-authored, or contributed to more than one hundred publications, including books on biculturalism and management.

Professor Manuel Mendonca has taught in McGill University's Faculty of Management and the Centre for Continuing Education since 1984. He received the 1994 Distinguished Teaching Award from McGill's Centre for Continuing Education. Before moving to Canada, he taught at St. Xavier's College, University of Bombay, India. His interests include cross-cultural leadership and management.

In this reading, Kanungo and Mendonca discuss the leader as a moral person, including how the leader's morals may be yoked to a higher source.

Sources:

McGill University (2009). *Manuel Mendonca*. Retrieved from http://people.mcgill.ca/manuel.mendonca/. getCITED. (2006). *Rabindra N. Kanungo*. Retrieved from http://www.getcited.org/mbrz/11058439

Selection from:

Kanungo, R. N. & Mendonca, M. (1996). Preparing for ethical leadership. In *Ethical dimensions of leadership*. (pp. 98-104). Thousand Oaks: Sage.

The Development of the Leader as a Moral Person

As discussed previously, charismatic leadership is essentially transformational in nature—that is, self-transformation of the leader and of the followers. Charismatic leaders readily recognize that the self-transformation ought to begin with one's self. In the context of ethical management, Blanchard and Peale (1988)[1] offer inspiring and practical principles of ethical power: purpose, pride, patience, persistence, and perspective. We briefly discuss these principles because charismatic leaders too can tap these sources of ethical power as they go about their task of self-transformation.

---

[1] Blanchard, K., & Peale, N.V. (1988). *The power of ethical management.* New York: Fawcett Crest.

Purpose

The critical set of behaviors of the charismatic leader is to evaluate the status quo; to formulate and articulate a vision that is discrepant from the status quo and to take the means—personal sacrifice, building trust among followers, and using unconventional behavior—to achieve the vision (Conger & Kanungo, 1987).[2] The charismatic leader often exercises his or her ethical power by subjecting the vision as well as the means to achieve it to the rigorous scrutiny of the purpose that it is intended to serve. What higher purpose does the vision serve? In the context of the business organization, it is universally admitted that the business must be profitable. Influential business magazines, such as *Forbes* and *Fortune,* and business textbooks blatantly suggest that the purpose of business is "to maximize profits and to maximize the wealth of those who own the business organization. It is a commentary on society that these attitudes and expectations largely go unexamined and unchallenged" (Watson, 1991. p. 34).[3] But the ethical leader stops to ask: Are profits a means or an end in itself? Corporations committed to a higher purpose "exist to provide society the goods and services it needs, to provide employment, and to create a surplus of wealth [profit] with which to improve the general standard of living and quality of life" (O'Toole, 1985, p. 49).[4]

The scrutiny of the vision in the perspective of its higher purpose will cause the leader to practice primarily the virtues of prudence and justice. Furthermore, the habit of questioning

---

[2]   Conger, J.A., & Kanungo, R. N. (1987). Toward a behavioral theory of charismatic leadership in organizational settings. *Academy of Management Review, 12,* 637-647.

[3]   Watson, C. E. (1991). *Managing with integrity: Insights from America's C.E.O.s.* New York: Prager.

[4]   O'Toole, J. (1985). *Vanguard management: Redesigning the corporate future.* Garden City, N.Y. Doubleday.

the purpose of one's actions in light of ethical principles demonstrates the strength of the leader's character that enhances the followers' perception of the trustworthiness of the leader.

Pride

The charismatic leader obviously needs to have high self-esteem. This self-esteem originates from a healthy pride in one's accomplishments as well as the esteem of one's followers. However, the leader's behaviors are not designed merely to gain the acceptance of the followers. For example, in formulating the vision the leader ought to take into account the needs and aspirations of the followers, but the leader ought not to allow the desire to be accepted by the followers to compromise the vision when such compromise will jeopardize the higher purpose. In other words, the leader does not look to the followers for affiliative assurance (Boyatzis, 1984)[5] to reinforce his or her self-love but rather for transforming the followers to accept and realize the vision.

The charismatic leader needs to exercise power over his or her followers but the origin of this power is the leader's identification with the objectives derived from the higher purpose. Consequently, in the exercise of such power the leader is seen as a helpful coach and mentor rather than a tyrannical dictator. As Donald Hall of Hallmark observed: "Being able to manage people is not standing over them with a whip but being able to understand people who work for them and around them and maximizing people's potential" (quoted in Watson, 1991, pp. 289-290).[6] Charismatic leaders exhibit healthy pride not vanity. The dividing line between

[5] Boyatzis, R. E. (1984). The need for close relationships and the manager's job. In D. A. Kolb, I. M. Rubin, & J. M. McIntyre (Eds.) *Organizational psychology: Reading on human behavior in organizations* (pp. 81-86). Englewood Cliffs, N.J. Prentice Hall.

[6] Watson. *Ibid.*

healthy pride and vanity is unbelievably thin because of the strong egoistic tendency in human beings, but charismatic leaders recognize that inordinate self-love is a human vice and not a virtue.

Patience

As the charismatic leader works toward the realization of the vision, he or she is certain to come across obstacles from the environment (internal or external) or from the reluctance of the followers to accept and be committed to the vision. The reasons for the latter might be lack of understanding of the vision and its positive features or simply a lack of trust in the leader. It takes time and effort to overcome such obstacles that are inevitable in a worthy and noble endeavor, hence, the need for patience. A patient person bears the present difficulties with calm and serenity because of his or her faith in the vision.

There are two aspects to this faith. The first aspect is the leader's strong belief in the truth and value of the higher purpose and in his or her vision of the future as the best way to serve that higher purpose. The second aspect relates to the strength of the leader's conviction in spiritual beliefs. When a leader believes in a higher purpose or a being representing the higher purpose (for some, that Being is God), the leader develops an inner realization that, in good time, the difficulties will be resolved. The faith referred to here is not fatalism that inevitably paralyzes action. Rather, both aspects of faith—the vision and the spiritual convictions—contribute to the leader's constancy of purpose that leads him or her to continue undaunted with what needs to be done in the unshaken belief that the present difficulties are part of the progress toward realizing the vision. This will particularly be the case with a leader who strives to exercise prudence and fortitude. As discussed in the first section, the practice of prudence enables one to properly assess all facts and circumstances surrounding one's decisions, and the practice of fortitude develops the capacity to act positively in the midst of difficulties. The relevance of prudence for charismatic leadership is reflected in the charismatic leader's need to be sensitive to the environment; the relevance of fortitude is demonstrated by the fact that the charismatic leader is called on to perform behaviors that involve great personal risks and sacrifices. As a result, the patient leader who is in the habit of practicing prudence and fortitude will not be inclined to resort to unethical practices when things do not go as planned.

Persistence

The power of persistence is best captured in Winston Churchill's bulldog-like perseverance—that is, to never, never give up. Persistence does not mean a stubborn obstinacy. Rather, the leader will not allow difficulties to weaken his or her resolve to stay the course; instead, he or she continues to take the steps necessary, even those involving personal risk and sacrifice, to achieve the vision. It is perfectly human to justify unethical practices when one feels overwhelmed by insurmountable internal or external difficulties. The practice of fortitude allows one to strive to overcome difficulties not because it is convenient or pleasant to do so, but because one's duty requires that it be done. This idea is forcefully expressed by John Hoyt Stookey of National Distillers (now Quantum Chemical) when he declared: "One of the things . . . that we mean by ethical behavior is that we will forgo profit in order to adhere to a standard of conduct. I believe that's a message a CEO needs to convey loud and clear to an organization and I find myself doing that" (quoted in Watson, 1991, p. 186).[7]

In a society in which both individuals and organizations are obsessed with and guided by short-term gratification, the practice of patience and persistence does become a

---

[7] Watson. *Ibid.*

real challenge. In his Spiritual Exercises, Ignatius of Loyola proposed that in situations when one is inclined to justify the neglect of one's duty with endless rationalizations, then the individual is advised not to debate these rationalizations, but simply to make the extra effort to do what one's duty dictates.

Perspective

"Perspective is the capacity to see what is really important in any given situation" (Blanchard & Peale, 1988, p. 69).[8] The habit of reflection is critical to acquiring a sense of perspective. And reflection is simply not possible unless one devotes some time each day to silence—a resource that has been recommended by wise men of all time and from all cultures, and yet the one resource that remains most untapped.

If I were a doctor and I could prescribe just one remedy for all the ills of the modern world, I would prescribe silence. For even if the word of God were proclaimed in the modern world, no one would hear it, because of the panoply of noise. Therefore, *create silence* (Kierkegaard, cited by Kreeft, 1990, p. 168).[9]

Silence is more than refraining from noise; it is the inner silence that allows one to reflect on the higher purpose, to question one's decisions in light of that purpose, and to seek strength not to betray it. It allows one to listen to the inner stirrings of the spirit and is needed to make distinctions, between right and wrong, to discern what one ought to do.

I am continually amazed at how clear my thinking becomes afterward, particularly if I'm faced with a big problem. It's as if the answer I am seeking exists somewhere already, just waiting for me to tune in to it. The solitude, quiet, and reflection are the tuning-in process (Blanchard & Peale, 1988, p. 76). [10]

---

[8] *Ibid.*

[9] Kreeft, P. (1990). *Making choices: Practical wisdom for every day moral decisions.* Ann Arbor, MI: Servant.

[10] *Ibid.*

The preceding discussion has touched on several suggestions available to charismatic leaders in their efforts to develop the inner strength they need to function as ethical, moral persons. The ascetical literature, however, emphasizes that the enduring effectiveness of these suggestions very much depends on their habitual practice and, more important, on a specific time the leader sets aside for the ascetical practice of "examination of conscience." No one will deny that individuals do not suddenly find themselves engaging in grave and serious unethical practices. On the contrary, examples abound that these are preceded by minor unethical lapses, which one rationalizes as being inconsequential or doing so because "everyone is doing it." The periodic examination of conscience prevents a person from, or at least alerts a person to the fact that he or she might be, treading the slippery slope of unethical behavior.

The Development of a Moral Environment

"To model love. I am the *soul* of this company. It is through me that our organization's values pass" (quoted in Blanchard & Peale, 1988, p. 89).[11] This was the response of the chairman of Matushita Electric when asked about his primary job. The statements of the vision, mission, and policies—however numerous, well-crafted, and articulated—are futile if the leader's actions and behavior are inconsistent with these statements. Actions speak louder than words; what the leader does and values sets the ethical tone and creates the moral environment of the organization. In the 1988 Touche Ross survey of key business leaders, deans of business schools, and members of Congress on ethical standards and behavior, "73 percent recognize the CEO's ability to influence ethical behavior" (Kangas, 1988, p. 11).[12]

---

[11]   *Ibid.*

[12]   Kangas, E. A. (1988). Introduction. In *Ethics in American business: A special report* (pp. 5-14). New York: Touche Ross.

Truly, the leader is the soul of the organization. For example, even in the relatively trivial area of employees' work attendance, the CEO's example has been found to be critical. In one organization, when the CEO regularly arrived at his office at 10:00 a.m., his executives came in at 9:45 a.m., but when his successor began work at 7:00 a.m., these same executives now came in at 8:00 a.m. or earlier (Stovall, 1988).[13] However, there are other more telling examples: One manufacturer continued to produce a product known to cause illness and death; on the other hand, Johnson & Johnson immediately withdrew Tylenol from the market, at enormous costs, even though the product was completely safe (Lank, 1988).[14] The actions of these CEOs sent clear, unambiguous messages about the ethical standards expected from their employees.

The higher purpose established for the organization by the charismatic leader becomes the starting point in creating the moral environment. The higher purpose and the values it represents convey to the followers what is acceptable and unacceptable behavior. However, to facilitate the employees' internalization of these values, the leader must develop specific codes of conduct for organizational members. The codes of conduct are useful and even necessary, but care needs to be taken in their development. For instance, in a survey of codes of conduct of more than 200 companies, the "most ignored item was personal character—it seemed not to matter" (Walton, 1988, p. 170).[15] In addition to the codes of conduct, the leader should identify areas and issues that might be particularly susceptible to unethical conduct and

---

13   Stovall, R. H. (1988). The Trinity Center roundtable—The ethics of corporate leadership. In *Ethics in American business: A special report* (pp. 28-29). New York: Touche Ross.

14   Lank, A. G. (1988). The ethical criterion in business decision-making: Optional or imperative. In *Ethics in American business: A special report* (pp. 47). New York: Touche Ross.

15   Walton, C. C. (1988). *The moral messenger.* Cambridge, MA: Ballinger.

develop internal policies and processes that specifically deal with them.

The leader should also create opportunities for employees to exchange ideas and experiences in the implementation of the code of conduct, as well as the difficulties they might likely encounter in acting ethically in certain situations, especially if ethical dilemmas are involved. Some organizations hold periodical retreats or discussion forums, which provide employees with the intellectual, emotional, and moral support necessary to maintain the high ethical standards expected of them.

Codes of conduct, related policies and procedures, and support structures are undoubtedly essential to the development of the organization's moral environment. However, in the final analysis, it is the charismatic leader's personal conduct that determines the effectiveness of codes, policies and procedures, and support structures. The moral environment cannot be created by the fiat of the leader. Just as Mother Teresa's work for the poorest of the poor is an external outpouring of her love for God, in much the same way, the organization's moral environment is a natural overflow of the charismatic leader's commitment to ethical principles and values that is expressed not only in terms of intellectual assent but also in his or her daily struggle to live by them.

Ohmann (1989)[16] cites the example of an executive whose policies and practices flowed naturally from his beliefs and values. This executive believed that his talent and resources are gifts entrusted to his stewardship for the "maximum self-development and useful service to one's fellows in the hope that one may live a rich life and be a credit to his Creator . . . It is against this frame of reference that the decisions of the moment easily fall into proper perspective" (Ohmann, 1989, pp. 66-67).[17] As a result, he provided employees with

---

[16] Ohmann, O. A. (1989). Skyhooks. In K. R. Andrews (Ed.), *Ethics in practice: Managing the moral corporation* (p. 58-69). Boston: Harvard Business School Press.

[17] *Ibid.*

opportunities to develop to the fullest of their potential. He held his employees accountable but, at the same time, coached them to performance levels that would justify the higher rewards. He viewed profits as a measure of the successful use of the potential of his employees. Instead of talking about employee communication programs, he spent most of his time in the field listening to his employees. He managed conflicts not by considerations of expediency or self-concern but by reference to what best served the organization's higher purpose. His basic values not only led to consistency in his decisions and behavior that made him dependable and trustworthy but also gave meaning and significance to even the otherwise routine and inconsequential activities of the workplace. The resulting moral environment truly reflected the soul of the organization and enabled its members to internalize its values, which became a firm and enduring foundation for their ethical behavior.

RUSS MOXLEY

1948-

Leadership and Spirit

2000

Russ Moxley is currently the president of Russ Moxley & Associates in Greensboro, North Carolina. Until 2002, he was a Senior Fellow and Director of the Center for Creative Leadership, a nonprofit research and educational organization also headquartered in Greensboro, North Carolina. Currently, he offers workshops in leadership development for corporations and non-profit organizations. Moxley's work at the Center for Leadership and Ethics at Greensboro College includes executive coaching and consulting with organizations interested in building a systemic approach to leadership development.

In the reading below, Moxley explores the leader's development of the inner life which permits him/her to understand and embrace the shadows within. The leader is then better able to reconcile the good and evil found in practical contexts.

Source:

Moxley & Associates, LLC. (2009). *Resume of Russ S. Moxley.* Retrieved from http://www.moxleyandassociates.com/resume.html

Selection from:

Moxley, R. S. (2000). *Leadership and spirit: Breathing new vitality and energy into individuals and organizations.* (pp. 129, 136-143). San Francisco: Jossey-Bass.

Chapter Six
Developing Our Inner Life

> Leaders, in the very way they become leaders, tend to screen out their inner consciousness.
> —Parker Palmer (1998b, p. 6)[1]

> We cannot afford the luxury of silence about the spiritual condition of our leaders. They themselves are experiencing stresses at a deep personal level which many of them cannot cope with; and they are taking action in their organizations that reflect their fragile and embattled spiritual condition.
> —Peter Vaill (1998, p. 217)[2]

Of all the "soft stuff" that executives and managers, and all of the rest of us, try to avoid, inner consciousness may be the softest of all. Inner consciousness cannot be quantified. It cannot be studied empirically. It cannot be experienced by any of the senses. It is not part of the curriculum at the Harvard Business School. It is hard to understand, much less appreciate. Managers and executives have enough problems and issues with which to wrestle; they see no need to go on an inner journey to find more. Plus, the part of the journey to our self that takes us in and down is the most difficult part to traverse, let alone complete. It is, then, rather easy to dismiss

---

[1]   Palmer, P. "Leading from Within." In L. Spears (ed.), *Insights on Leadership.* New York: Wiley, 1998b.

[2]   Vaill, P. *Spiritual Leading and Learning.* San Francisco: Jossey-Bass, 1991.

inner consciousness as not the right stuff to deal with. It is easier to operate on the belief that what you see is what you get . . .

Inner Life and the Shadow

We are a tapestry. On the front side of the tapestry that is us, the threads are woven together beautifully. From this side of ourselves, we cast light and foster connectedness. We trust others. We work collaboratively and develop partnership-as-leadership. This is the part of ourselves that we hope others see, the part we are glad to show in public. It is our persona. On the back side of the tapestry, there are knots—not pretty, but part of the essence of the tapestry. It isn't possible to have the front side without the back. From the back side (or, if you want, from the dark underbelly), we cast our shadows and foster disconnection. The dark underbelly is home to our fears, our envies, our dependencies, our anger—things often part of our unconscious. To the extent that we are aware of things lurking in the shadow, we try to repress them, or deny they are there, or project them on to someone else. For sure, we don't want to claim them as part of ourselves.

Jung told us that the shadow is part of each of us. We each "carry a shadow"; none of us is exempt. Throughout our lives, what goes on deep inside remains attached to us like a shadow. It is the part of us that we do not wish to be, the part that the ego tries to keep hidden from others. What exists in the shadow runs counter to our conscious ideals. As the stories I have told suggest, the shadow is home to our fears, anxieties, insecurities.

The paradox is that the more we try to hide the back side of the tapestry or escape the shadow, the more we are imprisoned by it. Jung told us what each of us must learn from our experience: our shadow becomes more beastlike if we try to deny it or hide it, and then this beast winds up hurting us and others deeply.

One part of our development journey is to, take an inner journey, identify the shadow, and find our whole self on the other side of it. Alan Briskin says that when we go in and down and find a shadow, it is like "finding a stranger in one's own home" (1996, p. 2).[3] It is a stranger we don't want to find there, and don't particularly care to meet. But it is a stranger who is our self, at least in part. Jung suggested that when we finally greet this stranger, our question should not be "How do I get rid of you?" but rather "How can I claim you?" or even "How do I embrace you?"

The shadow's companion is the persona, that part of ourselves that we show in public, that we let others know and see. It is our persona that makes polite and civilized discourse, even social relationships, possible. Often we delude ourselves into thinking that we are only the persona—our public self—that we want to be and want others to know. Because our persona is also part of us, we try to operate with the belief that "what you see is all there is."

So, what exists in the shadow? What strangers might we find on our inner journey? I have previously mentioned three of them in stories I told about the anger-based, fear-based, and approval-based executives. But there are others.

During the time I was responsible for management and organization development in a major corporation, one of my internal clients was responsible for a huge operation. He was a brilliant engineer, knowledgeable, forceful, influential, and by all external measures successful. Away from work, he was fun to be with, the life of the party in a relaxed and joyful way. He appeared confident and self-assured; he had no problems making tough decisions, confronting people whose work was unacceptable, even taking on corporate when he disagreed with a decision being handed down. Few people would have thought of him as having a problem with insecurity. But as I observed

<hr>

[3] Briskin, A. *The Stirring of Soul in the Workplace.* San Francisco: Jossey-Bass, 1996.

him over a period of several years, as I noticed how much he needed to let others know that he was the boss, as I realized how often he kept others in a one-down position (he wanted compliance, not collaboration) and how he used coercive power to keep them there, the more I began to think that if I could peel back several layers I would find an insecure, threatened man. He did not appear to know this about himself; it was part of his shadow. His shadow wasn't benign, it was toxic. It poisoned him, it poisoned others, and it poisoned relationships.

Other managers and executives share another particular type of insecurity or anxiety: I call it the impostor syndrome (I regret not knowing whom to credit for this phrase; I wish I had). Much of the work I do is feedback-intensive. It is helping managers and executives—all leaders in one way or another—get a good fix on who they are through various kinds of assessment. They learn about their strengths, their development needs, their impact on others, and their personal preferences—what makes them tick. It is leadership development as development of the person. It is leadership development from the inside out. Many share a fear that during the intensive assessment process they will be "found out," a fear that comedian Robin Williams described in a recent interview: "The essential truth is that sometimes you're worried that they will find out it's a fluke, that you don't really have it. You've lost the muse or—worst dread—you never had it at all. I went through all that madness early on" (Rader, 1998, p. 4).[4] Like other aspects of the shadow, this fear can feel like madness. It is madness that infects us, and it infects others.

Parker Palmer (though I have never met him, he is one of my favorite "teachers"; I like nothing better than to spend an afternoon engaging in discourse with him while reading something he's written—his writings invite dialogue) has identified five monsters that exist within the shadow of leaders (1998b).[5]

---

[4] Rader, D. "What Really Makes Life Fun." *Parade*, Sept. 20, 1998, pp. 4-5.

[5] *Ibid.*

First is the shadow of insecurity about identity, about one's worth as a person. For many of us (Palmer says he sees it especially in men), our identity is so tied to our title and our job, and our insecurity is so great, that if we were to lose our title or job we would lose our sense of self. How does this get projected? Palmer writes that "these leaders create institutional settings that deprive other people of their identity as a way of dealing with the unexamined fears in the leaders themselves" (p. 204).[6] It is difficult for men or women whose identity is tied up in a title, in the status symbols that accompany high positions of great authority, or in a particular job to move to a more collaborative, partnership model of leadership. For them, it would be like losing their identity.

The second shadow that Palmer sees in leaders is the inner fear that the universe is essentially hostile and life is a battle. "We talk about tactics and strategies, about using 'our big guns', about 'do or die', about wins and losses" (p. 205).[7] Because we fear that this is the way life is, we choose competition over collaboration; we create situations that are win-lose; and we develop relationships that are one-up, one-down. Because of this fear, individuals hang onto their coercive power (after all, they need it to win) and continue to favor hierarchy and bureaucracy more than community. This may be what is motivating the fear-based and insecurity-based executives described earlier. Like other aspects of our shadows, this fear may only be dimly recognized, yet it deeply affects how we relate and how we engage in leadership activities.

The third aspect of shadow Palmer names is "functional atheism." It is the deep-down belief that the "ultimate responsibility for everything rests with me . . . it is the unexamined conviction that if anything decent is going to happen, I am the one who needs to make it happen here" (p. 205)[8]: This belief, and

---

6   *Ibid.*

7   *Ibid.*

8   *Idem.*

the action we take based on it, obviously leads to stress and burnout for the individual, as well as leading to unhealthy and unproductive relationships with those with whom we work. Less obviously, it is not possible to enact partnership-as-leadership so long as an executive carries a deeply held convict that ultimate responsibility rests with him or her, that the buck must always finally stop at his or her door.

The fear of the natural chaos of life is the fourth inner reality that Palmer identified as lurking in the shadow. "I think that a lot of leaders become leaders because they have a lifelong devotion to eliminating all remnants of chaos from the world," Palmer writes (p. 206).[9] As soon as I read this, I knew he was describing me. As I suggested earlier, I try to control chaos in my own world, if not the entire world. I attempt to organize and structure everything; doing so protects my illusion that I am in control. I have worked with other executives who have the same fear. One was so fearful of ambiguity and chaos that she tried to develop a standard operating procedure for every possible situation that might arise in her department. She wanted nothing left to chance—or even to the judgment of other individuals. For those of us with this fear in our shadows, we project it by creating norms, policies, practices, and SOPs to cover every possible situation.

The final example of a shadow that leaders (read this as all of us) project on others, Palmer suggests, is the denial of death. This is demonstrated, he suggests, in how we try to keep everything alive, including projects, programs, and people who have been in a coma for years but have never been laid to rest. This fear is related to partnership in that we do not move to this practice of leadership until we recognize that we live in a postheroic age and that it is OK to let go of old ways of being leaders and doing leadership.

Read all this and it is easy to begin to believe that the shadow is the bad or evil side of us. It isn't. It is the

---

[9] *Ibid.*

comparatively primitive and unadapted side. Jung's way of saying this was that it contained more of our basic animal nature. But the shadow also helps us be more spontaneous, creative, and childlike. The shadow helps us experience strong emotions. It adds zest and vitality to life. It adds breadth and depth to life. Our hope and our task is not to rid ourselves of the shadow but rather to engage in processes in which we move things lurking in the shadow from the unconscious to our conscious and begin to embrace them. As we embrace them, we stop projecting them. We become more whole, freer to participate fully in the activity of leadership, more open to spirit working in and through us in shaping our identity. In our outer lives, we are better able to understand and accept others, including things lurking in *their* shadow, and we are better able to engage in partnerships.

The Journey Inward: Embracing Our Shadow

Learning to embrace our shadow is a journey down and in that inevitably leads to a meeting with a new part of ourselves, a journey for which there is no guaranteed rite of passage. It is a journey that some avoid all of their lives, or at least as long as their egos can repress the shadow or they can project everything negative onto others. Others start the journey and then turn back. To fully commit to an inner journey is a test of our courage. Jung said that "this confrontation [with self] is the first test of courage on the inner way, a test sufficient to frighten off most people, for the meeting with ourselves belongs to the more unpleasant things that can be avoided so long as we can project everything negative into the environment" (1993, p. 381).[10]

So, why take this journey? Simply, it is the only way to get to where we want to be. Let me remind you of a story as a way

---

[10]   Jung, C. G. *The Basic Writing of C. G. Jung.* (S. de Laszlo, ed.). New York: Modern Library, 1993. (Originally published in 1959).

of making this point. I love Old Testament stories. They are so real—real people struggling with real-life issues. One of my favorites is the story of the Exodus event. It is a story that can be read on several levels. On one level, it is a story of the journey that each of us must take, a journey from bondage through the wilderness to Canaan, a land flowing with milk and honey. Most of us would like to leave behind the things that imprison and bind us; we would like to get to the point where we don't project our shadow onto relationships and organizations. Our deep wish, though, is to find a way to do this—to get to the promised land—that does not involve wilderness wanderings. We are willing to walk around the wilderness, and often we walk up to its edge to see if there isn't some way around it. But we don't want to walk through it. Why not avoid the pain, the uncertainty, the trouble if we can? None [of] us likes to be torn and tattered by life's experiences. The Exodus story reminds us that there is no way around the wilderness; the way out is in and through.

The Exodus story also reminds us of several of the essential steps in the journey. First, we must acknowledge that the monsters in our shadows—our fears, our insecurities, our anxieties about the world, our dependency needs—keep us in bondage. Until we are aware of being imprisoned, there is no reason to move toward freedom. Sometimes we learn about how shadow constrains us when we experience particularly painful hardships: the loss of a friendship, a failure at work, a midlife divorce, a bout of depression. These experiences nudge us to begin the journey in and down. At other times, we become aware of bondage because of our active involvement in one or more spiritual disciplines. Yet other times, we begin the journey because the spirit that weaves through and permeates all of our experience is always at work within us nudging us toward wholeness. We have a slow but real dawning that the unexamined life is not as full and complete as it might be, and a sense that on the other side of the shadow we will find a more complete self.

The next step in the journey is engaging the wilderness, moving toward the shadow. It is tough to enter the wilderness, to begin the journey in and down, because we don't know what we will find there. But we do know that some monsters—some fears, anxieties, and insecurities—are terrifying. We know too that we will meet the things we hate about ourselves and usually project on others. This is a journey toward one of the most difficult but most important parts of self.

But even after we commit to the wilderness and begin the inner journey, questions remain. If the shadow exists primarily in our unconscious, how can we know it? If we don't know it, how can we move toward it, much less embrace it? Life offers clues about our shadows. We know we are getting close when we become aware of

- Things that tend to set us off. What slights cause you to overreact? When does your anger pop out to haunt you? What about your fears?
- What we don't like in others, especially others of the same sex. It is onto them that we most likely project the shadow.
- Those things we know about ourselves but try to keep hidden, the ways we don't want to be but deep down know we are.
- Our dreams (they are a rich source of clues).
- Feedback from others. Sometimes we learn the truth about ourselves from outside of us.

On the other side of the wilderness is Canaan, a promised land. This is the final step of the journey in and down; it is our intended destination. For our purposes, Canaan is what Thomas Merton called a "hidden wholeness," a place where we experience an internal sense of wholeness and true connectedness to others. It is the promise this place exists that makes the journey worth taking.

INDEX

C

Canaan, 422, 423

Carlyle, Thomas, 5, 39, 40

Casement, William, 16

Chaleff, Ira, 7, 10, 329, 330

Chao army, 265

Chao State, 265

character, 23, 31, 56, 62, 70, 78,
   111, 119, 120, 257, 260, 262,
   263, 295, 298, 313, 327, 343,
   362, 406, 411

charisma, 166, 276, 277

charismatic leader, 57, 166,
   172, 276, 277, 282, 404, 405,
   406, 407, 408, 410, 411, 412

circumstances of leadership,
   19, 20, 22, 23, 35, 50, 51, 57,
   79, 123, 168, 251, 258, 259,
   261, 262, 271, 273, 287, 340,
   355, 362, 408

citizen, 111, 134, 247

civilization, 156, 228, 229, 230,
   232, 235, 236

Clausewitz, Carl von, 5, 109,
   110

codes of conduct, 411

Codified thinking, 56

coercion, 46, 63, 64, 71, 377

collectivism, 297, 402

commonwealth, 30

communist, 389

community, 14, 15, 16, 45, 75,
   77, 78, 79, 80, 81, 82, 189, 190,
   191, 217, 218, 220, 279, 332,
   351, 365, 374, 395, 399, 419

compliance, 27, 418

constitution, 30, 37, 38, 39, 48,
   242, 243, 245

country, 16, 32, 39, 55, 100, 110,
   111, 123, 132, 220, 239, 242,
   245, 246, 247, 251, 282, 292,
   295, 298, 302, 304, 307, 311,
   313, 314, 320, 321, 369, 401

courage, 29, 85, 110, 120, 122,
   127, 129, 132, 143, 160, 245,
   258, 282, 332, 339, 421

crimes against humanity, 72,
   395

culture, 58, 63, 71, 169, 170,
   204, 213, 223, 225, 226, 227,
   231, 232, 234, 238, 253, 292,
   294, 295, 298, 305, 306, 307,
   311, 312, 313, 316, 320, 321,
   327, 332, 364, 365, 366, 388,
   395, 396, 397, 400, 402

D

Declaration of Independence, 48

Donaldson, Thomas, 400

dyad, 19, 23

E

earth, 36, 202, 237, 264, 274, 393

economy, 141, 251, 276

Edison, Thomas, 24

education, 14, 16, 32, 49, 54, 61,
   62, 67, 138, 143, 213, 220, 223,
   231, 232, 235, 237, 246, 247,
   279, 294, 308, 367, 372, 401

L

M

Edwards Brothers Malloy
Ann Arbor MI. USA
July 27, 2017